Anton C
adapted by 1

YOUNG CHEKHOV

Anton Chekhov (1860–1904), son of a former serf, graduated in medicine from Moscow University in 1884. He began to make his name first as a short-story writer, then in the theatre with the one-act comedies *The Bear*, *The Proposal* and *The Wedding*. His full-length plays are *Platonov* (written in 1878 but unpublished and unperformed in his lifetime), *Ivanov* (1887), *The Wood Demon* (1889), *The Seagull* (1896), *Uncle Vanya* (1899), *Three Sisters* (1901) and *The Cherry Orchard* (1904).

David Hare is a playwright and film-maker. His stage plays include *Plenty*, *Pravda* (with Howard Brenton), *Racing Demon*, *Skylight*, *Amy's View*, *Via Dolorosa*, *Stuff Happens*, *South Downs*, *The Absence of War* and *The Judas Kiss*. His films for cinema and television include *Wetherby*, *Damage*, *The Hours*, *The Reader*, and the Worricker Trilogy: *Page Eight*, *Turks and Caicos* and *Salting the Battlefield*. He has also written English adaptations of plays by Brecht, Gorky, Pirandello, Ibsen and Lorca.

ANTON CHEKHOV

Young Chekhov

Platonov
Ivanov
The Seagull

Adapted and introduced by
DAVID HARE

FABER & FABER

This collection first published in 2015
by Faber and Faber Ltd
74–77 Great Russell Street
London WC1B 3DA

Reptinted with amendments December 2015

Ivanov first published by Methuen in 1997
Platonov first published by Faber and Faber in 2001

Typeset by Country Setting, Kingsdown, Kent CT14 8ES
Printed in England by CPI Group (UK) Ltd, Croydon CR0 4YY

Adaptations © David Hare 2015

A CIP record for this book is available from the British Library

978-0-571-31302-0

4 6 8 10 9 7 5 3

Contents

Introduction

The presentation of these three plays in one season at the Chichester Festival Theatre in 2015 represents the fulfilment of a fifteen-year dream. In the late 1990s I was approached by Jonathan Kent to fashion a version of *Ivanov* for the Almeida Theatre. The resulting production was so outstanding that Jonathan's co-artistic director, Ian McDiarmid, suggested that I take a look at the six hours of ramblings which we in Britain call *Platonov*. As soon as I had started, I argued that we should revive *Ivanov* alongside *Platonov* and throw in *The Seagull* as well, since this far more familiar masterpiece represents the point to which the other two plays are heading. At the time practical difficulties prevented the realisation of such an ambitious project. Now, at last, after so many years, in a field in West Sussex, we will finally give audiences a chance to see the first progress of a playwright.

*

In a deliberately provocative essay the critic James Wood compares Chekhov with Ibsen, and, as critics will, finds in Chekhov's favour. Ibsen, Wood believes, orders life into three trim acts. The Norwegian thinks of his characters as envoys, sent into the world in order to convey the dramatic ironies and ideas of their author. The people in the Russian plays, by contrast, 'act like free consciousness, not as owned literary characters'. Wood rates Chekhov next to Shakespeare because these two alone, among the world's great writers, respect the absolute complexity of life, never allowing their creations to be used for any other purpose than being themselves. The special genius of the human beings you meet in Chekhov's plays and short stories is that they don't have to behave like people in a purposeful drama. 'Chekhov's characters,' Wood declares, 'forget to be Chekhov's characters.'

Who can deny that this is an alluring and obviously potent idea? Who doesn't love the notion that there once existed an author so free that he was able to summon up men and women who trail a sense of mystery as profound as human beings do in real life? Of course it would be wonderful if plays and books could be written which were seen not to reorder life, but which we were able to experience as if they were life itself. What a marvellous thing that would be! But behind Wood's apparently novel theory – boiled down: let's all applaud a writer who is not felt to intervene – you can hear the echo of another critical battle which has been raging for over a hundred years since Chekhov's death. Wood is firing a fresh round of artillery on behalf of that section of the playwright's admirers who value him as the ultimate universalist, the man too squeamish to say anything too specific about his own time and his own class. They think of their hero as a portraitist. But Wood ignores that other, equally vociferous section of admirers who prefer to believe that their man was as political, as social and as specific a writer as Gorky or Tolstoy. They think of him as a moralist.

It is my own conviction that we can't address these contentious questions unless we take time to consider those plays which Chekhov wrote, as it were, before he was Chekhov. *The Cherry Orchard*, *Three Sisters* and *Uncle Vanya* have been in the international repertory ever since they were written, sometimes giving more pleasure to actors who relish their ensemble qualities than to audiences who, in second-rate productions, find them listless. But less attention is paid to the playwright's earlier work. It is essential to see these vibrant and much more direct plays for what they are – thrilling sunbursts of youthful anger and romanticism – rather than for what they portend.

There is no duller and less fruitful way of looking at the key works of Chekhov's theatrical beginnings merely as maquettes for the later plays. Certainly, we can all amuse ourselves by drawing up lists of characters and plot incidents in *Platonov* which recur in *The Cherry Orchard* and *Uncle Vanya*. But as we tick off these motifs – the failed suicides, the mismatched lovers, the sales of the estates – then the danger is that we ignore equally powerful material and themes whose special interest is that they never occur again.

No, *Platonov* does not have the intricate, superbly wrought surface of *Three Sisters*. Who could possibly claim that so many hours of sometimes repetitive and overwritten speechifying exhibit the faultless literary control for which Chekhov later became known? But *Platonov* does have, in its very wildness, a sort of feverish ambition, a desire, almost, to put the whole of Russia on the stage, while at the same time focusing comically on one of its most sophisticated victims. Where is the parallel for this, not just in Chekhov's work, but in anyone else's?

The text of *Platonov* is so prolix that the most successful adaptations have, significantly, tended to be the freest. When Michael Frayn wrote his popular comedy *Wild Honey* for the National Theatre in 1984, he admitted that he treated the text 'as if it were the rough draft of one of my own plays'. When Mikhalkov made his 1985 film *Unfinished Piece for Mechanical Piano*, he reallocated lines, banished half the characters, abandoned the substantive plot, and shoehorned in ideas and images of his own. But my strategy, both more and less radical than that of my two gifted predecessors, was that I should try to stick, in architecture at least, to Chekhov's original plan. I would clear away massive amounts of repetition and indulgence,

I would recoin and rebalance much of the dialogue, I would hack determinedly through acres of brushwood, but nevertheless I would aim that the audience should see the play in something recognisable as the form in which Chekhov left it.

It was undoubtedly a risky undertaking. *Platonov* may seem an odd-shaped play. It can seem like a man who sets off for a walk in one direction, but who is then lured by the beauty of the landscape to another destination entirely. The first act has a gorgeous breadth and sweep which leads you to expect an evening in the company of a whole community. The second introduces an unexpected murder plot. By the time the third is under way, you are witnessing a series of extremely painful and funny duo-logues, all with Platonov himself as the common partner, and by the fourth, you are, with a bit of luck, adjusting yourself to a climax of feverish hysteria. No wonder commentators dismissed this ambitious story of steam trains and lynchings for 'uncertainty of tone'. A faithful performance of *Platonov* will test to the limit the idea that an evening in a playhouse needs to be held together in one governing style.

Even in my compressed version, enemies of the play will call it a ragbag. Let them. For me, something wholly original lies at its spine. The form, often accused of being undisciplined, can more truly be seen as a kind of narrowing, a deliberate irising down on to one particular character. Chekhov sets off to give us a broad-brush view of a society which is rotten with money, drink and hypocrisy. Capitalism is just arriving, and its practices, all too recognisable today, are sweeping aside a privileged class which no longer knows how to maintain its way of life. Ruling-class attitudes have survived long after ruling-class influence has gone. But then, once he has established the context of his vision, Chekhov goes on to embody the contradictions of this superfluous class in one single individual.

The schoolteacher Platonov has squandered his inherited fortune. Again, critics usually portray him as a small-town Lothario, seeking bored amusement in the pursuit of women. But if we examine what Chekhov actually wrote, we will find a hero who is, in fact, surprisingly reluctant to consummate his relationship with at least one of the women who are in love with him. Far from being a deter-mined seducer, 'the most interesting man in the region' is, on the contrary, a person to whom things happen – some-times at his wish, sometimes by accident. In his relation-ships, he tries not for easy conquest, but rather to discover in love a purpose and meaning which eludes him elsewhere. The tired, traditional notion of the provincial Don Juan suddenly breathes with humanity and contradiction.

It is hard, of course, not to see a wry autobiographical element in the twenty-year-old author's appraisal of a man whose main problem in life is that women find him irresis-tible. But no such identification can explain the confidence with which the women themselves are drawn. In the figure of the General's widow, Anna Petrovna, Chekhov creates one of the great heroines of the Russian stage – an edu-cated, intelligent and loving woman who can find no place in the world for her love, her intelligence or her educa-tion. In the compassion Chekhov extends both to Sasha, Platonov's religiously devout wife, and to Sofya, the idealistic young woman who is set on fire by Platonov's too-easy radical rhetoric, we find a degree of imaginative sympathy which would be remarkable in a writer twice or three times Chekhov's age.

In short then, we have a great example of Chekhov exposed – not, as in later plays, seeking to hide his per-sonality under the cover of his creations, but more, like Osborne through Jimmy Porter, willing to let his own passion and his own political despair spill on to the stage. This writer is not at all James Wood's stringless puppet-master, but rather a man unafraid by a mix of direct address, monologue, farce and tragedy to let us know how strongly he feels about the social decay around him. Perhaps because Rex Harrison played the part at the Royal Court in 1960 when he was almost twice the age the author specifies – he says twenty-seven, Harrison was fifty-two – there is an expectation in Britain of Platonov being played, when the role is played at all, by an actor who is far too old. But this play, above all plays, is a terrible tragedy of youth. Young Chekhov is hotter than old.

*

I've tried to be original. I have not introduced a single villain or a single angel (though I haven't been able to abstain from fools); nor have I accused or vindicated anyone. Whether or not I've succeeded I can't tell. Korsh and the actors are sure the play will work. I'm not so sure. The actors don't understand it and say the most ridiculous things, they're badly miscast, I'm constantly at war with them. Had I known, I'd never have got involved with it.

Chekhov's own words about his first performed play *Ivanov* chime neatly with Maxim Gorky's observation: 'How lonely Chekhov is. How little he's understood.' With hindsight we know that Chekhov was about to begin the process of banishing melodrama from the nineteenth-century stage, but as a result it has been easy and convenient to forget the fact that he once wrote an exceptionally good melodrama himself. Because he tended to disparage the play in his private correspondence, and because its early performances were so obviously disastrous, the author implicitly gave permission to anyone who subsequently wanted to label it as clumsy. Originally drafted in only two weeks, the play uses monologue and direct address. It features a hero who makes conspicuously long speeches. It satirises a certain layer of society in much broader strokes than those Chekhov later favoured. But what entitles us to think these techniques are not deliberate, and in their way just as skilfully deployed as the more muted strategies the author later adopted? Unless we can admit that *Ivanov* is not a lesser play, but simply *different* from his later work, then we will miss its significance.

Nothing has been more damaging to our feeling for Chekhov's plays than the way his admirers have tended to represent the author himself. I have often had to explain to enraptured young women that the object of their love is actually dead, and has been for a good long time now. Encouraged by suitably enigmatic photographs, we have tolerated the idea that the dramatist was some sort of all-purpose secular saint, living six feet above the rest of the human race, able to observe mankind's foibles with a medical man's detached and witty irony. Anyone who has bothered to establish the facts of his life would know how far off the mark this notion is. The real Chekhov is complex, testy and troubled. Indeed, to that tiresome school of academics who believe that literary criticism consists of marking off a writer's every line against a contemporary checklist of fashionable 'errors', the saintly Chekhov comes through with his halo looking distinctly askew.

When we hear this supposedly virtuous playwright saying that when he entered a room full of good-looking women he 'melted like a Yid contemplating his ducats' then we may begin to suspect that our man is not quite who he is commonly made out to be. When he elsewhere observes that the most complimentary thing you can say about a woman is that 'she doesn't think like a woman'; when we discover him in Monte Carlo, fretfully revising an infallible system and then losing five hundred francs in two days; when we catch him referring to his one-time Jewish girlfriend as 'Efros the Nose'; when we find him in Sri Lanka 'glutting himself on dusky women': then we are already waving a vigorous goodbye to the floppy-hatted and languorous stereotype.

A singular virtue of the play *Ivanov* is that it gives us a clear sight of this more robust Chekhov, and one who is happy to use some quite orthodox dramatic conventions – each act climaxes with what he calls 'a punch on the nose' – to tackle hotly contemporary themes. Here is a full-blooded writer, willing to address the ugliness of Russian anti-Semitism head-on, and dramatising a conflict from within himself in a way which is both deeply felt and funny. For once, his own feelings and thoughts are plainly on show.

It could hardly be otherwise. The dominating theme of *Ivanov* is honesty. It is hard to see how Chekhov could have written a play which asks what real honesty is, and – just as important – what its price is, without allowing access to his own personality. Although the play, like his later work, may be said to weave together a whole variety of threads, nothing is more striking in it than the deliberate contrast between the self-confident Doctor Lvov and the more cautious Ivanov. The play's defining argument is between a young doctor who thinks that honesty is to do with blurting out offensive truths, and the central character who insists with a wisdom which is notably pre-Freudian that no one can achieve honesty unless they have the self-knowledge to examine their own motives.

In this debate there is no doubt with whom Chekhov's sympathies lie. 'If my Ivanov comes across as a blackguard or superfluous man, and the doctor as a great man, if no one understands why Anna and Sasha love Ivanov, then my play has evidently failed and there can be no question of having it produced.' But for all his protestations of partiality, Chekhov makes sure to provide Ivanov with an opponent who is, in an odd way, as compelling as the hero, and sometimes almost his shadow. Chekhov leaves us to work out for ourselves whether honesty truly resides in judging others or in refusing to judge them.

Apart from the charge of technical immaturity, the play has also had to survive the impression that, in Ivanov himself, it presents a hero who is excessively, even morbidly self-pitying. Yet in saying this, critics ignore Chekhov's stated intention to kill off once and for all the strain of self-indulgent melancholy which he believed disfigured Russian literature. 'I have long cherished the audacious notion of summing up all that has hitherto been written about complaining and melancholy people, and would have my *Ivanov* proclaim the ultimate in such writing.' Far from idealising the so-called superfluous man, Chekhov seeks to send him packing. It was Ralph Fiennes who, at the Almeida in 1997, in a moment of striking revelation for the British theatre, finally played the part the way the author wanted, revealing Ivanov not as a landowner lost in useless introspection, but rather a man who found the whole Russian tradition of introspection and self-pity humiliating. As Fiennes portrayed him, Ivanov was not a stereotype. He was a man fighting with all his willpower not to surrender to a stereotype. He was determined to refuse the comfort of falsely dramatising his feelings. Viewed in this light, the play's tragic ending, which provided the author with so much difficulty, seemed to have a terrible logic.

Ivanov is a play with which Chekhov, for all his re-writing, never felt wholly satisfied. Yet as so often there are ways in which early literary struggle provides an infinitely richer experience than many works which we like to claim as mature.

*

Of all nineteenth-century plays *The Seagull* is most insistently modern. It is also the most adapted. I would not have dared to add to what is already a long list of brilliant adaptations unless I had wanted to tie these three plays together into a single experience, and to present the final play in an especially illuminating context. Because *The Seagull* deals with an artistic argument between the avant-garde and the traditional, it updates peculiarly well. Anya Reiss's recent transposition of the play to the Isle of Man in the present day – people go into town in Land Rovers, not on horseback – seemed to have none of the usual problems of doing what Jonathan Miller calls 'schlepping a play a hundred miles up the motorway'. On the contrary, it was triumphantly apt and alive. Those reviewers who complained of the presence of fridges, sunglasses and high-heels in Luc Bondy's stunning production for the Vienna Burgtheater, seemed blind to the beauty of what the director was doing: just nudging a play which is set on the cusp of change into a visual language which made it fresher and more immediate.

Presented, as on this occasion, as the climax to his work as a young man, then you may notice what is hardly apparent in a stand-alone production. The bones of the plot are pretty routine. A promising young woman is casually ruined by an older man, and cast aside. Her dreams and those of her despairing boyfriend are brutally destroyed. We are, if you care to notice, once more in the realm of melodrama, as we were in *Platonov* and *Ivanov*. For the third time, there will be a death in the final moments of the play. But now, in this climactic work, something new has arrived, which is not purely a matter of technique. Chekhov has found a sophisticated way of burying meaning deep in texture, of leaving as much unsaid as said. But also, instead of giving us single characters striving for individual self-expression, he has found a marvellous ability to suggest something beyond them, something inexpressible. His characters are starting to be victims of events and changes in themselves which it is almost impossible for them to recognise or understand. He is putting them under the eye of eternity.

Anyone who wants single-mindedly to obey the implications of Chekhov calling his play a comedy will find plenty of material in the characters' self-ignorance. At one level, Arkadina can't accept her career is on the slide; however much he discourses on the subject, Trigorin can't accept he's second-rate; and Konstantin can't accept that he can't write. But at another level, these truths are partial, speaking as much to the characters' fears as they do to the reality. And as the play deepens, then easy judgements become hard. Is Nina a good actress or is she not? Is Arkadina really a terrible mother, or is she not dealing with a son whose downward path is predestined and whom nobody can save from himself? Masha's decision to abandon all her romantic hopes and longings may seem expensive. But did she ever, at any point, have any real choice?

It is the unknowability of fate which pulls this play towards greatness. The balance in writing here has changed, but there is enough of Chekhov's early romanticism still showing to make it the most perfect, and most perfectly achieved, play he ever wrote. Are the characters victims of their traits, or are they choosing paths which might have led elsewhere? In *Platonov*, time is something which stretches ahead, meaningless. In *Ivanov*, it represents waste, like an abacus of failure. But in *The Seagull*, with its clever structure of inter-act jumps, time represents something infinitely more powerful: both the element in which we act out our own misfortunes, but also the reason for so many of them. This is a play about young people. Even Arkadina is only forty-three. But the whole set of characters seem to be struggling against some terrible force which strips them and robs them, however they behave. Angry at having to explain to a young woman how punishing his profession is, Trigorin launches into an affair for no other reason but because he can. Yes, of course, it has a terrible effect on Nina, its victim. But it also leaves Trigorin sadder, diminished, a husk.

The Seagull was famously a play made by a great second production. On its first outing, in an indifferent production, it flopped. This seems to me hardly a coincidence.

With *The Seagull*, Chekhov is for the first time beginning to write plays which crucially depend on how you do them. At the outset, as a short-story writer, he palpably condescended to the form of theatre, vowing each time never to go anywhere near a theatre again. But by the time he writes *The Seagull*, you can feel his increasing fascination with the form, and a new desire to advance the history of that form. He begins, in short, to take theatre seriously. On the surface, *The Seagull* is a play about theatre, and most certainly about art. For that reason perhaps it has a history of encouraging exceptional performances. It is a play in which actors as diverse as James Mason, Penelope Wilton, Vanessa Redgrave, George Devine and Carey Mulligan have all done among their greatest work. But the struggle to create something lasting and worthwhile in life is what really drives the play. Theatre is only the metaphor. Chekhov's own youth is ending and it is ending with a new determination not to knock away the past but to try, in however doomed a fashion, to find his way to some sort of future. It is a very long distance in this trilogy of plays from the character of the criminal Osip in *Platonov* who lives in the forest like a medieval thief to the young Konstantin dreaming of an art which has never been seen before. As we watch, or as we read, we are moving from the nineteenth century to the twentieth, and, implicitly to our own. We are seeing the birth of the new.

DAVID HARE

PLATONOV

adapted by David Hare
from a literal translation by Helen Rappaport

Note

*'If anyone still lives who needs proof of Chekhov's genius,
let him go and see* Platonov.'　　　　Kenneth Tynan

In the West, we generally believe that Chekhov wrote the
seven hours of material once called *Play Without a Title*
while he was a medical student, aged about twenty. His
brother Mikhail transcribed them, and the would-be
playwright offered the manuscript to the leading actress
Maria Nikolaevna Yermolova in the hope of a
production at the Maly Theatre in 1881. She turned it
down. The work was abandoned and never staged. The
text we have, lacking a title page, was discovered almost
twenty years after the author's death – in Moscow in
1923.

When the Soviet State Publishing House for Literature
brought out the collected works in 1933, the play was
taken – and is still believed by some – to be a reworking
of a teenage project, Безотцовщина, which Chekhov is
known to have destroyed. It was therefore given the title
Fatherlessness, even though fatherlessness is not
obviously one of the play's main themes.

There are references to performances in German in
1928, and in Czech in 1929, but the first widely noticed
production was in Stockholm in 1954. John Cournos
had made the first English translation in 1930 under the
title *That Worthless Fellow Platonov*, while in 1952 Basil
Ashmore called it *Don Juan (in the Russian Manner)*.
Jean Vilar's 1956 French production, *Ce Fou de Platonov*,
with Maria Casarès as Anna Petrovna, was wrongly

billed as a '*première mondiale*'. The first American text, *Firework on the James*, transposed the action to the deep South. By the time the play reached New York in 1960, it was in a different version entitled *A Country Scandal*.

It was only when Rex Harrison played Dimitri Makaroff's translation at the Royal Court Theatre, also in 1960, that the play acquired its familiar English title, *Platonov*. The first act, hitherto omitted, was now restored. Faithful translations by David Magarshack, for the BBC, and Ronald Hingley, for the Oxford Chekhov, have followed the same practice.

In 1984, Michael Frayn argued that *Platonov* was a misleading title – the play is about a group, not an individual – and that, anyway, no English speaker knew how to pronounce it (the name should be accented on the second syllable). Frayn called his own National Theatre version *Wild Honey*, and noted it was 'a different play, a new play'. Nikita Mikhalkov's 1976 film *Unfinished Piece for Mechanical Piano*, with Aleksandr Kalyagin as Platonov, made huge changes in storyline. In England, at the National Theatre, Trevor Griffiths used the film as the basis for his 1990 play *Piano*.

In 2001, the Almeida presented my more faithful adaptation. Aiden Gillen played Platonov. The opening night was on 11 September, to an understandably distracted audience. This reconceived version aims to advance a task which perhaps may always be unfinished.

Platonov in this English adaptation premiered at the Almeida Theatre, London, in 2001. It was first performed in this revised version at the Festival Theatre, Chichester, on 5 October 2015. The cast, in order of appearance, was as follows:

Anna Nina Sosanya
Nikolai Joshua James
Porfiri Jonathan Coy
Sergei Pip Carter
Bugrov Brian Pettifer
Platonov James McArdle
Sasha Jade Williams
Ivan Triletsky Nicholas Day
Maria Sarah Twomey
Yakov Nebli Basani
Vasili Mark Penfold
Sofya Olivia Vinall
Shcherbuk David Verrey
Osip Des McAleer
Kiril Mark Donald
Katya Beverley Klein
Marko Col Farrell

Director Jonathan Kent
Set Designer Tom Pye
Lighting Designer Mark Henderson
Music Jonathan Dove

Characters

Mikhail Vasilievich Platonov
schoolteacher, twenty-seven

Sasha Ivanovna
wife to Platonov, daughter of Colonel Ivan Triletsky

Nikolai Triletsky
doctor, son of Colonel Ivan Triletsky

Colonel Ivan Triletsky

Anna Petrovna
young widow to General Voynitzev

Sergei Voynitzev
son by General Voynitzev's first wife

Sofya Yegorovna
wife to Sergei

Maria Grekova
chemistry student, twenty

Porfiri Glagolyev
neighbour, landowner

Kiril Glagolyev
his son

Pavel Shcherbuk
wealthy merchant

Timofei Bugrov
merchant

Osip
horse thief

Yakov
servant

Vasili
servant

Katya
maid to Sofya

Marko
writ-server for the regional magistrate

Act One

June 1881. The estate of the late General Voynitzev in a southern province of Russia.

A blazingly hot day. An enormous green garden leading down to the river. A summerhouse beyond. Blankets, chairs and tables being prepared for lunch.

1 Anna Petrovna is playing chess with Nikolai.

Nikolai Any chance of a cigarette, *mon ange?*

Anna Take the lot if it means you won't ask again.

She hands the cigarettes across. He takes the chance to kiss her hand.

What's this? My annual check-up?

Nikolai It's not your pulse I'm after. Wonderful hands. Like kissing swan's down.

Anna Quarter past twelve.

Nikolai What are the chances of lunch?

Anna Not good. Chef got drunk to celebrate our return and he's still flat out on the kitchen floor. No doubt our guests will be starving.

Nikolai Well, if I'm anything to go by.

He contemplates his move.

Anna What are you doing? What's the point of playing if you don't think? Look, think, move. Frankly, the last thing you need is another meal. Look at you!

Nikolai I don't understand you, Anna. A woman of your sensibility who's not interested in food. A discerning stomach is as important in life as . . .

Anna Oh, not an aphorism, please!

Nikolai Why not?

Anna They're banned. As are jokes. Especially yours. Does no one tell you? Your jokes aren't funny.

Nikolai They go over your head.

He hesitates over a move.

Anna So. Is she coming today?

Nikolai Of course she's coming. She promised. She gave her word.

Anna Tell me, I'm interested, where do you put Maria Grekova?

Nikolai Where do I *put* her?

Anna Yes. In the scale of things. Serious? Not serious?

Nikolai What can I say? I call on her every day. We talk. We walk in the woods. Is it boredom? Is it love? All I know is that come the afternoon I miss her. I miss her terribly.

Anna Love, then.

Nikolai Perhaps. She's a nice girl.

Anna Oh yes, she's nice all right. Does she still study chemistry?

Nikolai Yes.

Anna That pointy little nose: She'll make an excellent scientist. Prim, proper and less humour than a dead horse. No, really. I like her. But I'm sorry for her, too.

Nikolai Why?

Anna Because I know you. You'll get her excited, you'll fill her head with nonsense, you'll bend her backwards over the chaise longue, then suddenly you'll stop and say. 'Oh God, commitment.'

Nikolai Yes, but how do I decide what's best? It's a big decision.

Anna Well then, be sure to ask around. Whatever you do, Doctor, don't rely on your own judgement. That's the worst mistake you could make.

Nikolai makes his move.

Nikolai She may not come anyway.

Anna Why not?

Nikolai Why do you think? Because Platonov's coming. Misogyny on wheels. For some reason he's decided she's stupid. So he uses her for target practice.

Anna I haven't seen him for six months. How is he?

Nikolai The schoolroom shutters were closed when I passed. On his own clock as always.

Anna Yes, but how is he? I'm longing to hear.

Nikolai I'm sure he's fine. When is he anything but?

2 *Porfiri Glagolyev and Sergei Voynitzev arrive, Porfiri already talking.*

Porfiri Oh yes, Sergei Pavlovich, in our day we treated women as gods. We regarded them as superior beings.

Anna Hold on, how did that get there?

Nikolai You put it there yourself.

Anna You're cheating.

Nikolai I'm not cheating.

Sergei What extraordinary days they must have been!

Porfiri looks round.

Porfiri Ah yes, ladies and gentlemen, the old days: they didn't just seem better. They *were* better. Last year in Moscow I went to the opera. A young man in the audience began to cry. All around, people sniggered as though there must be something wrong. As though to have feelings were wrong! As though to be moved were wrong!

Sergei Ridiculous.

Porfiri When I was young, people were not ashamed. When you cried, you cried. When you laughed, you laughed.

Nikolai Old days, new days, dear God, who cares? Who cares?

Porfiri When you loved, you loved. When you hated, you hated.

Anna suddenly gets up.

Anna I can't go on. Really! The smell of cheap scent is unbearable.

Nikolai Cheap? Very far from cheap, let me tell you.

Anna And I'd rather listen to what my dear neighbour Porfiri Glagolyev has to say.

Nikolai When she's winning you can't get rid of her. She starts losing and suddenly it's 'Porfiri Glagolyev!' If you don't come back at once, I shall claim victory.

Anna Claim! Claim!

She has gone to sit with Porfiri.

Sergei, do your dear stepmother a favour, give that idiot three roubles.

Sergei Three?

Nikolai Isn't this the way to live? Fleecing innocent women at games?

He takes Sergei's roubles.

Anna So, Porfiri Semyonivich, it's your view, is it, that women are superior beings? No doubt that means you enjoy great success with them?

Porfiri In women, Anna Petrovna, I discern all the virtues of the world.

Anna You discern them, yes. But are they there? You want women to be special and so you convince yourself that they are. But is it true?

Porfiri Anna Petrovna, one need only look at you.

Anna smiles. Sergei is back.

Sergei He's a romantic.

Anna Plainly.

Porfiri Is that such a bad thing?

Sergei I didn't say it was.

Porfiri This is what you all want nowadays. To remove the illusion from life. To rob it of romance. Very well, take romance away, but what then do you put in its place?

Anna Knowledge.

Porfiri In fact, Platonov put this rather well. I remember he once said: 'We have advanced in our attitude to women. But even advance turns out to be a kind of retreat.'

Nikolai Yes, well, that sounds like pure, unadulterated Platonov. What was he? Drunk?

Anna What do you think, my friend? What is your view of Platonov?

Porfiri Platonov, madam? Oh fascinating, of course. He's a brilliant man. But he exemplifies the modern vagueness, the modern malaise. No point, no purpose.

Anna He's kind. He's decent. Underneath.

Porfiri Oh yes, underneath, we're all kind, we're all decent. It's the surface that worries me.

3 Bugrov arrives, sweating profusely.

Nikolai And here comes our grocer friend, puffing like a steam train!

Bugrov Such heat, my friends! It must break soon.

Nikolai Everyone, please, the view from the high street: the heat will not last for ever. One day the heat will end.

Bugrov Thank you, Nikolai.

Nikolai On the contrary, thank you, Bugrov.

4 Platonov and Sasha arrive across the fields in Russian national dress.

Platonov Civilisation! At last! We have arrived at last!

Anna You're a ruthless man, Platonov. To have made me wait so long.

Platonov It was not at my wish. Never at my wish.

He kisses her hand.

Anna And Sasha! Dearest Sasha!

Sasha A pleasure to be here, Anna Petrovna.

Anna kisses Sasha.

Anna You survived the winter?

Platonov The two of us slept through the winter like bears, huddled in our den.

Anna It sounds enchanting.

Platonov goes round shaking hands.

Platonov And up next, the dodgy doctor, scribbling prescriptions and fake cures.

Nikolai Welcome my friend! And welcome, Sasha.

Nikolai kisses the top of Sasha's head.

Sasha What on earth is that smell? Is it scent?

Platonov And your brother has an expensive haircut by the look of it. I bet that cost a rouble or two.

Nikolai I never pay. Women stand in line to cut my hair.

Platonov Greetings, Porfiri Semyonovich . . .

Sergei Good Lord, Sasha, you really have filled out. Do you two do nothing all winter but eat?

Anna Come, sit down. Tell us what's been happening.

Platonov And I can't believe it. Can this be little Sergei? Anna, your stepson is changed beyond recognition. Where's the long hair? The short trousers? Youth's piping treble.

Sergei (*laughs*) He always does this. He always does it!

Anna Everyone, please, do sit.

Platonov Sasha, do you recognise the smell?

Sasha What smell?

Platonov The matchless smell of humanity! And there – look – remember, Sasha? – the chair in which I sat last year, discussing the meaning of life, day in, day out, with the beautiful Anna Petrovna . . .

Anna Was the winter really that bad?

Platonov *Bad?*

Sasha We got by. It was boring, of course.

Platonov Boring? The word 'boring' could never begin to convey it.

Sasha It was fine.

Platonov Just to see you, Anna Petrovna, after such an eternity, after such an Antarctic of boredom, just the sight of you: yes that is compensation enough!

Anna Then have a cigarette.

Platonov *Enchanté.*

They light up.

Sasha You got here yesterday?

Anna At ten o'clock.

Platonov I saw your lights at eleven but I didn't dare call.

Anna I can't think why not. We sat up talking till two.

Sasha is whispering in Platonov's ear.

Platonov You're right, my God, I forgot, you should have reminded me earlier. And you, Sergei, you didn't say a word.

Sergei What?

Platonov Marriage!

Sergei Oh yes. You're right. I forgot. I married. What can I say?

Platonov bows.

Platonov I would never have expected it. The irrevocable act! And performed at such speed!

Sergei It's true. One day in love, next day married. Quite a shock.

Platonov Forgive me, I've known you 'in love' once or twice, but it's the marriage bit that's new. Have you found a job?

Sergei To be honest, I have been offered a teaching job, but the pay's not what I'm looking for.

Platonov Ah yes, perfect excuse. 'Pay's bad, can't do it.'

Sergei Also: I'm interested in philosophy, the life of ideas.

Platonov What, three years out of university, is it, and now – what – you'll hang around for three more?

Anna You haven't explained, Sasha, why you were so late. Why you were so long coming.

Sasha Oh . . . well, Misha was mending the birdcage and I was in church.

Porfiri Not Sunday, is it?

5 Ivan Triletsky comes out to join them.

Ivan Well, well, well . . . if it isn't my very own daughter and my son-in-law. Greetings from Planet Triletsky. Has anyone noticed how extraordinarily hot it is?

All Everyone.

Platonov Good morning, Colonel. In good spirits, I see?

Ivan Never better. Praise the Good Lord for his protection.

They embrace. Then he kisses Sasha and sits down beside her.

Sasha Father.

Ivan A thousand times I've intended to come and see you both, and play with my little grandson.

Sasha He sends his regards.

Ivan Really?

Sergei I think she means metaphorically.

Ivan Ah well then, send mine back 'metaphorically'. I live for the day when I can take my own grandson shooting.

Anna Isn't he an angel? The Colonel is taking me out to shoot quail on St Peter's Day.

Ivan I can hardly wait. Goddess of hunting, the Divine Diana!

Ivan kisses her hand.

Anna The Colonel has a new double-barrelled shotgun.

Ivan English, of course, and lethal at a hundred paces.

Ivan smells her shoulder.

Ah, smell this woman! Smell her! May the Lord forgive me for what I say now, but emancipated women are the best. Guns in their hands, and the whiff of cordite on their flesh! Give this woman a pair of epaulettes and she will subjugate the world. Boadicea! Alexandra of Macedonia!

Platonov Drinking already, Colonel?

Ivan Drinking? What else should I do?

Platonov Doing the trick, is it? Loosening your tongue?

Ivan I got here at eight this morning. I had to do something. A bottle of Madeira before breakfast. Three glasses for this luscious Amazon and the rest for me.

Anna Wonderful. Thank you. Now everyone knows!

Nikolai turns to Bugrov.

Nikolai Bugrov, perhaps you can bring some of your merchant wisdom to answer the most pressing question of the morning.

Bugrov I can try.

Nikolai When are we going to get something to eat?

Anna Oh, please. Why can't you wait like everyone else?

Nikolai For I have seen a pie – yes, my dear Bugrov, such a pie, layered with the very flora and fauna of the world –

Anna What a bore he is! How rude he is!

Sasha He doesn't want to have lunch, he just wants to make trouble.

Nikolai Everyone's starving and I'm trying to make a joke of it. I don't think, fatty, you're in any position to criticise.

Platonov If it's meant to be a joke, why is no one laughing?

There is a silence. Anna looks round.

Anna I'm going to see to it now.

6 *Anna Petrovna gets up and goes into the house. Nobody speaks.*

Platonov Though I admit I'm a little peckish myself.

Sergei I really don't understand. Where on earth has my wife got to? I'm longing for you to meet her.

Platonov Why, yes. I was wondering . . .

Sergei What?

Platonov No, just a fancy.

Sergei What?

Platonov It might be amusing, that's all, if you didn't introduce us. Because in fact – probably she hasn't mentioned it – I once knew your wife. Slightly. When I was a student. See if she remembers me.

Sergei smiles.

Sergei This man knows everyone! He knows everyone! How on earth does he find the time?

7 *Sergei goes out, laughing. Maria Grekova, the young student, arrives.*

Platonov And now, Nikolai, this looks like the object of your affections.

Nikolai Maria Yefimovna! What a pleasure! What an absolute pleasure!

Maria gives Nikolai her hand, then nods to the others. Nikolai takes off her cape.

Maria Good morning, Nikolai. Good morning, everyone.

Nikolai Here. Let me help you with that. Tell me how you are. How are you feeling today?

Maria Oh. Pretty much as usual, thank you.

She sits in an agony of embarrassment. Nikolai sits next to her.

Porfiri Good morning, Maria.

Ivan My goodness, so this is Maria Grekova. Forgive me, I scarcely recognised you.

Maria moves her hand away.

Maria If you don't mind, I prefer my hand not to be kissed. I can't explain, but there's something about it I find creepy.

Platonov has got up to greet Maria.

Platonov Greetings, Maria Grekova, let me kiss your hand.

Maria snatches her hand violently away.

Maria What are you doing? Why don't you listen?

Platonov My mistake. You obviously consider me unworthy.

Maria I don't *consider* you anything. You know as well I do, you just do whatever you think will most annoy me.

Platonov Do I? Really? Why do you say that?

Nikolai Platonov, please leave her alone.

Platonov In a moment, I will. But first, about the bedbugs . . .

Maria If you start, if you start this again . . .

Platonov Isn't that what you're up to? Your latest scientific experiment. In the bedbug field, aren't you? Adding to the sum of human knowledge by distilling the essence of bedbug.

Maria Why do you do this? Why do you always do this?

Platonov My own area of research is the diagnostic hunt for a sense of humour. I look for it everywhere. I go to the ends of the earth, but in some people, no, I just can't find it.

She turns to Nikolai.

Maria You promised! You promised he wouldn't be here.

Platonov That was wrong of you, Nikolai. You lied.

Maria has begun to cry.

8 *Maria runs up the lawn. Anna Petrovna is arriving with Yakov and Vasili who prepare the lunch table. Anna shakes Maria's hand.*

Anna Ah, welcome, how wonderful to see you Maria Yefimovna. This is such a pleasure. What on earth's the matter?

Maria is crying into her handkerchief.

Nikolai I have to warn you. Do this once more and our friendship is finished.

Anna What happened? What's going on?

Platonov My friend Nikolai is in love. He plans to upturn the bedbug on her back.

Porfiri You must apologise, Platonov.

Platonov Apologise for what?

Porfiri You know full well.

Sasha Say you're sorry or I shall leave at once.

Porfiri Apologise, damn you.

Sasha I don't understand. Why do you do this? What do you do it for?

Platonov walks across to Maria.

Platonov Maria.

Maria Yes?

Platonov I am all contrition. No man on earth more abject than I. Lift your foot. Give me the dirt from beneath your sole. And I will eat.

Platonov takes her hand and kisses it.

Friends?

Maria Yes. Friends.

9 Maria buries her face in her handkerchief and then runs back into the house. Nikolai follows her.

Anna I must say, Mikhail . . .

Porfiri Sometimes you go too far.

Platonov You think so?

Porfiri Dammit, you go too far.

Anna It was wrong of you, Mikhail.

Platonov And haven't I said I was sorry?

10 *Sergei reappears with Sofya Yegorovna.*

Sergei And now, ladies and gentlemen, in person, the woman you've been waiting for. No less, no other than –

Anna Ah, at last, Sofya, please, sit down over here.

Sofya What a ravishing garden!

She sits down just a yard away from Platonov.

Porfiri Sergei . . .

Sergei Yes?

Porfiri Your beautiful wife has promised me that you will all come over to my place on Thursday.

Sergei If that's what she said, then that's what we'll do.

Nikolai comes back out.

Nikolai 'Oh women, women!' said Shakespeare. But wouldn't 'Oh God, women!' sum things up better?

Anna Where's Maria?

Nikolai In a darkened room.

Porfiri If you think this garden is ravishing, Sofya, you should see mine. It's superior in every way. My river is deeper, and I also have exceptional horses.

Anna We'll need to know how to get there.

Porfiri Oh . . .

Anna Through Yusnovka?

Porfiri No, that's miles out of the way. You go through Platonovka.

Sofya Platonovka?

Porfiri Yes.

Sofya It still exists?

Porfiri Yes. Why should it not?

Sofya I once knew its owner.

Porfiri Did you? Did you really?

Sofya Where is he now? Do you know what happened to him?

Sergei Give us a clue. Tell us his first name, and then we might be able to help.

Everyone laughs.

Sofya You're all laughing, but I've said nothing funny.

Anna Oh for goodness' sake, do finally recognise him, or he's going to burst.

Platonov stands. Sofya stands to look at him. A silence. Sofya reaches out her hand.

Sofya You've changed.

Platonov Yes, almost five years have gone by. Look at me! I know! As if my face had been eaten away by rats!

Sergei leads Sasha over to meet Sofya.

Sergei And this is Mikhail's wife, Sasha, sister to that well-known wit and gourmet Nikolai Ivanych.

Sofya shakes hands with Sasha, then sits.

Sofya I'm delighted to meet you. So you're married too? How much can happen in five years!

Anna Typical Platonov. He goes nowhere, yet he knows everyone.

Platonov How have you been?

Sofya I?

Platonov Yes.

Sofya My health?

Platonov Yes.

Sofya Not good. Everything else fine. You?

Platonov Oh. Well, as you see, a victim of fate.

Sofya In what way?

Platonov You always said you thought I was going to be Byron, if I remember. And I thought I was going run the country with my left hand. What happened? I'm a schoolmaster.

Sofya I don't believe you.

Platonov It's so.

Sofya But why?

Platonov If there were a simple answer.

Sofya You got your degree?

Platonov No. No. I quit without.

Sofya But you're still . . .

Platonov What?

Sofya You're still . . . part of the struggle?

Platonov Well, loosely.

Sofya I expressed myself badly. You still work . . . you work on behalf of other people. For their betterment, I mean. For progress. For emancipation. For women's liberation, for instance. Nothing stops you, I hope, pursuing ideas.

Platonov No. Nothing stops me. You're right. Nothing stops me. But nothing moves me either.

11 Pavel Shcherbuk arrives, riding whip in hand.

Shcherbuk Don't give oats to my horses, they don't deserve them.

Anna Ah, at last! My white knight has arrived.

All (*greeting him*) Pavel Shcherbuk.

Anna He even punishes his horses.

Shcherbuk kisses Anna and Sasha's hands, then Anna leads him to Sofya.

Shcherbuk Why not indeed? Punishment and reward, I believe in it. How else does a horse improve? How else does a horse know to do better? Horses need lessons like everyone else.

Anna takes him by the arm and leads him to Sofya.

Anna Pavel Petrovich Shcherbuk. Distinguished cornet of guards. Ex.

Shcherbuk Madam, once more I am the lonely Darwinist in a house full of liberals. Natural selection! The survival of the fittest! That's my creed.

Anna I'll start again. Shcherbuk: our friend, our neighbour and, most of all, our creditor.

Shcherbuk Thank you. More to the point, companion-in-chief and fellow adventurer with this dear lady's late husband, the General. Many hours spent happily with that incomparable gentleman in the conquest and subjugation of women.

He bows.

If you would. Your hand.

Sofya holds out her hand. Shcherbuk kisses it silently. He indicates Platonov.

27

And look at this lad. Whom I also knew in his green youth. Look at him now! What would you call him? Handsome? Full-grown? Why aren't you in the army?

Platonov Thank you. I have a weak chest.

Shcherbuk Says who? My God, I hope you haven't been consulting that appalling quack.

Nikolai Pavel, you are not to start. I forbid you to start.

Shcherbuk This man calls himself a doctor. I went in with a bad back, I came out with a bad back. I said to him, 'Why is yours the only profession in which there is no such thing as payment by results?'

Nikolai Platonov, you're closest. Hit him.

Sasha Father, you mustn't fall asleep. It's rude.

Ivan wakes briefly, shaken by Sasha, but then falls asleep again.

Shcherbuk Time was, I was a friend of your father's.

Platonov My father never lacked for friends. Friends and more friends. Leeching off him. The house full of them all day. Carriages parked in the drive. Carriage after carriage. Loaded with friends.

Porfiri Did you have no respect for them?

Platonov How can one believe in men whose great boast in life is that they do neither good nor bad, that they *are* neither good nor bad? But always lukewarm.

12 *Osip appears.*

Osip My privilege, Your Excellency, to congratulate you on your safe arrival. I wish you everything that you would wish from God.

Everyone laughs.

Platonov Here he is, back among us. Welcome, indeed!

Osip Thank you.

Platonov The fiend in human form. The walking dead.

Anna Now I think we may say the party is complete.

Osip I came only to pay my respects.

Anna Pay them by all means. And then leave.

Platonov This is rare. Someone must have wrenched open the graves. Normally you never see 666 out by day.

Osip (*bows*) I bid Your Excellency welcome. And also I congratulate you, Sergei Pavlych. May your wedding bring you happiness.

Sergei Thank you.

He turns to Sofya.

The family scarecrow.

Anna (*to Osip*) Tell them in the kitchen to give you a slice of pie. My God, look at his eyes, they're glowing. Tell me, just how much of our forest did you steal this winter?

Osip A few trees only. Three, maybe four.

Everyone laughs.

Anna Three! Maybe thirty, more like. How could you afford that watch? Gold? A gold watch, is it?

Osip It's gold.

Anna Did I pay for it? Was it paid for in timber?

Osip May I kiss your hand?

Anna Kiss.

Osip kisses her hand. Platonov then turns him round to display him.

Platonov Ladies and gentlemen, my pleasure to welcome one of the most interesting carnivores in the contemporary zoo. Osip. Horse thief. Parasite. Contract killer. Conceived in violence, and no doubt destined to end the same way. My God, look at that face. A ton of iron went into the construction of that face. When you look in the mirror, tell me what you see.

Osip A man. Like any other. No better. Perhaps a little worse.

Platonov Osip, the true spirit of Russia: the headless peasant, the fabulous warlord, up to his elbows in blood. And making the rest of us – the talkers, the non-doers – look pretty silly.

Osip Well, that's your view, not mine.

Platonov By the way, just asking, but why aren't you in prison at the moment? You usually are.

Osip Only in the winter.

Platonov Ah yes, of course, it's cold in the forest. That's when you fancy a nice snug jail.

Osip I'll tell you. Everyone knows I'm a thief, but they can't prove it. That's the problem with the ordinary Russian peasant. So cowardly, so stupid, that he can't be bothered, he doesn't have the *will* – the simple willpower – to gather the case against me. What does that tell you about the Russian peasant? He has no one to blame but himself.

Platonov Russia, you see? Even the thieves have theories. Doesn't that sum us all up? Thank you for that load of equivocating crap.

Anna Please!

Osip You think I'm the only one?

Platonov No.

Osip You think I'm the only thief here?

Platonov Not at all.

Osip If we're talking about thieves: Pavel Shcherbuk.

Platonov Ah well . . .

Shcherbuk Leave me out of it.

Osip Why? You're no different from me.

Platonov On the contrary. He's quite a lot different. He holds parties. People go to them. He gives money to charity. He buys up everything he can lay his hands on. He doesn't want one shop, he wants fifty shops. He wants a chain of shops. And a chain of bars. And a chain of hotels. His tentacles reaching out across the country. And for that people respect him. Shcherbuk has grasped the governing principle of Russian life. Crooks die in the forest but they prosper in the drawing room!

Anna Please, Platonov, you must stop!

Platonov Make enough money and no one will say a word against you.

Anna Stop! It's enough.

Sergei Calm down, Mikhail. (*To Osip.*) Osip, out! You bring out the worst in him.

Osip I bring out the truth in him.

13 Osip goes out.

Shcherbuk Please. If I'm to be lectured, it won't be by you. I'm a citizen. A father. Making a useful contribution. And what are you? A scoundrel, a wastrel. Born to wealth and threw it away.

Platonov If you're what's called a citizen, that makes 'citizen' a pretty dirty word.

Anna Please, I've already told you. Are you determined to spoil our whole day?

Sergei She's right. Anna is right.

Shcherbuk Morning till night, he pursues me. What have I done to him? The man's a phoney.

Sergei Please!

There's a silence. Platonov speaks quietly.

Platonov Nobody looks. Nobody thinks. Nobody sees. We go through life and we don't see. The honest man and the honest woman hold their tongue and say nothing. Why? Because we owe him money. Everyone owes him money. Decency flies out the window.

Anna This is last year's business. Let's not go over it again.

Platonov Fine.

Shcherbuk Fine.

Yakov appears and hands Anna a card.

Anna What's all this about? *Count* Glagolyev? Why all the ceremony? Of course, let him in.

Yakov goes. Anna turns to Porfiri.

Porfiri Semenych, your son is here.

Porfiri My son? He can't be.

Anna I thought he'd left us for ever. That's what he told us. He was leaving Russia for ever.

Porfiri He's abroad. Surely he's abroad?

14 Kiril Glagolyev comes in. A few moments later, Yakov appears.

Anna My dear Kiril, we're delighted to see you.

Kiril *Mesdames, messieurs, un honneur de vous revoir.* I cannot tell you how uncomfortably hot it is in Russia after Paris. *Et je dois dire,* what an extraordinary city Paris is.

Sergei Please. Why doesn't our Frenchman sit down?

Kiril I've just dropped by, that's all, for a quick word with my father. Which I'm afraid to say isn't going to be entirely pleasant.

He turns to Porfiri.

Porfiri Kiril. What's this?

Kiril You know what it is. You know full well.

Anna Why don't you just sit down and tell us about Paris?

Kiril I can tell you three things about Paris. It is a great city. It is a modern city. A sparkling city which makes Russia seem like the medieval backwater it is. But one further thing: it is a city in which it is impossible to survive without money.

There is a response from everyone to this.

Anna Oh I see . . .

Porfiri Now I see . . .

Anna Here we go . . .

Yakov Lunch is served, madam.

Kiril turns appealing to the whole group.

Kiril Six thousand! Six thousand he sends me! You really think a man of my standing can survive in Paris on six thousand a month?

Porfiri Of course. Why not? It seemed quite adequate.

Kiril Do you have no idea, do you have any idea, you pitiful idiot, of how much you need to be a gentleman in Paris?

Nikolai I think you should calm down, Kiril, or else we'll call the police and get you charged with impersonating a count.

But Kiril stands, shouting at his father.

Kiril Give me my money! Give me my money!

Anna Everyone, luncheon is ready. Come now, Monsieur le Français, let me take you to lunch and you can tell us about Paris.

Nikolai Lunch at last, my God.

Bugrov You could actually starve to death waiting for lunch in this house.

Nikolai To lunch! Food! Food, everyone. At last we eat.

Anna leads Kiril out. Everyone goes.
Platonov offers Sofya his arm.

Platonov Yes. It's as bad as you think it is. A world made up only of the utterly third-rate. That's who we are. That's what we are. What beautiful eyes you have.

He smiles at her as they go to lunch.

Shcherbuk I told you.

Porfiri And you were right.

Shcherbuk A phoney, through and through. A thorough-going phoney. Someone needs to deal with him.

Sergei is waking Ivan Triletsky.

Sergei Ivan Ivanych, it's lunch.

Ivan (*jumps up*) What? What's happening?

Sergei Lunch. That's all. That's all that's happening.

Ivan Lunch. Splendid.

15 *Ivan and Sergei go, so only Shcherbuk and Porfiri are left on the lawn.*

Shcherbuk I have a question. Is it really going to happen?

Porfiri If I knew what you're talking about, then maybe I could tell you.

Shcherbuk You're going to marry her?

Porfiri I haven't asked her.

Shcherbuk But you think there's a chance?

Porfiri How can I say? Nobody can know the soul of another.

He goes. Shcherbuk alone.

Shcherbuk He doesn't seem to realise. A marriage isn't just between two people. The woman owes me, for God's sake. She owes me money. If she marries Porfiri, then I get to be repaid.

16 Anna Petrovna leaves the table to call Shcherbuk to lunch.

Anna Shcherbuk, you're joining us?

Shcherbuk In a moment. First, I wonder, could I make a small suggestion?

Anna As long as it's quick.

Shcherbuk I was hoping you might make progress towards repaying your debt.

Anna That's not exactly a 'suggestion'. How much do you need? A rouble? Two?

Shcherbuk Anna, I can paper the walls with your IOUs.

Anna Is this still the sixty thousand? Why do you go on like this? What on earth do you need the money for?

Shcherbuk What do I need it *for*? I need it because it's mine, that's why I need it.

Anna You only have our IOUs because you wangled them out of the General when he was dying.

Shcherbuk Who was the General's best friend? Who closed his eyes when he was dying?

Anna Dying and drunk, I may say.

Shcherbuk Please tell me: what's the point of an IOU if you never pay up?

Anna Let me just explain to you, I know you find this difficult to grasp, that's what an IOU is. It means I owe you money. That's what it means! Sue if you like, it doesn't bother me at all.

Shcherbuk Another question.

Anna What this time?

Shcherbuk I need you to tell me: do you have feelings for Porfiri Glagolyev?

Anna Why do you ask? Oh I see. Money again. You want me to marry him, do you? What, just so your pockets can once more be stuffed to overflowing?

Shcherbuk looks at her a moment.

Shcherbuk You should be careful, Anna. You're proud and arrogant. Pride is a sin.

17 Shcherbuk goes to table. Anna stands for a moment. Then Platonov joins her.

Anna Oh it's you.

Platonov Let me kiss your hand.

He kneels and kisses her hand.

Throw them out. Cast them all out.

Anna If I could.

She shakes her head.

The text for today is decency. The sermon will be given by Mikhail Platonov.

Platonov Forgive me. I got carried away.

Anna What does it mean to say we want to be decent? How can we be decent when we're in debt? One word against these people and they can cut me off and leave me for dead. And they would do it too. I owe them all money, every one of them. Oh yes, decency's a fine thing. But if I have to choose between decency and losing the estate –

Nikolai calls from the table.

37

Nikolai You two, why don't you come and eat?

Anna You and I, we'll go riding this afternoon. Don't you dare go away.

She puts her hand on his shoulder.

Why don't we live? Why don't we live just a little?

She goes out. Platonov looks across to the table.

Platonov Just as I thought. She's wondering where I am. Looking round with those beautiful velvet eyes. Just the sight of her. Among these terrible people. How lovely she is. And how unchanged!

18 Sergei comes across, wiping his mouth with a napkin.

Sergei Come on, where have you got to, Platonov? Come and drink Sofya's health.

Platonov I've been looking at your wife, Sergei. You're a fortunate man.

Sergei Well, not until now. But in this one thing.

Platonov My only regret is that you never knew her before.

Sergei Why does that make you sad?

Platonov Why? She's beautiful now. But once she was even more beautiful.

Sergei More?

Platonov Yes.

Sergei I don't believe you.

Platonov It's true. Her eyes.

Sergei Her hair.

Platonov Yes. And what about my own wife? There she is, sweating and flustered, hidden behind the vodka bottle. Her blunt, peasant features blushing red. In agony, as always, over my behaviour.

Sergei Forgive me, but, tell me, are you happy with your wife?

Platonov She's my wife. That's all you need to know. Without her, I'm lost. One day you'll understand family. How important family is. I wouldn't sell Sasha for a million roubles. Think about it: she's stupid and I'm worthless. Put it another way, we're perfectly matched.

Nikolai comes back, slapping his stomach with satisfaction, carrying a bottle.

Nikolai Come on, a little drink, everyone, to celebrate the homecoming.

Platonov One thing I meant to ask . . .

Sergei Yes?

Platonov That advertisement today in the paper.

Sergei Oh yes.

Platonov An auction? Are things really that bad?

Sergei I don't think they're bad. As I understand it's not a proper auction, it's more some sort of commercial fiddle. Porfiri will buy the estate and that way the bank will leave us alone. And we'll pay him interest. Or something. It's sort of technical, I think.

Platonov Whose idea is it?

Sergei Oh. Porfiri's. Wasn't it?

Platonov But ask yourself: why's he doing it? What's in it for him?

Sergei I can see what's in it for us. We keep the estate and we pay Porfiri money. The advantage being we're shot of that blasted bank.

He takes Platonov by the arm.

No more business, come on, let's all drink and be friends.

He takes Nikolai by the other arm.

What do we say? I'll tell you what we say. We say, 'Let the world go to hell.' Does money matter? No. People matter. As long as we're alive and Sofya's alive and Anna Petrovna's alive, that's what matters.

Anna Oh, just look at them! The team of three.
    (*Sings.*) 'Find me a harness for my three fine horses . . .'

Nikolai (*sings*)
    'My horses gallop in a team of three . . .'

The men raise their glasses and sing.

Men
    'Find me a harness for my three fine horses
    My horses gallop in a team of three
    Speed my horses through the darkening forest
    Ride through the night and return to me

    'Nothing in my heart I have not shown you
    Nothing in my soul you cannot see
    Fly the course, advance, surrender
    Ride through the night and return to me

    'Shallow is the grave I'll one day sleep in
    Certain is the death I know must be
    Drive my horses to embrace our ending
    Ride through the night and return to me.'

Act Two

Evening. A few days later. From the house can be heard laughter and music from violin and piano. A waltz, a quadrille. The sound of skittles – balls rolling and cries of 'Four!' and 'Five!' Yakov, Vasili and other servants, all in black frock coats, all drunk, are lighting lanterns as guests move through the garden.

1 Nikolai, in a peaked cap with a cockade has his arm round Bugrov.

Nikolai Be fair, be fair to me, Timofei. I'm only asking for a loan.

Bugrov I don't have it. You know I don't have it.

Nikolai You do. I know you do, Timofei Gordeich. It's only a loan. You needn't worry. There's no danger you'll ever get it back.

Bugrov Just remind me, what branch of medicine was it you specialised in?

Nikolai The same as most doctors.

Bugrov That's what I thought.

Nikolai Presenting the bill.

Bugrov gets out his wallet.

Bugrov You do love a joke, don't you?

Nikolai Well, I do.

Bugrov Especially at a working man's expense.

He starts counting out notes. Nikolai looks enviously at his wad.

One, six, twelve . . .

Nikolai My God, and they say Russia's bankrupt!

Bugrov hands Nikolai the notes.

What about that one, look, with its little eyes staring up at me?

Bugrov (*handing it over*) All right, that one as well.

Nikolai Thank you, Timofei Gordeich! May you live many years and die even fatter than you are. No, really, I've been meaning to mention. You sweat all the time, you drink, your veins are standing out like hosepipes. You do seem to be on the way to an early grave.

Bugrov Thank you.

Nikolai That's just my opinion. You can always get a second. Though I have to say, by and large, doctors all take the same view of bad-tempered, bilious little grocers with high blood pressure. You're one of the few things we agree upon.

He puts his arm round Bugrov.

Just joking. No offence. You won't die tomorrow. Isn't it always the crooks who live longest?

Bugrov That isn't funny.

Nikolai What's this I've heard? That you're buying up Sergei's IOUs?

Bugrov Where did you hear that?

Nikolai What's the idea? That Anna Petrovna is going to take pity on him and give her stepson the family mines? And, that way, you'll get your hands on them?

Bugrov I think you're out of your depth, Nikolai.

Nikolai looks at him a moment.

Nikolai You're a great man, aren't you? But you're also a crook.

There's a silence.

Bugrov I'm going to take a nap. Wake me for supper.

2 *Bugrov walks off to the summer house. Nikolai smells his money.*

Nikolai Smells of peasant. The rich smell of peasant. How many people did he swindle to amass that much? What shall I do with it?

He sees Yakov and Vasili in frock coats.

Over here, lads. Yes, you. The undertaker's assistants.

He gives them a rouble each.

One for you. And one for you.

Yakov / Vasili Thank you, sir.

They bow.

Nikolai You're both absolutely legless, aren't you? There you are. And don't spend it all at once. And don't spend it on drink. Or women. And bow.

They bow.

And out.

They go. Sergei is passing.

Do you want three roubles?

Sergei takes it, pockets it and goes out without speaking.

You might at least say thank you.

3 Sasha comes in with Ivan.

Sasha Oh God, is there no end to this? My father drunk. My husband drunk. My brother drunk.

Ivan What are you saying?

Sasha Do you have no shame? If you're not frightened of what people think, aren't you at least frightened of God?

Ivan God? Yes. I'm frightened of God.

Sasha At your age. When a man is meant to set an example.

Ivan I wanted to be a general.

Sasha I know.

Ivan I deserved to be a general.

Sasha I know. Generals don't drink.

Ivan Generals drink. Like everyone else. They drink when they're happy. You, Sasha, you've turned into your mother. The same walk. The goose, bottom-loaded. No, really. You know I love you. I loved her too.

Ivan kisses Sasha.

I miss her.

Sasha I know. I know you do.

Nikolai Have a rouble.

Ivan Well, I will, thank you, son. I wouldn't take it from anyone but you.

Nikolai Sasha?

Sasha Five, please. Mikhail only has one pair of trousers. He has to sit naked while I do the wash.

Nikolai gives Sasha five roubles.

Nikolai Where are you going?

Ivan I'm taking her home. Waddle, waddle. Then I'm coming back to enjoy myself.

He looks at Nikolai a moment.

Am I frightened of God? That's what she asked. How can you live my life and not be frightened? I've lived only for possessions. I've put money before everything else.

Nikolai Well, then, it seems rather sad you've ended up with so little.

Ivan It is. It is sad. I'm one of the men Christ threw out of the temple.

He stands a moment, drunk.

Has anyone seen Sasha?

Nikolai She's over there.

Sasha Give him his hat, Nikolai.

Nikolai takes the cap off and puts it on his father.

Nikolai There you are, old soldier. Left turn and go on your way.

Ivan Left turn it is. Run it up the pole and salute. Come on, Sasha. I'm going to carry you home.

Sasha Don't be ridiculous.

Ivan I used to carry your mother.

Sasha Put your cap on straight.

Sasha adjusts Ivan's headdress.

Ivan Yes?

Sasha Yes.

Ivan Can I not carry you? Sasha, please let me carry you.

Sasha Father. You're not young any more.

4 *Sasha puts her arm round Ivan and goes out. Shcherbuk and Bugrov come from the house, arm in arm. Anna appears in the distance, watching events.*

Shcherbuk Put fifty thousand in front of me, and of course I'd take it. Of course I'll take it!

Bugrov Would you? I wouldn't.

Shcherbuk As long as I knew I wouldn't be caught. You're honestly going to tell me you'd walk past fifty thousand roubles?

Bugrov I'd walk past it. I'm an honest man.

Nikolai I'm giving out roubles. Do you want one?

Shcherbuk I'll have one if it's going.

He gives one to Shcherbuk.

Nikolai Bugrov?

Bugrov Well . . . if you insist. Just the one.

Shcherbuk The honest man!

Anna calls from far away.

Anna What about me? Don't I get a rouble?

Nikolai No. You don't get a rouble. You get five!

He heads her way. Anna disappears.

Shcherbuk Has she gone?

Bugrov nods.

If there's one thing I hate it's a liberated woman. Have you been watching Porfiri? Sitting there, staring at her, doggy-eyed.

Bugrov He'll get her.

Shcherbuk You think?

Bugrov Not that I envy him any more than you do. All that education, all that spirit . . . What a nightmare!

Shcherbuk I know.

Bugrov Try living with that!

Shcherbuk Don't.

Bugrov puts his arm round Shcherbuk.

Bugrov Come on, let's go see the servants.

Shcherbuk Oh God, yes. Anything rather than this lot . . .

Bugrov Is there a man alive who, in his heart, doesn't prefer doing it with servants?

They both sing as they go.

Shcherbuk / Bugrov
'When servants serve, they serve with willing,
When servants serve, they serve all night . . .'

5 Shcherbuk and Bugrov go. Sergei and Sofya reappear.

Sergei Tell me. Tell me what you're thinking.

Sofya I don't know. I don't even know what I'm thinking.

She sits.

Sergei I don't understand. All I want is to be a good husband.

Sofya You promised me. You promised me you wouldn't ask questions.

Sergei I'm not asking questions.

Sofya Oh Sergei, can't we just go? Can't we get up tomorrow and go? Can't we live abroad?

Sergei We'll go tomorrow.

He kisses her on the cheek.

I hate this place as much as you do. Do you think it doesn't get to me too? Germany, England – they're small countries, the people live close to each other, so ideas spread quickly. Belgium. But here, the mud is so thick, in spring, in autumn, you can't even get to the next village. Ideas get bogged down. But to be fair, there are good people. You never speak to Platonov. I've noticed you go out of your way to avoid him. Why? This place lacks culture, you say. He has culture. Oh it's so easy to look down on people, isn't it? But don't you think we have to give them a chance?

Anna reappears in the distance.

Anna Has anyone seen Sergei?

Sergei I'm here.

Anna Sergei, I need you a moment.

Sergei looks at Sofya a moment.

Sergei My darling, we'll leave tomorrow if it's what you want.

He goes into the house. Sofya alone.

Sofya I see his lips moving. My husband's lips move, but they make no sound. For days on end I never think of him. I married . . . I married only a few months ago.

Platonov shows me no mercy. Everywhere I go he pursues me. And I know . . . just the sight of him, the smell of him. I know: just one step and I'm lost.

6 *Platonov appears from the house. He's a little drunk.*

Platonov Alone?

Sofya Yes.

Platonov Avoiding the herd?

Sofya What makes you say that?

Platonov smiles.

How dare you? How dare you say that?

Platonov What?

Sofya 'Avoiding the herd'.

Platonov Oh.

Platonov sits next to her.

When we first met, you seemed pleased to see me. Now when I speak to you – that's when I can find you, that's when you're not running from one room to another – the incredible vanishing woman – when you do stay long enough for me to speak in your presence, then all you do is look to the floor and honour me with one croaky 'Yes'. Do you mean it as a joke?

Sofya No.

Platonov What then?

Sofya looks at him a moment.

Sofya Yes, I admit, I avoid you.

Platonov Ah.

Sofya Here, in this region, people respect you. People speak well of you. They consider it a privilege to listen to you talk.

Platonov I think that may be putting things a bit high.

Sofya And yes, when I arrived, I was happy to join the circle, the adoring circle.

Platonov And now?

Sofya No.

Platonov What changed?

Sofya I came to find you unbearable.

Platonov Unbearable?

Sofya I can think of no other word. You speak all the time of the past as if some obligation were upon us. Tell me, what obligation exists? The girl loved the student, the student loved the girl. So? Isn't it the oldest story in the world? And isn't the history of the world that people move on? What right do you have to come near me – these sudden bursts of shouting, you clutch my hand, you follow me about, you stare at me – as if the past licensed you. But the past is gone. And to what end? What is the point of this pursuit? Where would you wish it to lead? It's as if you are waiting.

There is a silence.

Platonov Finished?

He gets up and makes to leave.

Sofya What? What are you doing?

Platonov I'm going.

Sofya Don't go.

Platonov Don't? You want the unbearable to stay?

Sofya looks at him resentfully.

I see clearly now. It's me that got it wrong, not you.

Sofya In what way?

Platonov I didn't notice you were a coward.

Sofya does not reply.

So it turns out that every man you meet who is in the least bit out of the ordinary, who shows any sign of life or of vigour, represents a threat?

Sofya No.

Platonov Yes.

Sofya How dare you call me a coward?

Platonov Where is your steadfastness, Sofya? Where are your roots? Yes, I spoke to you when we first met, I approached you because I imagined you a rational woman.

Sofya You have no right. You have no right to talk to me like this.

Platonov It's a problem, is it? Persecuted, are you? So much in demand? What, men no sooner look at you, is that right, than they want to take you away from your husband? My God, the insufferable burden of being so vain as always to imagine that everyone desires you.

Sofya 'Imagine'?

Platonov Platonov loves you, does he? The crazy Mikhail Platonov is in love with you, is he? How sweet that must be.

He turns and goes.

Sofya Where are you going? Where are you going?

She has shouted after him but he has gone.

How dare you? How dare you speak to me like this?

She stands a moment, shocked.

We need to talk more.

7 *Sofya goes into the house. Osip starts taking down lanterns and putting them in his pocket.*

Osip Garden parties. Who do they think they're fooling? As if holding garden parties made you respectable.

Vasili has appeared and is watching Osip.

Vasili Hey, what's going on? Those lanterns aren't there for your benefit, you know.

Osip Aren't they?

He grabs Vasili's hat from his head.

You think it's a good idea? Taking me on? You think that's sensible, do you? Murder me, why don't you? Spit in my face.

He throws the hat high into the tree.

Then down. Down on your knees. Where you belong, on your knees, old man.

Vasili kneels.

Vasili This isn't right. It isn't right, what you're doing.

Osip And if anyone saw us: a gentleman in a frock coat, kneeling before a thief. This is the future. This is how things will be.

8 Shcherbuk comes from the house. Osip at once takes off his cap. Vasili goes to a bench at the side where he begins to weep.

Shcherbuk Come over here. Stand some paces off. I don't want to be seen with you.

They go to a darker corner of the garden.

The schoolteacher. Platonov.

Osip Yes?

Shcherbuk I don't want him killed. Maim him. Can you do that? He's a good-looking man. Cripple, but not kill.

Osip We can do that.

Shcherbuk How much will that cost? Hold on, there's someone coming.

9 They go off to a dark place at the back, as Platonov arrives, laughing with Maria.

Platonov What did you say? I can't believe it. I didn't quite catch what you said.

Maria Didn't you?

Platonov Why don't you say it again?

Maria All I said was – and it's not likely you'll take offence, because after all, you say much worse things, you say much harsher things –

Platonov Do I? Do I, my beauty?

Maria Please. You mustn't.

Platonov I mustn't what?

Maria You mustn't call me a beauty. I know I'm unattractive. I know it. Aren't I?

Platonov I'll tell you in a minute. You go first.

Maria Well what I said was: it seems to me possible either you're a scoundrel, or else you're a sort of genius, one or the other.

Platonov laughs loudly.

Platonov So that is what you said. I thought so. Oh my poor stupid girl . . .

Maria Hold on . . .

Platonov You're just like all the others.

Maria has sat down. Platonov kisses her.

Maria Wait. No. Just a minute. What is this?

She gets up. Then she sits down again.

Why did you kiss me?

Platonov 'Genius!' she says! 'I'll say something shocking,' she thinks. 'Something to provoke him.'

Maria I didn't think that.

Platonov You think I'm a *genius*? Are you out of your head?

He kisses her again.

Maria What does this mean? Are you in love with me?

Platonov (*mimicking*) 'Are you in *love* with me?' she asks.

Maria You do love me, don't you? Or you wouldn't have kissed me.

She begins to cry.

Oh my God, you're in love with me. Aren't you?

Platonov Am I? No. Truthfully? No. I can't love stupid women, it's a failing of mine. Oh, and now, look, she's gone pale. Oh my goodness, look at her. She's flashing her eyes. Right! Change of tactic, change of direction! Hold on, she's getting up . . .

Maria Is this your idea of fun? Is this your idea of being funny?

Platonov (*putting his hand up*) Watch out. Slap coming.

10 Maria moves off, as Nikolai comes back, now wearing a top hat, and looking up to the sky.

Nikolai The cranes are flying! I never saw the cranes flying this early.

Maria Nikolai Ivanych, I demand: if you have any respect in the world, either for me, or for yourself, then cut yourself off from this man.

Nikolai From Platonov?

Maria Yes.

Nikolai Don't be ridiculous. He's a friend of mine. He's also my revered brother-in-law.

Maria It's jokes, isn't it? It's nothing but jokes all day.

Nikolai Well, one does one's best.

Maria Does it never occur to you that there are times when the jokes have to stop?

Nikolai I can't say that has ever occurred to me, no.

Maria When I've been assaulted!

She has shouted at the top of her voice.

Maria When all this man wants is to make women cry! Mission accomplished! She's crying again! You all think

55

he's deep – a tortured soul! Our own local Hamlet! – when he's just a cheap provincial bully. Cruelty is cruelty. Well, if you can live with that, Nikolai, you're welcome to it. At least we'll know where we stand.

11 *Maria goes. Nikolai stands a moment.*

Nikolai Did you get all that?

Platonov The drift. I got the drift.

Nikolai I must say. Even I can see there is something confusing.

Platonov How?

Nikolai In you. Half of me respects you, thinks you the most intelligent man I've ever met. The other half wonders why you waste your time persecuting young women.

Platonov She's so stupid! She's so incredibly stupid! I don't understand how on earth you can put up with her.

Nikolai Mikhail, a revolutionary notion, take it on board: it's actually none of your business.

Platonov Isn't it? Why not?

Nikolai And what's more – in theory I'm in love with her.

Platonov In theory?

Nikolai I am! I am in love with her!

He gets up.

And somebody tell me what's happened to Anna Petrovna? What's going on?

Platonov Is anything going on?

Nikolai There are times, I can see, when there's this

generalised malice in you, it's secreted by your glands, it oozes out of you. Finally, though, it's undignified.

Platonov Why? Tell me, why is it undignified?

Nikolai Because a man like you should fight in his own class.

Platonov We're all so much less than we ought to be.

There is a silence. Osip makes to go.

Osip And if you try and swindle me, I'll come after you, I warn you.

Shcherbuk Be quiet. Get on with the job.

Shcherbuk and Osip go. Nikolai gets up.

Nikolai And somebody tell me what's happened to Anna Petrovna? What's going on?

Platonov Is anything going on?

Nikolai You must have noticed. Sighs, tears, groans, hysterical bursts of laughter . . .

Platonov Oh . . .

Nikolai Is she in love?

Platonov It doesn't seem likely. Who is there to love round here? More like she wants to shoot herself.

Nikolai Now it's your turn to be ridiculous. You know full well. Women don't shoot themselves. They take poison. Everyone knows that.

Platonov smiles.

Oh look who it is. The counterfeit count.

He has bumped into Kiril Glagolyev and he now puts money in his hand.

Nikolai Here's three roubles, my man. Good luck to you.

12 Nikolai goes out. Kiril frowns and shouts at the departing Nikolai.

Kiril I've got money! What are you saying? You think I'm broke?

He shakes his head.

One of the strangest people I've ever met. And one of the stupidest. Of course in Paris you never meet people like him.

Platonov Ah yes, Paris.

Kiril Have you been?

He sits down next to Platonov.

Shame. Well, if you come, just look me up. The whole culture is different. One way of putting it: the whole place is less like a pit bog. And the women look less like pugs.

Platonov frowns.

Platonov Tell me, is it true, this rumour that your father wants to buy more property?

Kiril The only thing I have heard about my father is that he seems set on courting Anna Petrovna. She's intriguing, I admit. I look at her and I find myself thinking: is it natural, or what?

Platonov Is what natural?

Kiril Well, obviously, is that her natural . . . whatever? Or is it corsetry? It's impressive, whichever it is. You'd be able to tell me.

Platonov Would I?

Kiril From what I've heard. That's what everyone says.

There is a silence, Platonov quiet now.

Platonov Count, you insult me.

Kiril All right, there's no need to take it so badly. Most people would be flattered. Though from what I've heard Anna Petrovna is desperate for money. And I'm told she's willing to do anything for it.

Platonov looks, ice cold.

Platonov Why don't you ask her?

Kiril What? I'm sorry?

Platonov If that's what people tell you.

Kiril is staring.

Kiril It's great. It's a brilliant idea. Thank you. You wait – you watch. I'm going to ask her. And I'll bet you anything I get the answer I want.

He runs towards the house, but as he reaches it Anna Petrovna comes out. At once he starts bowing and scraping.

Oh well, perhaps not at this very moment. Pardon me, Your Excellency. No wish to intrude. I'm on my way.

13 Kiril goes hurriedly out, avoiding Anna, who moves towards Platonov.

Anna What are you doing out here?

Platonov Oh, it's cooler.

Anna Isn't it a marvellous evening? The sky clear, the air fresh, the moon bright. Shame we can't sleep under the stars.

She sits down next to Platonov.

Is that a new tie?

Platonov It's new.

Anna When I was young, I slept on the grass.

There's a moment's silence.

I'm in such a good mood. At last everything is right. I think today I'm more in love with you than ever. You've been so perfect today. You haven't offended a single guest.

Platonov And tonight you have never been more beautiful.

Anna You know that Porfiri Glagolyev is asking to marry me? My money troubles would be over. At a stroke. I'd endow your school. Would you like that?

Platonov Very much.

Anna But you don't want me to marry? Mikhail, surely. You can't.

Platonov doesn't answer.

Are we friends you and I?

Platonov Certainly we're friends.

Anna It's a short step, isn't it? Between a man and a woman. A short step on from friendship.

A moment, then they both laugh.

Platonov Ah, that's it.

Anna We're human, aren't we? Love is a noble thing. Why are you blushing?

Platonov Let's go and dance.

Anna No.

Platonov I want to dance. Why can't we dance?

Anna Because when I dance it will be with someone who knows how.

There is a silence.

Well?

Platonov Well what?

Anna Who's going to speak first?

Platonov shakes his head.

Platonov It isn't worth it, Anna.

Anna Not worth it?

Platonov No.

Anna Why not? If you were free, I'd marry you. I'd marry you tomorrow.

Platonov is silent.

Perhaps you don't realise: at a moment like this it's rude to say nothing.

At once Platonov leaps up.

Platonov Let's forget it, please. Let's pretend it never happened.

Anna Why?

Platonov Why? Why do you think? For the obvious reason. Because I respect you.

Anna Oh . . .

Platonov And the respect you have for me is the most valuable thing in my life. Oh, believe me, I'm not against adventure. The odd grandiloquent passion: fine. But to have some squalid, dishonest liaison with you – with you of all people – the one intelligent, attractive, free woman I know.

Anna We're talking about love.

Platonov Yes. That's exactly what we're talking about. I love you, Anna. It's *because* I love you. Please, don't tell me that our love has to be crammed into one demeaning category. It's bigger than that. It's bigger!

Anna gets up, angry.

Anna Leave me. Come back when you know what you're saying.

Platonov Please.

He grabs her hand and kisses it.

And also let's face it, we can't altogether ignore it: I am slightly married.

Anna Oh, you are?

Platonov Yes.

Anna Really? You say you're married and yet you also say you love me? You claim to love me?

Platonov Yes. Well?

Anna If you love me, why mention your wife?

Platonov can't answer. He moves towards her to whisper in her ear.

Platonov I wouldn't lie to you. If I could lie to you, Anna, I would have been your lover long ago.

Anna Liar! Out of here! I'm telling you. Out!

Platonov You're not really angry. I know you. I know when you're angry.

He goes. Anna alone.

Anna Strange. The strangest man. 'Our love can't be crammed into a category.' He sounds like a male novelist making love to a female novelist. If he has his way, we'll talk, we'll never act. Very well. Tonight. It's tonight or never. It's gone on too long. It's hurt me too much.

14 Porfiri Glagolyev comes into the garden.

Porfiri Ah, there you are, at last I've found you . . .

Anna Porfiri Glagolyev. Sit down, why don't you?

Porfiri sits.

Porfiri I wanted to ask. You haven't answered my letter.

Anna No.

Porfiri I was wondering why not.

Anna I didn't know how. To be honest, I don't know why you need me.

Porfiri Well, I hope I've made it plain, I wouldn't *need* you . . .

Anna No . . .

Porfiri Not in the strict sense. As I said in the letter, I would be happy to forgo conjugality.

Anna Yes, you did say that. Those very words.

Porfiri It's a soulmate I need, a housekeeper.

Anna It's odd, Porfiri Semyonych, but the truth is, I can't make much sense of your proposal. If I were as kind, as clever, as rich as you I'm not sure I'd want to take on someone who would be merely a friend in a skirt. Why would I want that?

Porfiri Anna, you represent my last hope of achieving something worthwhile. Will you not at least consider me?

Anna No. And don't ask again.

She looks away.

Take no offence. My refusal has no significance. If we all possessed everything we loved, it would leave no room for our dreams.

She laughs.

There you are. You've lost a woman, but acquired some philosophy. You're in credit.

15 Maria returns, arguing violently with Nikolai.

Maria Never. Never in my life was I so insulted. And you stand aside! You do nothing!

She begins to cry again.

Nikolai What are you suggesting? You want me to pursue the man with a club?

Maria Why not? You think I wouldn't swing a club in your defence?

Nikolai Oh really! What can I do? What am I meant to do? I'm not one of nature's club-swingers!

Maria Very well then, we will never speak again. I never wish to speak to you again.

She bursts into tears.

Nikolai And so she goes on! Like diseased cattle! The staggering, the shouting, the crying. So it goes on!

He goes out.

Maria Cattle, he calls me. I'm the innocent party!

She turns to Anna.

He kissed me.

Anna When?

Maria He pushed me against a table and called me a fool. Tomorrow I shall go the Regional Head of Education to demand the dismissal of Mikhail Platonov.

Anna shakes her head.

Anna Do yourself a favour. Forget what he did. Take my advice. I promise you, in a day or two you and I will meet –

Maria No . . .

Anna – we'll sit in the garden together and have the best day of our lives picking his character apart.

Maria No!

Anna Trust me. I'm an expert.

Maria What's his secret? Tell me. What is it about him? One rule for the rest of us? Another for him? Everywhere, a conspiracy that somehow, for some reason, Platonov will always be forgiven. Well, no. Tomorrow I will end his career.

She goes out. Kiril appears from the house.

Kiril Ah, there you are, Father. You're needed inside.

Porfiri Who needs me?

Kiril For goodness' sake go inside and then you'll find out.

16 *Porfiri goes into the house.*

Anna When your father is dead, you'll regret the way you treated him.

Kiril You think so? I needed him out the way. I have something important to ask.

He makes a big smile.

A simple question. Yes or no?

Anna What?

Kiril Yes or no? That's the question. Dress it up how you like but that's the question.

Anna I have no idea what you're asking.

Kiril Don't you? If I opened my plump wallet, would you?

Anna Petrovna gets up, furious.

Anna At least I credit you with frankness.

She just looks at him.

Kiril Ah for a moment there I thought you were going to hit me.

Anna I was.

Kiril Please. Do it. In my experience, when a woman hits you, it means she's about to say 'Yes'.

Anna looks at him, cold now.

Anna Get him out! Somebody get him out of here!

Kiril Why? What have I done? Surely, come on, it's a joke. You recognise a joke. Don't you have a sense of humour?

He pursues her out.

17 *Platonov appears, talking with Sofya.*

Platonov Yes, so that's how it is. I'm a schoolmaster. A job for which I may say I am completely unsuited.

He sits.

I live in a world where evil triumphs, evil runs rampant through our land, and what do I do? In theory I'm twenty-seven years old. And yet already I'm indifferent to everything except the pleasures of the flesh. I watch other men work, I watch them work and suffer, they work themselves into the grave, all so that I can eat, and yet I feel no shame. Only the thought of death touches me, death moves me because I fear we will die having accomplished nothing. Oh Sofya, tell me, how can we be born again?

Sofya does not answer.

Believe me, I don't care a whit for myself, but I care for you. Where is the person I loved? Where is her courage? Her commitment? Her daring? No, truly, you must listen. Why do you imagine you're ill all the time? You're sick. You're pale. What happened? What turned you from a fine young girl into a woman frittering away her very existence?

He takes her hand.

Tell me, in the name of all that's decent, what on earth made you marry that man?

Sofya He's not a bad person.

Platonov Don't lie to me, Sofya. Don't lie!

Sofya once more tries to get up, but he restrains her.

Sofya He's my husband. I must insist . . .

Platonov I don't care who he is, I'm speaking the truth! You, you, of all people, why did you not choose a man who would work, who would suffer, who was willing to suffer for the things he believed?

Sofya Be quiet. People will hear.

Platonov Let them hear! Let the whole world hear what I say!

Guests pass across, looking. Now Platonov suddenly becomes quiet.

I loved you, Sofya. I loved you more than anything on earth. If you'd met someone earlier, someone worthy of you, then you might have raised yourself up. But if you stay here in this place, with this man, you'll only sink deeper.

Sofya covers her face with her hands.

Life! Why don't we live as we should?

Sofya Leave me alone. It's too much. Leave me alone.

Sofya gets up and moves away, her hands still covering her face. There is noise and excitement now from inside the house.

18 Sergei comes running out of the house, other guests following.

Sergei Ah the very people I'm looking for. It's firework time. Yakov, let's get everyone down to the river.

He speaks to his wife.

Have you decided? Are you coming?

Platonov She's not coming. She's going to stay here.

Sergei Good for you, Platonov. It's damp by the river, I was concerned for her health. You're a great man, you can talk anyone into anything. I'm going to light the fireworks.

He runs out. For a moment Platonov and Sofya are alone.

Platonov Anyone? Anything?

Sergei (*off*) Where are you, Anna? Platonov!

Platonov goes on looking at Sofya as he calls to Sergei.

Platonov I'm coming. Don't light them without me. I'm coming.

Platonov turns and runs out. Anna Petrovna comes running out of the house.

Anna Wait, Sergei, not everyone's ready. Fire the cannon but don't light the fireworks.

She stops, looking at Sofya.

What's wrong, Sofya? Is something wrong?

Platonov (*off*) This way, my lady. This way to the fun.

Anna Coming!

She runs out. Sofya is alone.

Platonov (*off*) Who wants to come on the river? Sofya, do you want to come in the boat?

Sofya What should I do? Somebody tell me what I should do.

Platonov (*off*) The boat's waiting.

19 *Sofya runs out. Porfiri and Kiril come from the house.*

Porfiri You're lying! You must be. By God, I know it. You're lying!

Kiril Of course I'm not lying. For God's sake, why would I lie? It's what happened. I kissed her. She asked for three thousand. It's true! We settled on a thousand. 'I'll do it for one,' she said.

Porfiri Kiril, you're talking about a lady.

Kiril So?

Porfiri A lady's honour is sacred.

Kiril And my honour? You think I'm not telling the truth?

Porfiri stares at him.

Give me a thousand. It's what she asked for.

Porfiri It's a joke.

Kiril No. And you wanted to marry her!

He laughs.

As God is my witness! Give me the thousand, then watch. Watch when I give it to her. On this very bench. What more do you need?

There's a pause. Then Porfiri takes his wallet out and throws it on the ground. Kiril stoops to start counting out money.

Sergei (*off*) Anna, it's time. Nikolai, are you going up to fire the gun?

Nikolai (*off*) That's what I'm doing, damn you.

In the distance Nikolai is seen climbing up on to the roof of the summerhouse. The sound of Bugrov screaming.

Nikolai Oh my God!

Bugrov That's my face. You're treading on my face!

Kiril runs off. Bugrov appears, holding the side of his face.

Nikolai Sorry, old man.

Shcherbuk I can't find the matches. Anyone seen the matches?

Porfiri I worshipped her. God forgive me, I worshipped her.

Bugrov He trod on my face! The bastard trod on my face!

He reels away into the night.

Porfiri Help! Someone help me! Help! Help!

20 *Porfiri has a stroke and falls off the bench. Sofya comes running back, her hair messed up, her face pale now.*

Sofya I can't! I can't! It's more than I can bear! I can't even breathe! A new life at last!

Sergei (*off*) Watch out! Here we go!

The fireworks go off. The sound of a boating song in the distance.

'The sudden roaring of the flooding river
The swell of the tide as it rises high
The splash of the oars as they hit the water
The flash of the lightning as it splits the sky

'Across the darkening heart of the country
The dazzling river cuts like a knife
Feel its strength as it carries us onwards
The power of the river giving us life.'

SCENE TWO

A clearing in the forest. Night. On the left-hand side, the village school. Through the clearing, a railway line which turns right by the school, disappearing way into the distance. A row of telegraph poles.

1 Sasha is sitting by the open window. Osip is in front of it, his gun slung over his shoulder.

Osip You want to know what happened? I'll tell you. She was bathing in the river. She'd lifted her skirt. She cupped her hands and put water on the back of her neck. Then she began to drink. She saw me watching: 'Never seen anyone drinking before?' I said, 'Your Excellency, there's a girl in the village, Manka, and she's thought round here to be the most beautiful girl alive. But next to you, she's a camel, she's a donkey. If I kissed you now,' I said, 'I might very well die.' 'Kiss me,' says Anna Petrovna. And I kissed her, just between her cheek and her neck.

Sasha And what did she do?

Osip 'And now go,' she says. 'You smell,' she says. 'Wash more often.'

Sasha She's brazen.

She hands him a bowl of cabbage soup.

Take your cap off to eat. And don't forget to say grace.

Osip takes off his cap.

Osip Ever since that day, I can't sleep. I close my eyes and she's still there. I take her presents. I shoot partridge, quail. Once I brought her a live wolf. If she'd said 'Kill yourself', I'd have done it.

Sasha When I met Mikhail, the same thing. Before he told me he loved me, I would have committed the great sin. The sin of self-killing.

Osip Yes. That's how it is.

He drinks from his plate.

Sasha Why don't I see you in church, Osip?

Osip I can't go anywhere by day. Too many people in a church.

Sasha Why do you go on? Why do you go on hurting the poor?

Osip It's not something you'd ever understand. I've never met a woman like you.

Sasha I think I can hear my husband.

Osip (*smiles*) I don't think so. No, I don't think so. Chances are your husband's still with the General's widow.

Sasha Oh no, I don't think you've got that right.

Osip Haven't I?

There's a pause.

Sasha If you'll pardon me, I think we may have talked enough for tonight.

Osip Saint Alexandra! What did Platonov do? Say prayers, light candles to find a wife like you?

He bows.

Alexandra Ivanovna, goodnight.

Sasha (*yawns*) On your way and God be with you.

Osip I'm going.

He moves away.

If you need me, ask the birds. Any passing lizard, ask for Osip, he'll know where I am. Look, see that tree stump glowing. My mother always said a tree stump shines where a sinner is buried, so that people may know to pray for him. Over there, another. And another. There are so many sinners in the world.

2 *Osip goes. We hear him whistling in the forest as Sasha comes out of the schoolhouse with a candle and a book.*

Sasha Misha's been gone for so long. I hope he doesn't catch cold. Someone's coming. It's Misha. At last.

She blows out the candle, then calls out.

Quick march! Left, right, left, right, left right . . .

3 *Platonov appears from the forest.*

Sasha You're such a hopeless drunk. Come here.

She wraps herself round him.

Platonov Why aren't you in bed, my little germ?

Sasha Because I wanted to stay up for you.

She sits down beside him.

You are very late.

Platonov Has the express gone through?

Sasha Only the goods train.

Platonov Ah well then. Not yet two.

Sasha I got back at ten. Little Nikolai was screaming his head off. What happened after I left?

Platonov We ate, we danced and then Porfiri had a stroke.

Sasha A stroke?

Platonov Yes. Did you miss it? It was only a mild one, much to his son's disappointment.

Sasha It must have been terrifying.

Platonov I suppose.

Sasha Poor Anna Petrovna. What an extraordinary woman she is. All evening I thought: how fine she is! And how rare!

Platonov puts his head in his hands.

Platonov Oh, Sasha . . .

Sasha Mikhail, what's wrong? What have I said? What's wrong?

Platonov I'm unworthy, I'm ashamed.

Sasha Misha, what are you talking about?

Patonov shakes his head.

You love me, you say. Day after day, you tell me. You find something in me, you say.

Sasha Of course. I love you.

Platonov But what? What is it you love? What is it in me you love?

Sasha You're my husband.

Platonov Only that? Because I'm your husband? No better reason?

He laughs and kisses her on the forehead.

Oh my dear, beautiful little fool! I don't deserve you. What bliss it must be to know nothing.

Sasha Thank you.

Platonov Does happiness really depend on ignorance? We made a child. You and I. We made a child together. How is it possible? You're so precious, so sweet. I should keep you in a glass case.

Platonov tries to kiss her, but Sasha resists, angry.

Sasha No! I won't! Why should I kiss you now?

Platonov Why not?

Sasha Why did you marry me if you think me so stupid? Get to bed. You're drunk.

4 *Sasha gets up, angry, and goes into the schoolhouse. Platonov alone.*

Platonov Drunk? Yes. Now. And when I spoke to Sofya, was I drunk then? What wrong did her husband ever do me? But there I stood, peddling my usual theatrical bilge. 'Sofya, you should be with a man who has suffered for what he believes. You should be with a worker.' Just imagine it! Sofya! With a worker! And her eyes, as I spoke? Trusting! Burning, as if I were speaking the truth! In a country full of crooks, I do nothing wrong. I don't take bribes. I don't steal. I don't beat my wife. And yet I live a life entirely without value.

5 The sound of horse's hooves. Then Anna Petrovna appears, dressed in a riding habit and carrying a whip.

Anna You're awake. I knew you'd be awake. God gave us the winter for sleeping. Why sleep now?

She stretches out her hand.

And yours?

Platonov reaches out his.

Platonov For some reason I can see you've taken it into your head to be rash . . .

Anna In my old age, you mean.

Platonov Old women can be forgiven everything, but pardon me, I'd hardly call you old.

Anna Thank you.

Platonov You're young. Your life is ahead of you.

Anna No. My life is not ahead of me. I want it now.

There's a silence.

Platonov Why do you look at me like that? What craziness was it made you step this way?

Anna I didn't step, dear. I rode.

Platonov Come to take the fortress by storm?

Anna You know full well: things have to be resolved. Aren't you ashamed? Aren't you ashamed to deny me? Deny me in autumn, when the rain comes and the mud. Deny me in the winter, in the frost. But on a night like this . . .

She puts her arm round him, and they kiss deeply.

Platonov If only I could make you happy! You deserve to be happy. But I'll do to you what I've done to all the others.

Anna How conceited you are. The lady-killer. Our local Don Juan!

She laughs.

And how handsome you are in the moonlight.

Platonov I know myself too well. If I had one ounce of honour in me, I would leave you right now.

Anna Then do.

She laughs again.

Ah, very well, now we see. Look at you, stricken as if at some terrible misfortune. What are you? Frightened? Frightened of love?

Platonov No. I'm not frightened. It's just . . .

Anna looks, as if at last understanding him.

Anna What is it? Anything to talk, anything to keep talking?

Platonov No!

Anna You love a woman. She loves you. It's a fine night. Why do we need to talk? Tomorrow we'll talk, tomorrow we'll solve the world's problems. And maybe even our own. Smoke me like a cigarette and throw me away.

She has moved closer to him. Platonov grabs her arm.

Platonov Please. It's the last time I'll ask. For your own sake, don't do this.

Anna throws herself round him.

Anna I no longer care. You're mine. You belong to me.

Destroy me, destroy yourself. Ring out, victory bells.
You're mine.

She throws a black handkerchief over her head.
Platonov laughs.

Platonov The mad woman! The mad woman desires me!

Anna At last he understands!

They both laugh, but before they can go on Anna
hears someone approaching.

Hold on, there's someone coming. Quick. Quick.

6 *Nikolai has appeared and is knocking on the*
schoolroom window.

Nikolai Sasha! Sasha! Are you awake?

Sasha opens the window.

Sasha Is that you, Nikolai? What do you want?

Nikolai I need a bed. Put me in the classroom, I'll sleep
on the floor.

He rubs his head.

I can't tell you. I'm in a terrible state. I'm seeing double.
I can't even see which window to climb through. Good
thing I'm not getting married today or I'd commit bigamy.
And, Sasha, you seem to have two heads.

Sasha Well, I don't. Come on.

Nikolai starts to climb in.

Nikolai, the shopkeeper's wife is out looking for you.
She's desperate. Her husband's had a haemorrhage.

Nikolai Oh, him. He'll be fine. He's always complaining.

Sasha Ouch! You're treading on my foot.

Nikolai disappears through the window, but now there is the sound of more people approaching.

Platonov Oh God, what is this? The Champs Élysées?

7 *Shcherbuk and Bugrov appear, tired and drunk.*

Shcherbuk Yes indeed, sir, Pavel Shcherbuk in person. Survival of the fittest! Where the hell are we? Does anyone know?

They laugh.

Ah, by God, what looks like a house of education, no less. Do you think we should call on our friend, the schoolteacher? Or do you think he's still occupied, making free with the General's widow?

Bugrov I'm feeling terribly ill.

Shcherbuk Has anyone warned him? What happens to people who go near the General's widow?

He makes an annihilating gesture.

Boomph! Next thing you're down with a stroke.

Bugrov Boomph!

Shcherbuk I mean, I'm just asking, but has anyone seen our coats? Did the girls take them from us?

He laughs.

Oh Lord yes, we drank some champagne, didn't we? Didn't we drink some champagne?

Bugrov We did.

Shcherbuk *My* champagne, I may say. Like everything else in her house. Mine!

Bugrov Yours.

Shcherbuk I mean, finally, when it comes down to it. The clothes on her back? Mine. Sergei's stockings? Mine. The food on their table?

Bugrov Yours.

Platonov (*to Anna*) I can't take this. I can't take this any more.

Anna (*to Platonov*) Listen.

Shcherbuk yells into the night.

Shcherbuk Everything for sale! Everything must go! That's it. Tomorrow, the reckoning. Tomorrow, I call in my debts.

They start on their way.

Bugrov Too classy for me.

Shcherbuk Who?

Bugrov The widow.

Shcherbuk Oh.

Bugrov I like peasant girls.

Shcherbuk I know. I know you like peasant girls. You've just had a peasant girl.

Bugrov They should have a road here. That's what I'd do. If it were up to me. I'd put down a nice road.

Shcherbuk Gravel?

Bugrov Could be. Could be gravel.

8 Shcherbuk and Bugrov disappear into the distance, still talking. Anna and Platonov come out from behind the trees.

Anna Have they gone?

Platonov They've gone.

Anna So?

Platonov takes her arm a moment.

Platonov Anna, one thing. You have to know this: I'm only coming because my body tells me to. My body is weak. And for no other reason.

Anna turns and hits him with her riding crop. Sasha appears at the window.

Sasha Mikhail. Mikhail, is that you?

Platonov Oh Lord . . .

Sasha Ah, there you are. Who's that with you?

She laughs.

Anna Petrovna, I hardly recognised you. What are you wearing?

Anna Hello, Sasha.

Sasha Have you been out riding?

Anna Yes.

Sasha What a wonderful idea.

Anna I thought so.

Sasha smiles.

Sasha Misha, can you come in for a moment? My brother isn't well. You come in too, Anna Petrovna. I'm going to go to the cellar, get us all some milk.

Anna Thank you. I have to go home.

She whispers to Platonov.

I'll wait. Don't be long.

Sasha Misha, will you come and help?

She disappears. Platonov looks at Anna ruefully.

Platonov Stay here. I'll put her to bed and then I'll be back. Don't worry. I won't be long.

9 *Platonov goes indoors. Anna alone.*

Anna Well, it won't be the first time he's deceived her.

Osip steps out of the shadow. Anna turns.

Who is it now? Who's there?

Osip bows.

Osip.

Osip The same.

Anna You've been watching? You've watched everything?

She takes Osip's chin with her hand.

Anna You're pale. What's wrong?

Osip What do you think is wrong?

Anna smiles.

Why do you smile? I revered you, like a saint. If you'd ordered me through fire, I'd have gone. If you'd asked me to kill, I'd have killed. I loved you. And you waste yourself on this man?

Anna looks at him a moment.

Anna Very well. Tomorrow. You can visit. Bring me birds from the wood. And not a hair on Platonov's head to be touched. Do you hear me?

Osip is weeping now.

There are tears in your eyes.

She looks at him a moment.

Anna When Platonov comes out of the school fire a warning shot. Fire in the air to let me know he's back. You'll do it?

Osip nods.

Osip Only he won't come.

Anna You wish.

10 *Anna smiles and runs out. Osip beats his cap against the ground and cries.*

Osip I'll kill him. In the name of God, I'll send him to hell.

11 *Osip goes into the wood as Platonov pushes Nikolai out of the schoolhouse.*

Platonov For goodness' sake, man, what sort of doctor are you? Do you have no conscience? The shopkeeper may be dying for all you know.

Nikolai That's what happens when you're a doctor. It isn't all keeping people alive, you know. You do lose some.

Platonov At least go and see!

Nikolai This is Russia! The distances are very great.

Platonov is pacing, indignant now.

Platonov Medicine has a purpose. The purpose is to relieve suffering . . .

Nikolai Fascinating stuff, a fascinating discussion, but do you think we might leave it till the morning?

Platonov You are not going to sleep! I forbid you to sleep!

Nikolai What is it? Gone two? I mean, thank you, to be reminded of the finer points of medical ethics, but just at this moment . . .

Platonov What God do you serve? Tell me. What God do any of us serve?

Nikolai Well, that's a rather larger question, if I may say so. All right! I'll go. Do you hear me? I'll go!

He has yelled back suddenly. Now he steadies himself.

Isn't that what you wanted?

Platonov Go!

Platonov stamps his feet, enraged now.

12 Nikolai goes. Platonov alone.

Platonov To go or not to go? That is the question. What do I do? I thought I'd changed. A woman speaks to me, says one word, and I set out once more on yet another squalid dishonest romance. Why? Men struggle over questions of world-shattering importance. Nothing shatters my world except women. Caesar had the Rubicon and I have women. The worst two words in the language: ladies' man.

Sasha appears at the window.

Sasha Misha, are you still outside?

Platonov Yes, my precious.

Sasha Why don't you come in?

Platonov Darling, I need the fresh air. My head's splitting. You go to sleep.

Sasha Goodnight.

She closes the window.

Platonov The humiliation of deceiving someone who trusts me so completely! I've made up my mind. I'm going to bed.

13 Just as Platonov heads for the schoolhouse, Katya appears.

Katya Sir.

Platonov What is this? Katya, it's you. What are you doing at this hour?

Katya I'm delivering a letter.

Platonov A letter?

Katya Yes.

Platonov From whom? From Sofya? Are you mad?

Katya My mistress said at all costs to be quick.

She hands the letter to him. Platonov looks at her, irritated. Then he lights a match to read.

Platonov 'Am taking first step. Come take it with me. Am born again. Come take me. Am yours.' Hmm. Reads more like a telegram. 'Will wait till four at the summerhouse near the four pillars. My husband drunk and shooting. All yours. S.'

He turns to Katya.

She gave you this?

Katya Yes.

Platonov In person? Are you sure it's for me?

Katya Well, I wouldn't get the wrong man, would I?

Platonov Go back. Thank you.

14 Katya smiles to herself and goes. Platonov alone.

Platonov And now. It comes to this. All my useless eloquence, my silver tongue, and where does it lead? A woman driven to distraction. I shall leave. I shall ignore it. Quick march to the furthest corner of the earth to begin a life of penance and hard work.

He is silent a moment.

On the other hand, you'd have to say: it's interesting. A woman like that. Incredible hair. Wonderful complexion.

He lights another match.

Love! Is this love? Is this what I've been waiting for? A new life. A new beginning. No, change of plan, I won't, I'm not going to do it. I'm a father. I have a son.

He shouts.

Sasha, I'm coming to bed.

There's a pause. Platonov shouts again.

No I'm not.

He sets off, exhilarated.

Go, smash, trample, defile!

15 Sergei and Kiril come running in with shotguns across their backs.

Sergei Ah, there you are, the very man we've been looking for.

Platonov Me?

Sergei embraces Platonov.

Sergei Well? Coming shooting?

Platonov Shooting?

Sergei I'm drunk. Yes. For the first time in my life. God, I didn't know what I'd been missing. And Sofya had this wonderful idea. She sent me off to shoot game.

Kiril Come on, we have to hurry. It's getting light already.

Sergei Listen. What about this? We've just decided. We're putting on *Hamlet* tomorrow.

Platonov Are you, by God?

Sergei Sofya as Ophelia, Nikolai as Horatio and you can be Claudius. The role of Hamlet is taken. *C'est moi.* Hey, where are you going?

Platonov I've got an appointment.

Sergei At this time? Who with?

Platonov A mutual friend.

He goes out. Sergei shouts after him.

Sergei Rehearsals at ten!

Kiril Let's get going.

*16 Kiril and Sergei go out, Sergei spouting lines from
Hamlet: 'Nymph, in thy orisons be all my sins
remembered . . .', 'To be or not to be, that is the
question . . .', etc., way into the distance. There is the
sound of an approaching train as Osip appears.*

Osip Where is he? Which way did he go? Where is he?
Platonov! Platonov!

*He calls out, then goes to the schoolhouse and breaks
the window.*

Mikhail Vasilich, are you there?

Sasha appears at the window.

Sasha What's going on? What's happening?

Osip I'm looking for your husband.

Sasha He's not here.

Osip Isn't he? Then he's with the General's widow.

Sasha What are you saying? What do you mean?

Osip It's what I told you. It's what I warned you from
the beginning. I saw them. Here. Kissing. I saw them
kissing.

Sasha It's a lie. I tell you, it's a lie.

Osip It's not a lie. I saw it with my own eyes. And that's
where he's gone. To the General's widow. I was to give
her a signal. Well, here it is.

He fires the gun into the air.

Do you hear me? Do you hear me now? And when I find
him, I'll kill him. I'll cut his throat.

The lights of a train appear as Osip jumps across the embankment. Sasha comes out in her nightdress, her hair down.

Sasha He's gone. He's deceived me and he's gone. Oh God, I don't want to live.

She lies down on the rails.

Forgive me, God. Forgive me for this. My son! Nikolai! My son! Help me, somebody help me!

She changes her mind and tries to clamber out of the path of the train, but her dress is caught on the rail. Osip jumps towards Sasha.

Oh my God, my God . . .

Osip takes her up in his arms and carries her into the schoolhouse. The train passes.

Act Three

Three weeks later. Morning. A room in the school.
Doors on the right and left. An upright piano, a chest of
drawers, chairs, a divan upholstered in oilcloth, a guitar.
Bachelor chaos.

1 Platonov is asleep on the divan by the window, his
face covered with a straw hat. Sofya comes in and shakes
him awake.

Sofya Wake up, Mikhail Vasilich, wake up. What on
earth are you doing, with that horrible hat?

She takes it off.

Look at him, I can't believe it! His shirt filthy, his chest
naked to the world . . . Mikhail, come on, it's time to
get up.

Platonov What?

Sofya Wake up!

Platonov What's happening? Who is it?

Platonov sits up. Sofya holds a watch in front of him.

Sofya Look at the time.

Platonov I'm looking.

He lies down again.

Sofya Platonov!

Platonov What is it?

Sofya I said look at the time.

Platonov Half past seven. Are you back again?

Sofya We had an arrangement, if you remember . . .

Platonov And what arrangement was that?

Sofya To meet at the hut at six.

Platonov Did I say six?

Sofya Does it mean nothing to you? Does your word mean nothing to you?

Platonov Well, it does when I'm awake. It's keeping my word while I'm asleep I've never quite mastered.

Sofya shakes her head.

Sofya You really are turning into the most undesirable person. Have you ever turned up on time for any of our meetings?

Platonov You'll just have to give me a moment to think about that one.

Sofya How many times now have you let me down?

Platonov Well, I think that may be a rephrasing of the same question.

Sofya What is this? What is happening to you? You are the man who reawakened my whole spiritual life. I come to you, I find you, your hair uncombed, your breath stinking of alcohol . . .

Platonov leaps out of bed, furious.

Platonov Leave me alone!

Sofya Are you drunk already?

She begins to cry.

Sofya Why do you speak to me like that?

Platonov Like what?

Sofya You address me as if I were some kind of peasant, a servant girl, nothing more.

Platonov I'm not going to do this, I refuse to talk to you if you're just going to cry.

Sofya I never cried in my life until I met you!

She turns to him.

Just three weeks since that night, and here I am, I'm a skeleton, I'm a smudge, waiting for you to say something kind. Where is the happiness you promised me? Platonov, think. You're a decent, intelligent man. Come, sit down. Sit in this chair and ask yourself. What are you doing to me?

Platonov shakes his head.

Platonov All right, I'll tell you. What I've done is, I've robbed you of your family, your peace of mind and your future. That's what I've done. I've taken them from you as surely as if I were your bitterest enemy. And all in the interests of a meaningless affair.

Sofya I give myself to him, and he calls it meaningless!

Platonov It scarcely matters, does it? What matters is what your husband is going to think.

Sofya What, that scares you, does it? You scared of Sergei, are you?

Platonov No. Not at all.

Sofya Well?

Platonov I'm scared *for* him. What he'll do when he knows.

There's a silence.

Sofya You're scared he'll find out?

Platonov Profoundly.

Sofya He's found out. I told him.

Platonov No.

Sofya Yes. This morning. Why do you look so horrified?

Platonov Did you mention my name?

Sofya Of course. I went to him. I've let it go for too long.

Platonov And how did he react?

Sofya Oh, he reacted like you, just the same as you. My God, if you could see yourself at this moment! Consumed with fear. It's revolting, you look revolting.

Platonov What did he say?

Sofya Just like you, he thought I was joking. 'You're joking,' he said. Then, when he realised, he turned pale, he fell to the floor, he crawled across the floor on all fours, the same repulsive expression on his face that you have now . . .

Platonov clutches his head.

Platonov Oh my God, what have you done?

Sofya What have *I* done?

Platonov Yes!

Sofya What are you suggesting? Are you seriously suggesting that I should let him carry on in his ignorance?

Platonov Well, of course!

Sofya You think you could honourably live with such a thing? With such deceit?

Platonov Quite easily!

Sofya Mikhail, I'm an honest woman. I cannot live with dishonesty.

Platonov He falls to the floor, he crawls on all fours, and you call that honest? You think it honest to break a man's heart?

Sofya It's what had to be done.

Platonov You realise what this means? You've cut yourself off from your own husband for ever! And for what? For a man you will one day leave.

Sofya Never.

Platonov Yes! And probably quite soon. Chances are.

He turns, gesturing dismissively.

All right, so, very well, it's your business. I defer to you. Do as you wish. Whatever we do, let's do it quickly, that's all.

Sofya We leave here tomorrow.

Platonov Fine.

Sofya We go in the morning.

Platonov Fine.

Sofya I've already written to my mother to tell her we're coming.

There is a slight pause.

I've told her about you.

Platonov Good idea. How did she take it? Found on all fours, was she?

Sofya Oh, Mikhail, you must see, this is our chance. This is our chance to make a new life. This is the moment when I can take you away to a life with no grimy shirts – this hopeless waste and idleness. It's what you said. We'll work. We'll bake our own bread, we'll sweat, we'll toil with our own hands till they're calloused and raw.

Platonov I'm all for it, believe me, but with respect, Sofya, you've never worked in your life. What work? There are women all over Russia and no jobs to be had.

Sofya Trust me, Mikhail. It was you who helped me be born again , and all I want is the chance to repay you. We'll go tomorrow. Yes? We'll spend the day getting ready and tonight we'll meet at the hut at ten. You'll be there?

Platonov Yes.

Sofya Promise you'll be there.

Platonov I've said.

Sofya looks at him, then laughs.

Sofya Oh Mikhail, I believe. I believe! Tomorrow we'll be different people, we'll start again, a better life. Here. Feel. Feel!

She laughs and holds out her hand. Platonov kisses it.

I'll see you tonight.

There is a slight pause.

Platonov Eleven, did you say?

Sofya Ten. I said ten.

Platonov See you then.

Sofya Put on some decent clothes for the journey. And I've got money, we can dine on the way. Mikhail. I'll expect you at ten.

*2 Sofya runs out. Platonov alone. He goes to the
cupboard and, without noticing, pours himself a drink.*

Platonov 'I'll expect you at ten.' 'A new life!' And how
many women have promised me that? God, that reminds
me, I must write to Sasha, it's the very least I can do.
And then, with a bit of luck, goodbye to it all. Cheers!
'A new life! A new man!' Did I just have a drink?

> *He gets a letter from the windowsill and lies down on
> the divan.*

And now, let me see, the letter from Anna Petrovna. The
hundredth in the present sequence. 'Why do you never
answer my letters? You are thoughtless, tactless and
cruel . . . I miss you.' What beautiful handwriting.
Lovely little commas. A literate woman is a beautiful
thing. This time I'll have to write back or else she'll turn
up at my door.

*3 Marko, a little old messenger, has appeared. Platonov
gets up.*

Platonov Well, good morning! Are you looking for
someone?

Marko I'm looking for you, sir. I have a summons for
you.

Platonov That's very sporting. Who sent you?

Marko I've come from the Regional Magistrate.

Platonov Excellent. What can it be? An invitation to a
party, do you think?

Marko has handed him the summons.

'In the case of criminal assault, Maria Grekova, brought
against Mikhail Vasilievich Platonov . . . '

He breaks out laughing.

Oh, very good. Bravo, bedbug. When do you think it's scheduled for?

Marko The hearing is set for the day after tomorrow, sir.

Platonov Perfect. Tell her I wouldn't miss it for the world.

Marko You have to sign, sir.

Platonov goes to sit at the table.

Platonov Pencil do?

Marko Fine.

Platonov Old soldier, are you?

Marko That's right, sir. Discharged after Sebastopol. A Sergeant of Artillery.

Platonov Artillery, eh? Were the guns any good?

Marko They weren't bad, sir. Round bore. And then the bullets came out the end.

Platonov Here you are. I've signed five times, that should do you.

He hands the summons back.

It's a shame it's the day after tomorrow, because I'll be gone by then. Pity. It would almost be worth holding on for.

Marko hesitates a moment.

Marko I was wondering, sir . . .

Platonov Yes?

Marko I've walked ten miles.

Platonov Yes, of course. Careless of me. But I can't give you money, I'm afraid. I do have some tea. It's better for you. Here. How do you want it?

He has opened the cupboard and got out a tea caddy.

Marko I'll have it in the pocket, thank you sir.

Platonov The pocket? Are you sure? You don't think it'll smell?

Marko It didn't smell at Sebastopol, sir.

He holds out his pocket and Platonov pours the tea in.

Platonov Say when.

Marko When.

Platonov Ah, the old contemptibles. You are a marvellous body of men. Well, most of you are.

Marko Only God is perfect, sir.

Platonov takes the summons and sits down to write on it again.

Platonov If you could just do one more thing for me . . .

Marko Anything.

Platonov (*writing*) 'Beautiful one, sadly I shall not see you in court, for tomorrow I leave town for ever. Live happily. Never forgive me.'

He turns to Marko.

Do you know where Maria Grekova lives?

Marko It's about eight miles, sir, if you cross by the ford.

Platonov Fair enough. Five roubles, all right? I'll pay you tomorrow. Tell her, no reply is expected. Can you remember that?

Marko I think I can, sir.

Platonov Then on your way. Good luck, soldier. Keep fighting.

Marko And you, sir. You fight. You fight like hell.

4 *Marko goes out. Platonov alone.*

Platonov Maria Grekova: at last a woman with the courage to treat me as I deserve. Who knows? Perhaps it'll catch on.

He lies down on the divan and covers his face with a handkerchief.

The truth is, it's Sasha I'm sorriest for. I mean, if I'm honest the poor thing hasn't got a chance without me. The way she just went! Took the child, walked out, not a single word.

There's a silence.

Still. I wish we'd said goodbye.

Anna Petrovna appears at the window.

Anna Are you there? Can I come in?

Platonov leaps up, desperately straightens his clothes and tidies his hair.

Platonov Oh my God, what shall I do? What on earth shall I say?

Anna Mikhail Vasilievich . . .

Platonov A quick drink, I think, to sharpen my wits.

He goes to the cupboard and takes a drink from the bottle.

Or dull them.

*5 Anna comes in. Platonov is trying to close the cupboard.
He turns, guiltily.*

Anna Well, well . . .

Platonov gestures towards the lock.

Platonov I've got a problem with the cupboard.

Anna I'm sorry?

Platonov It won't lock. I can't lock the cupboard.

*He drops the key and picks it up. Then walks across
to her.*

Good morning.

Anna And you won't look me in the eye?

Platonov No. I'm too ashamed.

He kisses her hand.

Anna Ashamed? What are you ashamed of?

Platonov Well, it's quite a long list.

Anna You haven't seduced anyone, have you?

Platonov In a sort of way. I mean, you could say. Yes.

Anna I see. Do I know her? Don't worry, I'll find out
eventually, I promise you.

She sits down on the divan.

Platonov Look, I mean, if I could just make a distinction
here. There's such a thing as conversation . . .

Anna Yes . . .

Platonov Which I like. I like conversation. But there's
also interrogation, which, forgive me, I'm less keen on.
No questions. No more questions!

There is a moment's silence.

Anna Why don't you answer my letters?

Platonov There we are. Exactly the point I was making!

Anna You haven't come to see me for three weeks.

Platonov No.

Anna Well?

Platonov I've been ill.

Anna You're lying.

Platonov All right, I'm lying. We'll agree, I'm lying.
What's the point of this?

Anna Do you realise you stink? Platonov, what's going
on?

Platonov Nothing's going on.

Anna The house is filthy, your clothes are filthy, your
eyes look like two plates of borscht. This is like last year.
Last year all over again. You seduce them in the summer,
then you spend the whole autumn drunk. Come on, tell
me where it's hidden.

*Platonov points to the cupboard. Anna Petrovna
unlocks it.*

My God, what's this? A distillery? Which one have you
been drinking?

Platonov All of them.

Anna The sooner your wife comes back to you the
better. Is that what you want? Do you want her back?

Platonov All I want is for you to stop asking questions.

Anna takes a drink from the bottle.

Anna Not bad actually. It really isn't bad. And there's one for you. We'll have one drink and then we'll throw the bottles out. Cheers!

Platonov Cheers!

They both drink.

Anna At least, in a minute. We'll throw them out in a minute.

Anna pours two more and they drink again.

Platonov Cheers!

Anna Cheers!

She goes and sits down.

Come and sit over here and tell me how much you've missed me.

Platonov Every minute of the day.

Anna Well, there you are. So why didn't you come and see me?

Platonov The usual reasons.

Anna What are they?

Platonov Guilt.

Anna (*dismissive*) Oh . . .

Platonov Conscience. But now you're here, I must say I do begin to feel better.

Anna You don't look it. You look like an actor, playing the part of the lovelorn. All romantic thinness and longing. I tell you, that sort of thing does nothing for me. I don't read those novels and I don't live that life. You should live as a man lives.

Platonov Remind me. How do men live?

Anna Men wash more often than you. And they come and visit me.

There's a silence. The two of them look at each other. Then Platonov shakes his head, answering her unspoken request.

Platonov I'm not leaving this house.

Anna Please.

Platonov No.

Anna Come over to my place.

Platonov No.

Anna At least come for a walk. Get out. Meet some people.

She waits, sensing Platonov has something important to say.

Platonov I haven't told you, I'm going to go away.

Anna I don't think so.

Platonov I'm leaving tomorrow.

Anna reaches for the bottle and takes a swig.

Anna It doesn't sound very likely to me.

Platonov No, but it's true. At the moment I can't tell you why. And I can't tell you, as it were, with whom. Because of whom. But nevertheless. That worthless drunk Platonov, whom everyone despises, will finally do what everyone has wanted. He will vanish from the earth.

Anna looks up at him, tears coming into her eyes.

Anna Oh my God, you mean it. You really mean it this time, don't you?

Platonov Yes. And no doubt, Anna, in ten years' time, in twenty, you and I will meet –

Anna Don't . . .

Platonov We'll pass one another in the street, and we'll stop, and we'll laugh together, and then perhaps we'll cry, as old people do, remembering . . .

Anna pours him another drink.

Anna Have a drink. I don't mind you talking nonsense if you're drunk. How can you be leaving? How can you be going?

Platonov That's what I'm doing.

Anna Will you write? Promise me you'll write.

Platonov I won't write. Of course I won't. How can I write?

Anna (*shakes her head*) Without me. You wait. You'll be lost without me. You're hopeless without me.

The tears are pouring down her face now.

I think I'm drunk. I think I'm just a little drunk.

Platonov goes to the window.

Platonov Please, Anna, leave me now. I beg you. Make it easy. If you could see yourself. The way you're looking at me now . . .

Anna All right. Very well. I'll leave you.

Platonov Leave me.

Anna Goodbye.

She holds out her hand. He kisses it.

I'll see you again.

Platonov No. That's the whole point. You won't.

Anna looks at him a moment.

Anna So shall we have a drink then? Why don't we? Why don't we have a drink before we part?

Platonov Yes, all right. We'll have a drink.

Anna pours them both another drink.

Anna Cheers!

Platonov Cheers!

They both drink.

Anna You don't think you might possibly stay? I mean, I'm just asking. You know, if you did, we might even have a good time. We might even have some fun. And God knows, that would be a first in this region . . .

Platonov Yes, it would.

Anna It would set records in this region.

Platonov That's right.

Anna And if we're going to drink, then for God's sake let's do the damn thing properly, let's not tipple, let's not *sip*: let's drink.

She pours them another drink.

Let's face it, you die if you drink, and you die if you don't. So, on the whole that means you might as well. Cheers!

Platonov Cheers!

They both drink.

Anna I want to ask you something, Mikhail. Tell me honestly. Do you think I'm a drunk?

Platonov Well . . .

Anna Do you think I should have another? Maybe I shouldn't, because then my tongue will be tied, and what will I talk with? What will I talk with then?

She smiles, her eyes filling with tears again.

You see, I'll tell you something, if you really want to know something, I'll tell you. What it's like being me. And how there's no hell on earth worse, I swear, there's nothing worse on earth than being an educated woman. Because, you see, it's very hard, if you live in this region, to know just what precisely an educated woman is *for*. If I'd gone away, if I'd become a diplomat or the head of a school, in a place which isn't here . . . oh well then. And it's not helped if she's what people call an immoral woman as well. That doesn't help either. You see, a dog is needed. You understand? A cow is needed. A horse is needed. You know what to do with them. But I'm not needed.

There's a silence.

Of course, if I'd had children. Do you like children?

She gets up.

Don't leave this place. Please don't. You see, if you leave, there's nobody else, there's really nobody. We've had a lot of fun here, haven't we? Just at the moment, I need a holiday, I need a rest. I need to be a wife and a mother.

Platonov stands looking out of the window.

Could you say something? Could you just say something?

Platonov shakes his head.

But you love me, don't you? You do love me?

Platonov I'll kill myself if I stay here.

Anna Yes, but you love me, don't you?

Platonov Everybody loves you, Anna.

Anna I don't understand. You must be going mad. Here we are, we're in love with each other. What more do you want?

Again, Platonov doesn't answer.

Why didn't you come? Why didn't you come that night?

Platonov turns, suddenly vehement.

Platonov In the name of God, in God's own name, will you please help me? Will you please go?

Anna All right, I'm going, I'm going . . .

Platonov Please go, because if you don't I'll tell you everything, and then I know I shall just want to kill myself.

Anna I'm giving you my hand. I'll call by this evening.

Platonov No.

They embrace.

For the last time.

Anna My darling.

Platonov Off you go and good luck.

He closes the door and bolts it. There is a silence. Then Anna calls from behind the door.

Anna (*off*) Mikhail, I promise, I'll come back and see you again.

6 Platonov puts his fingers to his ears, then takes them down.

Platonov She's gone. It's over.

He opens the door, but she's gone.

She's an astonishing woman. You know I'll say this and I'll only say it once, but I wouldn't have minded. I really wouldn't have minded if she'd stayed five minutes longer. In fact, you know . . . I'm thinking: why not? Maybe I should have a word with Sofya. Ask her, why not? Ask her outright: how about delaying? Not for long, just a couple of weeks and then I could go somewhere with Anna. Sofya can go to her mother's, she'd like that, she was saying only recently how much she loves her mother. And she needs a rest, God knows, from the look of her. Could work. Could work pretty well actually. Hey, it's a good idea!

A knock at the door.

And it's only two weeks.

7 Platonov opens the door. Osip is standing there.

Osip Mikhail Vasilich.

Platonov My goodness. To what do I owe the honour?

Osip You'll find out soon enough.

Platonov Well, make it quick and then on your way.

Osip comes in. Platonov closes the door.

Osip I'm here to say goodbye.

Platonov You're going away?

Osip No, you are.

Platonov Well, I must say, you are extraordinarily well-informed.

Osip Thank you.

Platonov I suppose you couldn't also tell me where I'm going?

Osip Yes, I can. To hell.

Platonov Ah. And is it your job to send me there?

Osip More like, I just buy you the ticket.

Platonov You mean you're working for someone else?

Osip takes out a 25-rouble note.

Osip Shcherbuk gave me this.

He tears up the note.

Platonov Well that's an extraordinarily noble gesture. Thank you.

Osip It's nothing to do with nobility. I don't want anyone thinking I killed you for the money.

There is a moment. Neither man moves.

You could always make a run for it. The door's over there and I'm nowhere near.

But Platonov is holding his ground.

Platonov It's the smile, you see.

Osip What?

Platonov It's the idiot grin that I find incredibly annoying. As if killing people were fun. I look at you and I just want to hit you.

Osip Then hit me. Go ahead. Go on. Hit me.

Platonov goes up to Osip and hits him, surprisingly hard. Osip staggers.

Platonov Well, there you are, yes? Rather harder than you expected, yes? I've wanted to do that for some time.

He hits him again. Osip staggers again.

Osip Have you? Have you indeed?

Platonov My God, what a disgusting creature you are! What have your victims ever done to you? What harm have they ever done you?

Osip Spit in my eye.

Platonov No.

Osip Spit in my face.

Platonov I wouldn't waste the spit.

He goes up to Osip, enraged now.

Go on, then. Kill me. That's what you're here for! Kill me! Well?

Osip trips Platonov and they fall fighting on the ground.

Oh no, you see, it's me that's going to kill you.

Osip turns him over on his stomach, twisting his arm, and then takes a knife from his belt.

Platonov Oh God, that's my arm! God Almighty, that's my arm!

Osip Oh, don't want to die, eh? Don't feel like dying?

He raises the knife to kill him.

Platonov For pity's sake, don't stab me. In the name of God, I'm a father! I'm a husband! Have pity!

8 Sasha comes running in.

Sasha What on earth? What on earth's going on?

Osip turns and sees her, at once gets off Platonov.

Osip All right, I won't do it in front of her. Not in front of her. Take the knife! Take it!

He hands Sasha the knife.

And tell him from me: he won't get away.

Osip jumps out of the window. Sasha stands aghast. Platonov writhes on the ground.

Platonov Oh my God, oh my God, what's he done to my arm?

Sasha Are you all right, Misha?

Platonov I'm fine. Just give me a hand.

Sasha What was he doing? What's going on? I told you to have nothing to do with him.

She helps him towards the divan, where he lies down.

Platonov I'm fine, honestly. I promise.

Sasha puts a pillow under his head.

Oh Sasha, is it you? How wonderful, it's you.

Sasha It's me, but why have you closed your eyes?

Platonov It's all right. I'm all right, don't worry. So you came back? You came back to see me?

He smiles at her and kisses her hand.

Sasha No. Not at all. I only came because little Nikolai is ill.

Platonov What's wrong?

Sasha I don't know. A kind of fever. High temperature. He has a rash, and he doesn't sleep. Oh Misha, I'm so frightened . . .

Platonov Don't be frightened. Have you sent for your brother? Has your brother seen him?

Sasha Oh, he saw him, yes.

Platonov What did he say?

Sasha You know what he's like. He stayed five minutes. Told me not to worry.

Platonov I do think he is the only doctor on earth who won't bother even to treat himself when he's dying.

Sasha What can we do?

Platonov Pray.

There's a silence.

You're at your father's?

Sasha I am.

Platonov You told him?

Sasha I did.

Platonov About us?

Sasha Oh Misha, what shall we do about little Nikolai?

Platonov God wouldn't do that. He wouldn't. God wouldn't take our son.

There's a silence.

You've got to take care of him, you know. He's a very special boy. He's a Platonov, after all. I suppose he could always change his name. No seriously, I've been thinking how much he means to me.

He examines his arm. Sasha starts to cry.

Oh God, my arm's turning sort of purple. That's right, laugh. Oh I see, you're not laughing. You're crying. Don't cry, little pup. I do love you, you know. I love you very much.

Sasha Is it over? The affair?

Platonov 'Affair'! Honestly, what a bourgeois expression.

Sasha You mean it's not over.

Platonov It'll be over soon.

Sasha But when?

Platonov Look at me, for goodness' sake. You can see I'm exhausted. And if you think I look terrible, you should see her! My God! It's taking its toll on her, I can tell you. The joke is, we're completely mismatched. She's so appallingly naive, sometimes I just want to scream. No, really, I think you can be pretty sure. Sofya and I aren't going to be together very long.

Sasha gets up, then staggers.

What's wrong? What are you doing? What's happening?

Sasha Sofya?

Platonov Well, it hardly comes as news to you, does it? I mean, I have to say, I do have to say, my arm really is hurting now.

Sasha I thought you were with Anna.

Platonov With Anna? Who on earth told you that? What a ridiculous idea!

Sasha With Sergei's wife?

Platonov Well, in a sense.

Sasha When I thought it was the General's widow, then, yes, you're right. In a way, it didn't matter. But with another man's wife! Well, may you be happy with her!

Platonov I don't want to be happy! I want to be with you!

Sasha Thank you.

Platonov For goodness' sake, come on now, be reasonable, Sasha, I'm your husband, I'm the father of your child.

Sasha But that's what I'm saying! How could you? How could you do this?

Platonov I know. Look, it's not something I'm proud of. But on the other hand, it's not a novel, you know. This is life. In life it's possible to forgive.

Sasha sits. Platonov goes over to her and kisses her on the head.

I have to say, be fair, what is it you do every night?

Sasha I go to church.

Platonov Quite. You kneel, you light candles, you say interminable litanies for people you don't even know. Think of it this way: all your churchgoing has been a sort of rehearsal. Here's the moment where a little loving kindness would actually be of some use. A little forgiveness would go a long way.

He embraces her.

I know I've done wrong, I'm Sofya's lover, possibly Anna's lover, too – that isn't quite clear yet – I haven't always lived up to my own high standards. But nobody's going to love you as I do. Who else is going eat that soup you make? No, I mean it. Really. Of course you have the right to leave me. You do. But, be fair . . . can you really face life without me?

Sasha I don't understand. My life's in ruins and all you can do is joke about it. Let me go!

She wrenches herself away.

This is the last time you'll see me. You'll never see me again. In future the Colonel will bring you our son.

She shakes her head.

May God forgive you. You've ruined our lives.

9 *Sasha looks a moment at Platonov, and then goes out. Platonov alone.*

Platonov The cheek of it! The nerve! My God, the sheer brass nerve! Just because she goes to church! What a louse! What an *insect*! What is this? Open season? I mean, please, if you're dissatisfied with any detail of your life . . . My God, I need a drink. I need it desperately. Can anyone explain: why am I feeling so ill?

He walks to where Anna left the bottle. As he does so, Sergei appears at the door. They are both still a moment.

Sergei You know what you've done, I suppose?

Platonov No. Tell me.

Sergei You've killed me.

There is a silence.

Platonov Drink?

Sergei No thank you.

Platonov pours his and walks slowly to the far side of the room.

Platonov Go on.

Sergei Talk about unequal distribution. Please! Look what the gods gave you . . .

Platonov I know.

Sergei Charm, intelligence, good looks. Oh yes, they were really handing it out, the day you were born. The day you were born it was à la carte. And me? Well, no, mine was a different kind of day. My day, it was weakness and stupidity. On my birthday, they handed out superstition and asthma. One gift only they've given me. Ever. One stroke of fortune in my entire life.

He turns, about to break down.

And of course my dearest friend had to take her too.

Platonov I'm going to ask you to leave . . .

Sergei As if things were not unequal enough!

Platonov I'm going to have to ask you to get out of here!

Sergei I'm going, don't worry. I came to challenge you to a duel, but now I'm here all I want to do is cry.

He looks a moment at Platonov.

Have I lost her? Have I lost her for ever?

Platonov Yes.

Sergei shakes his head, sobbing.

Sergei All right I'm going, you don't need to tell me, I'm going.

Platonov Please do.

Sergei Just do me one favour. Give her back. I beg you, give her back. She's mine. You don't need her. You have lots of women. I have one.

Platonov As God is my witness, I'm going to shoot myself unless you leave my house at once.

Sergei I'm going. I'm going.

He leaves. Platonov is alone.

Platonov Somebody tell me. What is this? What have I done? I should stay away, for the rest of my life I should stay away from other human beings. I'm contaminated. Just kill myself. Why not?

He strikes himself on the chest, then starts screaming.

Oh Jesus, Jesus . . . Sasha! Sasha! I beg you, come home!

10 Platonov runs to the door, but before he gets there Porfiri Glagolyev comes in. He is well wrapped up and carries a crutch.

Porfiri Ah, excellent, the very man I came to see. I hope I'm not disturbing you.

Platonov What?

Porfiri Though from the look of you . . . I must say you do look very unwell.

Platonov I'm drunk.

Porfiri At this hour? In some curious way your condition suits my purpose. Possibly you may think this a strange enquiry, but upon your reply depends my whole future.

Platonov Fire away.

Porfiri As you know I have always held our mutual friend Anna Petrovna to be, in a sense, an ideal of womanhood. Are you going to fall over?

He reaches out to support Platonov.

Nobody knows Anna Petrovna better than you. I have come to ask you: is she worthy to be the wife of a respectable man?

There is a moment's silence, Platonov staring at him.

Platonov Everything in the world is rotten. Everything is filthy. Everything is mean.

He faints on Porfiri, then falls to the floor. Then Kiril comes in.

Kiril What's happening? What's going on?

Porfiri I've been a fool, Kiril. I've lived a life of ideals. There's no love in the world, there's no faith, there's no trust.

Kiril looks at him, not understanding.

We're going to Paris.

Kiril Paris?

Porfiri I'm coming with you. If we're going to sin, let's sin in style. Let's wallow like that creature wallows.

He points at Platonov inert on the floor, then raises his arms above his head.

'Everything is rotten. Everything is filthy. Everything is mean.'

Porfiri puts his arm round his son.

Come on, let's live as other people live. You can be my teacher.

Kiril I love it. My father taught me to read. I'll teach him to live.

Porfiri We'll go. We'll go tonight.

Kiril In Paris everything is possible.

Porfiri Paris! Paris! Let's go!

They go out.

Act Four

The following morning. Again, the garden of the Voynitsev house, fields stretching away into the distance. An oppressively hot day, rain in the air.

1 Sofya is with Katya.

Sofya All right, calm down, there's no need to be hysterical.

Katya I'm telling you, madam: the furniture's smashed, the windows are wide open, the schoolhouse door has been wrenched from its hinges. Something terrible has happened.

Sofya Yes, but what? What exactly has happened?

Katya Well, it's not clear, is it? Either he's done some terrible harm to himself, or else he's fled altogether.

Sofya Did you go to the village?

Katya Of course.

Sofya Well?

Katya Nothing. Nobody knows anything.

Sofya What can I do? What on earth can I do?

Katya What's sad is, he used to be so amusing. He used to be such a humorous man. Until he met you, madam. Now you see him, he's like a fish on a slab. Oh madam, why don't you stop?

Sofya Stop? Why don't I stop what?

Katya It's not worth it, is it? Love. You don't eat, you don't drink, you don't sleep, the only thing you do is cough.

Sofya Will you go back? Go back to the school, will you, and look for him again?

Katya Don't you think you should go to bed, madam? You haven't slept all night.

Sofya I will. I promise. We'll do a deal. If you go back to the school, I'll go to bed.

Katya Or better still, madam, why don't you walk the ten miles and I'll . . .

She stops, deliberately.

Sofya What did you say?

Katya I said I'm going, madam. See you later.

2 *Katya goes. Sofya is left alone.*

Sofya He promised. I waited all night at the hut and he never came. So much for love. It's obvious. He doesn't love me.

Sergei arrives, not expecting to see Sofya.

Sergei You?

Sofya Yes.

Sergei I wasn't expecting you. I needed to sleep.

Sofya It's my fault. I came out here to be quiet.

Sergei No. Don't go in.

Sofya stays seated.

Odd, isn't it? Suddenly to be strangers together.

There's a pause.

So you're leaving?

Sofya Yes.

Sergei When?

Sofya Today. We'll leave today.

Sergei Well, I wish you happiness. Don't they say that happiness is always built on the misfortune of others?

Sofya Was there something you wanted?

Sergei I'm sorry?

Sofya You asked me to stay.

Sergei looks at her a moment.

Sergei I wanted to apologise. For last night. It was unpardonable. My behaviour. I ask your forgiveness.

Sofya You have it.

Sergei My mind's become a fog, it's become a sort of jungle. I can't find my way through any more. I see a light somewhere, a gleam of light somewhere in the distance and I hold to that. I live for that.

Sergei gestures round the garden.

Sofya Sergei . . .

Sergei Here I am. In the grounds of my family home. Of what was once my father's home. Major-General Voynitsev, of the suite of His Imperial Majesty, Knight of the Order of St George. A great and glorious man. 'Oh I wonder, may I introduce my ex-wife?'

Sofya Sergei, you must stop. You must stop all this. You said all this last night.

Sergei I'm going mad, I know I'm going mad.

Sofya What more can you say? What do you want? To make me feel guilty? To punish me?

Sergei Sofya, you must let me speak!

He has raised his voice.

He doesn't love you. You know he doesn't love you. You've wrecked your own life and you'll ruin his. And why? Because you were there. Because you were sitting in a garden one afternoon. So he took you. Whim! Caprice!

Sofya suddenly gets up and walks away.

And now you're crying.

Sofya Yes! I'm crying!

Sergei And why? Because what I'm saying is true.

Sofya shakes her head, barely able to speak. Then she turns, in agony.

Sofya Where's Platonov? Tell me where he is. Where is he?

Sergei I have to tell you, Sofya: Platonov has gone.

Sofya Where?

Sergei I gave him a thousand roubles and he went.

Sofya It isn't true!

Sergei No! You're right! It isn't true! I'm lying! Everything I say is a lie.

Sofya I hate you.

Sergei Do you know what it is? Do you know what it is to be betrayed? I'm going mad. Oh, yes, Platonov is alive, walking, breathing, still among us, and best of all, unhappy, suffering as you suffer – I have that at least, I have that compensation. He steals you and it doesn't make him happy.

A moment, then Sofya speaks to herself.

Sofya You're heartless. All of you. You're all without love.

Sergei Sofya. Help me. Give me some relief. Tell me one thing. It's still . . . it's still to happen, isn't it? It hasn't happened yet, has it?

Sofya I'm his. I'm already his.

She gets up to go. Sergei grabs at her.

What are you doing? Let go of me.

Sergei How dare you? How could you? How could you?

3 Anna Petrovna comes into the garden. She stops a moment. Sergei lets go of Sofya's arm. Sofya adjusts herself.

Sofya Anna Petrovna. Excuse me. I have to go.

There's a moment's silence. Then Sofya goes out. Anna Petrovna looks at Sergei.

Anna So. You've heard the news?

Sergei Yes.

Anna You know what has happened.

Sergei nods.

I've always been told, in life one should never trust one's enemies. But better advice: don't trust your friends.

Sergei Yes.

Anna Porfiri. He promised.

Sergei Yes.

Anna He promised he would go to the auction.

Sergei Why didn't he? Where was Porfiri?

Anna This brilliant commercial opportunity! The solution to our problems!

She shakes her head.

Why on earth did we agree to it? We could have lived out our days in the way we always have. In debt and who cares?

Sergei Why didn't he go?

Anna The servants say he went off to Paris instead. To Paris! Porfiri didn't even go to the auction!

Sergei I can't believe it.

Anna The estate has been sold.

There is a silence.

The Lord gave, and the Lord hath taken away. Blessed be the name of the Lord.

She turns to Sergei, tears in her eyes.

Oh Sergei, what shall we do with you?

Sergei With me?

Anna You know you're going to have to find work. Sergei, you can teach. You're not a bad man. You have ideals, you talk of doing good. You have a wife.

Sergei I had a wife.

Anna (*shocked*) Sergei . . .

Sergei A woman lay at my side. A woman slept beside me. *Acting* my wife!

He looks at Anna.

Yes. That's right. Think of the worst thing and that's what it is.

Anna No.

Sergei It's true.

Anna I don't believe you. Who would do that? No one would dare.

Sergei Oh wouldn't they?

Anna Do you know who it is?

Sergei Isn't it obvious? How many times have you heard people say? 'Oh,' they say. 'There's only one interesting man in the region . . .'

Anna stands, stunned.

Anna No.

Sergei Then go and ask her!

Anna No.

Sergei What is it? Diabolical visitation? Was she ravished by a spectre? Ask her! Why not? If you don't believe me, why don't you ask her?

There is a silence. Anna sits.

Anna No need. I'll take it on trust.

4 *Bugrov appears from the house.*

Bugrov Ah, pardon me. Excuse me, Anna Petrovna. There was no one to announce me.

Anna turns away.

Anna This is just awful.

Bugrov I know. The heat. Unbearable.

He wipes his brow. Neither Sergei nor Anna looks at him.

All your servants have gone to the village. It seems our friend Osip has been killed.

Sergei Osip?

Anna So it's true.

Bugrov He was safe in the forest. But he chose to make an appearance in the village. In life, one mistake is enough.

Bugrov stands waiting for a response.

He was killed near the well. A group of peasants got together and beat him to death.

Sergei Bugrov, what do you want us to say? He was evil. It's what he deserved. I feel nothing for him.

There's a silence. Bugrov shifts.

Bugrov This is a difficult visit.

Anna Oh please!

Bugrov To get to the point: It's in my name. But I didn't buy it.

Anna No one imagined you did.

Bugrov No.

Anna Quite.

Bugrov I don't have the wherewithal.

Sergei Please! This is insufferable!

Bugrov shifts again.

Bugrov Pavel Shcherbuk presents his compliments and asks me to tell you: please, stay on as you like . . .

Anna Thank you.

Bugrov In fact, if you wish, you may stay until Christmas. There will be some changes. While these are going on, lest these inconvenience you, he's suggesting perhaps you might move into a wing. After all, the house is not short of rooms.

He smiles.

Also, the mine . . .

Anna No. We don't wish to sell it.

Bugrov As you know, the mine remains your property. Shcherbuk instructs me to say . . .

Anna What would he give for it? Chickenfeed? You can tell him from me there's no question of selling the mine.

Bugrov The point he makes is: as you know, Sergei here has issued a large number of promissory notes. If you don't sell the mine, Pavel Shcherbuk will sue Sergei.

Sergei It's Anna's property. My stepmother will not lose the estate because of me.

Bugrov I'm sure that's commendable. But I have IOUs as well, remember? And I would also . . . as it were . . . sue your family.

He shifts.

Nothing personal. It's purely business.

Anna Thank you, Timofei Gordeich. We have heard what you say.

Bugrov You mustn't worry. You have until Christmas.

He walks away. Anna is looking away. Sergei is quiet.

Sergei It's my fault.

Anna No.

Sergei If I have to, I shall live simply. I'm sure there's a way. After all I no longer have a wife to support.

Anna moves away, shaking her head.

Anna You say that as if it's already been decided.

Sergei Well, hasn't it?

Anna Of course not. He's only seduced her. It's only seduction!

Sergei Only?

Anna You really think a man like Platonov is going to spend his life with a woman like that? A boring little prig like Sofya? I mean, with respect.

Sergei What are you suggesting? She'll come back to me? You think I'd take her?

Anna Do you know for a fact . . . Have they actually . . .

Sergei Yes. I asked her.

There is a silence.

Anna No. She's showing off, that's all. It's Platonov. Talks up a storm. Trust me. He doesn't actually go through with it.

Sergei He went through with it.

Anna Well, there's no proof.

Sergei suddenly loses his temper.

Sergei Of course there's no proof!

5 Maria Grekova comes into the garden.

Maria Oh my dear friend, Anna Petrovna, I hope you'll forgive me, I hope you don't mind my barging in.

Anna Not at all.

Maria My mother always said, in life everything's a matter of timing.

She laughs nervously and gives her hand to Anna.

I desperately needed to see you. Forgive me, Sergei Pavlovich.

She leads Anna to one side and hands her the summons. She talks in a whisper.

Read it. You see. His writing.

Anna starts to read.

Anna Well?

Maria You have no idea what I've done. I went to the Director of Education. Because of my allegations, Mikhail Vasiliev is being transferred. That's before I got his message. You see what he's written?

Anna I do. And?

Maria looks at her.

Maria I was hoping . . . well, I was hoping you might send for him.

Anna I?

Maria I've become convinced that I've done him a terrible wrong.

Anna You must wait inside. I was talking to Sergei. It's urgent.

Maria Of course. I'm sorry. Don't be angry.

She kisses Anna.

Anna I shan't.

Maria I was so sure what I wanted. I wanted justice. But sometimes don't you think love is more important than justice?

Anna just looks at her.

Anna I think, wait in the library.

Maria Of course.

She goes into the house.

Anna I'm going to talk to Sofya. Nothing is decided. Nothing is yet decided.

Sergei You say!

Anna Sergei, wait for me here.

6 *Anna goes into the house. Sergei alone.*

Sergei What can I do? There's no end to my torment. Unless I choose to end it myself.

Platonov comes through the field with his arm in a sling.

No, I don't believe it. No.

Platonov Please. I don't ask you to forgive me. I've not come here for forgiveness. I have come to be of help.

I have an offer to make. Sergei, I want you to live. If the price you require is my own death, then ask for it. You need only ask. I speak as your friend.

Sergei I want nothing. I ask nothing.

7 *Anna Petrovna comes back out.*

Anna I heard his voice.

Platonov Anna.

Anna Yes. Sergei has told me what happened. Is he speaking the truth? It's true?

There is a silence.

And what's so contemptible, you didn't even love her!

Sergei Anna . . .

Anna You were just bored!

Platonov I think it would help if we try to be civil.

Sergei Anna, ask him why he's come here.

Anna You just play with people!

Sergei No, really! Ask him!

Anna It's not hard to guess.

Sergei Soft soap. Soft talk. That's what he's here for. We're not going to listen to his nonsense.

Platonov 'We'? Who is this 'we'?

He turns to Anna.

Anna, just now I offered to atone for my sin. I think I did mention to Sergei I was willing to shoot myself.

Sergei Is that what you call 'atone'? *Words? Promises?*

Violent now, Sergei points across the fields.

Across those fields – look – in the village, Osip has atoned. That's what I call atonement!

Platonov I heard.

Sergei Down by the well a Russian has atoned for his sins!

Platonov Listen at least. Listen to what I say. I've lain awake all night, in anguish. We've both lost our wives. Without our wives, we're both finished. Both of us know that.

Sergei You come here – how dare you! – you ask for our sympathy. As if you were just one more victim of your own depravity!

Platonov shakes his head.

Platonov You know, I'm still a human being.

Sergei Coming from you!

Platonov Being unhappy doesn't give anyone rights. You don't have the monopoly. Oh, you lovers of humanity, you all spout such fine words, until you're confronted with a real human being.

There is a silence.

Anna Sergei, he's right. He came in good faith. Just once only perhaps, life gives us one chance to behave well. Not when we wish. When we must. Take your chance.

Sergei stands a moment, unsure.

Are you all right?

Platonov No. It's my arm. I'm in agony. I'm shaking with cold. I think I'm going to die.

Sergei If it helps, Mikhail: let's part as friends.

Platonov By all means.

They embrace. Platonov makes to lie down.

The truth is, I have to tell you, I'm desperate to sleep, but I don't seem able. If someone could find me a blanket or something . . .

Anna Mikhail, you can't sleep here. Go back to your home. I promise I'll send someone over to look after you.

Platonov I just need some water.

Anna Sergei.

Platonov Thirsty.

Sergei hands Anna a carafe which she gives to Platonov. He drinks from the carafe.

I'm really not well.

Anna puts her hand on his brow.

Anna I'll send for Nikolai.

Platonov (*softly*) I feel bad, Your Excellency.

Anna (*smiles*) Oh yes? And how do I feel?

8 *Sofya appears from the house.*

Sofya I heard he was here.

Anna Sergei . . .

She looks at Sergei tactfully for them both to withdraw.

Sofya So you'd better tell what's been happening.

Platonov What's been happening is that I've decided it's over.

Sofya You decided? *You* decided? When did you decide?

She looks at him in disbelief.

Platonov Sofya, you're married.

Sofya So?

Platonov You're a married woman. Pick up the life you had, and try to return to it.

Sofya I can never return!

Platonov Learn! Learn from your mistake.

Sofya suddenly shouts at him.

What about me? What happens to me?

Platonov looks at her, pleadingly.

Platonov I died. Years ago, I died. I can't say how many. Two, was it? Or three? One night, I cleaned my teeth, I pulled the sheet up over my ears and when I woke up, I was dead. Oh, no apparent change of condition. I got up, kissed my wife, went to work. No external symptoms. We're all around, have you seen us? Everywhere you go. The appearance of life and nothing else. We perform the functions, we go through the motions. But on our breath, a sweet scent of decay. Bury me in the forest so I don't infect the air.

Sofya And last week? Were you dead last week? When you kissed me? Were you dead when you made love to me?

She suddenly becomes hysterical.

Let me out of here! I'm going to kill myself! Let me out!

At once Anna Petrovna and Sergei come running back.

Anna What's going on?

Sergei What's happening?

Sofya I can't! I can't live in this world.

Anna Calm down. Sergei, quick, get her some water. Sit down over here.

Anna has tried to lead Sofya to a chair but she breaks free.

Sofya And you! You turned him against me. It was you that did it. You're worse than he is. You're worse.

9 Nikolai comes in quickly, Yakov vainly trying to announce him.

Nikolai Where is he? Take me to him. Lead me to him at once.

Yakov (*half in, half out*) Nikolai Triletsky . . .

Nikolai For God's sake, everybody knows who I am! This house becomes more pretentious by the minute.

Yakov goes indoors. Nikolai walks, furious, over to Platonov.

Anna Nikolai . . .

Nikolai And here he is. Sitting here as if nothing has happened. Ready no doubt to give his greatest performance.

Platonov Nikolai?

Nikolai Ladies and gentlemen, for the last time, prepare yourselves to watch Mikhail Platonov in the sickeningly familiar role of Innocent Party.

His anger is real, chilling.

Ready, are you? Costume in place? Hair and make-up adjusted? Audience stilled?

Anna For God's sake, Nikolai, tell us what's happened.

Nikolai Sasha has poisoned herself.

Platonov No.

Nikolai Yes. She has taken sulphur and poisoned herself. Anything to do with a certain shock-haired philosopher? Or was he nowhere near the scene of the crime?

He has taken out a note, which he hands to Platonov.

Read this.

Platonov No!

Nikolai Read it!

Platonov 'Suicide is a sin . . .'

Anna My God!

Platonov 'Praying for suicides is a sin. I am a sinful woman. Little Nikolai, may God bless you as I bless you myself. Misha, cherish your son. Live according to God's law. The key to Misha's chest of drawers is in my woollen dress . . .'

He looks up.

I must go to her. I must see her at once.

Nikolai See her? You think you deserve to see her?

Platonov Me? You think I wanted her dead?

Nikolai turns round, like a lecturer.

Nikolai You see, everybody! Observe, everybody! The actor's most valuable faculty. He summons up tears!

Effortless, you see? The actor's indispensable gift for crying at will.

Platonov For God's sake, man, you think I'm not moved? My wife is dead and you think I'm not moved?

Nikolai Very good, you see. Students, take note. The rising inflection, here brilliantly deployed. No greater master. 'You think I'm not *moved*?' Denoting emotion! Implying emotion! Superbly cast as ever. The very slightly ruined good looks, the deep pencil lines around the mouth . . .

Platonov Leave me alone! For God's sake, leave me alone!

Nikolai What a fine man! Destroyed his wife and to no purpose! God save us from the intellectuals. Because they're always the stupidest of all!

Anna Leave him, Nikolai. It's enough. Leave him.

Nikolai Enough? What, you think *enough*? I've spoken what? for thirty-five seconds? You think that's enough if she were dead?

Anna Isn't she?

Platonov Nikolai, you said she was dead.

Nikolai Platonov's favourite topic. My shortcomings as a doctor. I called by this morning. It was pure chance.

Platonov You mean she's alive?

Nikolai Yes. She took sulphur and poisoned herself.

Platonov laughs and embraces Nikolai.

Platonov Oh my God, she's alive. Thank God she's alive.

Nikolai Yes, dangerously ill, but alive.

Platonov Thank God.

Nikolai I found the note by her bed.

Anna Why did you scare us like that? You gave her something?

Nikolai Of course.

Anna What did you give her?

Nikolai looks at Anna, serious.

Nikolai Believe it or not, I gave her what she needed.

There is a silence. Then Platonov suddenly leaps up and kisses Nikolai on the cheek.

Platonov Oh Nikolai, Nikolai . . . I have to be honest, I do have to say, I've never had much faith in medicine, but for once in your life, you actually did something!

Anna But is she all right? Is she going to survive?

Platonov Of course she'll survive.

He moves round, manic.

Forgive me all of you, please forgive me for everything . . .

Nikolai And now so cheerful! Look at him! Look at him now!

Platonov kisses Anna's hand.

Platonov Anna Petrovna, forgive me. Everyone forgive me!

He turns, holding his head.

Oh God, now it's me that's not feeling too good. I think it's a chill. Can someone get me some water?

Anna Sergei, get him water, please.

Platonov And, I can't explain, there are visions. I keep seeing toy soldiers marching by, all wearing chintz and with little pointy caps which keep flashing. You don't have any quinine, do you?

Nikolai I don't think quinine's what you need.

Platonov Don't you?

Nikolai I think more like a whack round the head.

Platonov Water, I need more water!

Nikolai (*feeling Platonov's forehead*) He's ill. I don't know what's wrong with him but he's very ill.

Anna We need to get him into town.

Platonov What's interesting, Anna, is that there's a very small piano crawling across your breast. Is there any chance you'd let me play a little Chopin?

10 *Platonov laughs uncontrollably, then gulps back more and more water, as Ivan comes across the fields. He is in his dressing gown, drunk, naked to the waist and carrying a revolver.*

Ivan Lead me to the man! Lead me to him! Make way! Make way!

Nikolai Oh, for goodness' sake, this is the limit.

Ivan My daughter, my only daughter!

Nikolai Go home. What on earth are you doing with that gun?

Ivan And am I to die unshriven?

He has addressed this question to the whole group.

Nikolai What on earth is he on about?

Ivan Mikhail, I have come to implore you: in the name of Jesus Christ, go to her, calm her, reassure her. Tell her you love her, and that you will always be her husband. For if she dies in sin, I too shall not be absolved.

Platonov Had a drink already, Colonel?

Nikolai Who told you she was dying, Father?

Ivan You're young, all of you. Only the old know what it is when judgement is close.

Nikolai Come, Father. Give me the gun. Please. Come inside.

Ivan Only the old know the terror of the end.

Nikolai takes the gun from Ivan and puts it down on a chair. Then leads him out.

Platonov My mouth's dry. Why is my mouth still dry?

Suddenly Sofya moves forward to address Platonov.

Sofya Mikhail, it is you who did this. What has happened today has been your doing.

Anna Not just at this moment, Sofya. Not just at this very moment, I think.

Sofya You have cast us aside like trash.

Anna Sofya . . .

Sofya You have destroyed us. Now you alone can raise us back up.

She pauses a second. Nikolai has returned.

It isn't too late. Take me back, Platonov. Take me back.

Platonov Well, I mean, if there was anything I felt I could do . . .

Sofya Save me, Platonov! Save me!

She drops to her knees.

Anna Sofya, never give them that. You're a woman. Never drop to your knees.

Sofya Somebody tell him, please. Somebody tell this man what he must do!

Anna goes to pull Sofya up.

Anna Nikolai, Sergei, I need help, we need to get her to bed.

Sofya Tell him what he must do!

Nikolai I have a sedative I can give her.

Anna I must say, I wouldn't mind a little chloroform myself.

Sofya is now screaming 'Tell him what he must do' as Sergei and Anna drag her away.

Come on, Sergei, pull yourself together. Show some courage.

Sergei Don't you think I'm trying?

11 *Nikolai, Sergei and Anna take the hysterical Sofya out. Platonov is left alone.*

Platonov A cigarette, please, someone, and a glass of water.

He sits up, tries to focus.

And now, a sort of planetarium. Wispy cirrus, and then Saturn diaphanous beyond. A big yellow ball, moving. Sort of like an orange, floating in broth.

143

He gets up and heads towards the table where the revolver has been left.

Ah good. Perfect. The necessary instrument.

With his left hand Platonov lifts a revolver to his temple.

And if I did it? *Finita la commedia!* One smart ape less on the earth!

He pauses, the gun suspended.

No, I don't think so. I want to do it, but nature says no. Lord God Almighty, I'm thirsty.

12 *Maria has appeared.*

Platonov Well goodness me, my sainted enemy.

Maria Mikhail.

Platonov What are you doing? You don't happen to have water concealed about your person?

Maria What? Oh no.

She smiles nervously.

I got your letter.

Platonov Yes, I was pretty pleased with it. It was one of my best.

Maria I thought so too.

Platonov I wonder, do you think you might take me home with you? I wouldn't need a bed. I'd be happy in the barn.

Maria Come with me. Come.

Platonov tries to focus on her.

Platonov I think in that case I might kiss your cheek.

Maria Oh really!

Platonov You're doing that thing, that red thing . . .

Maria What red thing?

Platonov What's it called . . .

Maria Blushing?

Platonov That's right. You're blushing.

Platonov reaches out and touches her cheek.

That's the very spot where I pointed my revolver.

Maria I'm sorry?

Platonov Just now. Before you came in. In that soft place. Between muscle and bone.

Platonov's hand is held a moment against her cheek.

I love everyone. I've tried to. I really have loved them. You think I've gone mad?

Maria suddenly puts her head on his lap. Platonov kisses the top of her head.

13 Sofya comes in and sees Platonov sitting with Maria's head in his lap. Sofya picks up the discarded revolver. Maria gets up at once.

Sofya Enough! It can't be allowed!

Maria What's going on? What's happening?

Sofya fires the gun at Platonov. She misses. Maria at once interposes herself between Platonov and Sofya. Maria shouts for help.

Quickly. Someone come quickly!

Sofya Out of the way.

She pushes Maria out of the way and at point-blank range shoots Platonov in the chest.

Maria Quickly!

Platonov What? What is this?

14 *Platonov falls to the ground. Anna Petrovna, Sergei, Nikolai and Ivan come running from the house. Anna snatches the gun from Sofya and throws her down on to the ground.*

Anna Platonov!

Sergei covers his face and turns away as Nikolai loosens the buttons on Platonov's frock coat.

Nikolai Mikhail Vasilich! Can you hear me?

Anna Nikolai, for God's sake, help him.

Nikolai Water!

Maria gives Nikolai the carafe.

Maria Save him! Please save him.

Nikolai drinks the water himself and puts the carafe aside. Ivan drops to his knees.

Ivan Didn't I say I was done for? Finished. Didn't I say that? God be my witness. I am.

Yakov, Vasili, Katya come from the house. Marko appears from across the fields.

Marko If you please, I'm from the Regional Magistrate –

Anna Platonov . . .

Platonov sits up and looks round.

Platonov (*points at Marko*) Give that man three roubles.

He falls back and dies. Nobody moves. Anna looks round.

Anna He's just hurt. It's all right. It isn't serious. Everyone. Why is everyone staring?

Maria moves away and sits at the table. Anna takes Platonov in her arms.

Ivan He rests with the saints.

Nikolai He's dead.

Anna No, no, no . . .

She cradles Platonov in her arms.

Nikolai Father, go and tell Sasha. She needs to know. The rest of you: there's nothing to see. Life is worth only a kopeck. And Misha has spent his kopeck.

He kneels and weeps.

Oh my friend, my dear friend, who shall I drink with at your funeral?

Sergei Nikolai, what can we do?

Nikolai Plainly, we were meant to take care of him. Plainly, we didn't.

Anna Be calm now, Sofya. The worst is over. Nikolai, I'll deal with Sasha. Leave her to me.

Anna hugs Platonov tighter.

Anna Platonov! My life!

Nikolai To work now, Sergei. We must look after Sofya.

Sergei Yes. As you say.

Sergei goes across to Sofya.

Ivan God has forsaken us on account of our sins. Why did you sin, you stupid old man? I killed God's creatures, got drunk and swore. I judged my fellow men. So the Lord lost patience and struck me down.

IVANOV

adapted by David Hare
from a literal translation by Alex Wilbraham

Note

Ivanov is the first play Chekhov actually completed. It was drafted in under two weeks in 1887. At the time Chekhov was known primarily as a comic short story writer, and the play was commissioned by Korsh's theatre in Moscow which specialised in farce. The management was surprised by the seriousness of the play Chekhov delivered. There were only ten rehearsals. The production was shown in a double bill with a French farce and the first night was famously unsatisfactory. According to the author, the actor playing Shabyelski got all his lines wrong in Act One. In Act Two the drunken party guests were indeed drunk. They improvised extensively, and some furniture was knocked over. Chekhov left, vowing never again to have anything to do with the theatre. The *New Times* commented, 'No author of recent times has made his bow to such a hotch-potch of praise and protest.'

It was when the Alexandrine Theatre in St Petersburg wanted to present the play in 1889 that Chekhov began some serious rewriting, mainly of Acts Two and Four. In particular, he worked on the ending, which had never satisfied him. In spite of the author's own doubts, *Ivanov* this time played triumphantly.

For many years, *Ivanov* had an unhappy record in Britain. Komisarjevsky directed the premiere in Barnes in 1925. John Gielgud played in his own production at the Phoenix Theatre in 1965, with Yvonne Mitchell as Anna and Clare Bloom as Sasha. The title role was later taken by Derek Jacobi, John Wood and Alan Bates. In 1997

Jonathan Kent directed this present adaptation at the Almeida Theatre, with Ralph Fiennes playing Ivanov, and the play was for the first time accepted to belong alongside Chekhov's four better-known works. It was also the first English-speaking production of Chekhov to be invited to play at the Maly Theatre in Moscow. The version was then presented in 1998 at the Lincoln Center Theatre in New York with Kevin Kline and Hope Davis.

Ivanov in this English adaptation premiered at the
Almeida Theatre, London, in 1997. It was first performed
at the Festival Theatre, Chichester, on 1 October 2015.
The cast, in order of appearance, was as follows:

Ivanov Samuel West
Borkin Des McAleer
Anna Nina Sosanya
Shabyelski Peter Egan
Lvov James McArdle
Kosykh Brian Pettifer
Avdotya Beverley Klein
Gavrila Mark Penfold
Babakina Emma Amos
Zinaida Lucy Briers
First Guest Col Farrell
Third Guest David Verrey
Lebedev Jonathan Coy
Sasha Olivia Vinall
Pyotr *and* **Guest** Nebli Basani
Ensemble Mark Donald

Director Jonathan Kent
Set Designer Tom Pye
Lighting Designer Mark Henderson
Music Jonathan Dove

Characters

Nikolai Ivanov
a regional councillor

Mikhail Borkin
the steward of Ivanov's estate

Anna Petrovna
Ivanov's wife, nee Sarah Abramson

Count Matvyei Shabyelski
Ivanov's uncle

Yevgeni Lvov
a young country doctor

Zinaida Savishna
wife to Lebedev

Marfusha Babakina
a young widow and heiress

Avdotya Nazarovna
an old woman of no known profession

Kosykh
an excise officer

Pavel Lebedev
chairman of the local council

Sasha
daughter to the Lebedevs, aged twenty

Gavrila
servant to the Lebedevs

Pyotr
servant to Ivanov

First Guest

Second Guest

Third Guest

Fourth Guest

Visitors, men and women

The action takes place in a province
in Central Russia in the late 1880s

Act One

The garden of Ivanov's estate. On the left is the facade of a house with a terrace. One window is open. In front of the terrace is a wide semicircular area from which paths lead to the right and straight ahead. On the right-hand side there are small benches, tables and chairs. On one table a lamp is already lit. Evening is drawing in. The sound of a duet for cello and piano, coming from indoors.

1 Ivanov is sitting at the table reading a book. Borkin, the steward, appears from the depths of the garden, in big boots and carrying a gun. He is high on drink. He goes quietly up to Ivanov, and when he is near aims the gun at his head. Ivanov jumps up.

Ivanov My God, what on earth are you doing?

Borkin (*very quietly*) Bang!

Ivanov Misha, honestly, you know what my life's like . . .

Borkin (*laughing*) I know, I do know . . .

Ivanov Why do you do it? Why do you do these things?

Borkin (*conceding*) All right I promise . . .

Ivanov You seem to get some sort of pleasure . . .

Borkin . . . I'll never shoot you again.

Ivanov Thank you. I'm trying to read.

Ivanov has sat down again. Borkin sits down beside him and takes off his cap.

Borkin My God, it's so hot. You wouldn't believe it. I've covered fifteen miles in under three hours. I'm exhausted. Feel.

Ivanov Later.

Borkin Come on, feel. Here.

He has taken Ivanov's hand and put it on his chest.

An irregular beat. There. Boom-boom-boom-*boom*. It's a murmur of the heart. I could drop dead any moment. Then what would you feel?

Ivanov I'd feel nothing.

Borkin No really. I'm asking. Tell me.

Ivanov I'd feel I could finish my book.

Borkin Sweet fellow, I really am asking. Tell me the truth: would you be upset?

Ivanov Only one thing upsets me. The smell of stale vodka.

Borkin You can smell vodka? Amazing. Or maybe not, after all. In Plesniki I ran into the presiding judge. Do you know him? We had eight glasses each. What a great judge! Though if you ask my opinion, drinking is bad for you. In the long run. That's my opinion. Drinking is harmful. What's your view?

Ivanov Oh for God's sake, this is unbearable. Do you have no idea of what this is like?

Borkin I plead guilty, your honour.

Ivanov gets up to go.

No, stay there. Please. Such cultured people! You're not even allowed to speak to them.

Ivanov turns back.

Oh, just one thing. I need the eighty-two roubles.

Ivanov What eighty-two roubles?

Borkin Tomorrow. (*Reminding him.*) The workmen? The roubles?

Ivanov I don't have it.

Borkin Oh, well, thank you. I'll tell them that, then. That's marvellous. Let me rehearse. 'I don't have it.' How was that?

Ivanov I have no money. Wait till the end of the month. That's when the council pays me.

Borkin You tell them. You go and tell them. I'd love to hear you. 'I don't have any money. The council hasn't paid me yet!' I'd love to hear you tell them that!

Ivanov What do you want me to do? There's no point in asking me. What is this? What on earth is the point?

Borkin What is it? What *is* it ?

They are beginning to lose their tempers.

It's me asking when we're going to pay our own workers. Call yourself a landowner? Oh yes, 'progressive farming techniques'! May I remind you: you own a thousand acres of land, and yet you don't have a rouble in your pocket. It's like owning a cellar full of wine, and losing the corkscrew. What am I meant to do? I'll take the troika tomorrow and sell the wretched thing. Why not? I sold the oats before they'd even been harvested. Tomorrow I may as well sell the corn. It's fine. Do you think it bothers me? Ay-ay-ay! If you're looking for someone who gets bothered, you've come to the wrong man.

2 *Borkin has begun to pace up and down. Now the voice of Count Shabyelski comes from indoors.*

Shabyelski (*off*) You're impossible to play with. Your touch is appalling, and you've got the ear of a fish!

At once, Ivanov's wife, Anna Petrovna, appears at the open window.

Anna What's going on? Misha? Why all this stamping about?

Borkin Tell me how you live with your darling Nikolai and manage to not stamp about.

Anna I meant to ask, can we have some hay put on the croquet lawn?

Borkin Oh just . . . leave me alone!

Anna Well, really. What a tone to use to a woman! And when I gather you're so keen to attract one as well!

She turns cheerfully to Ivanov.

Shall we go and turn cartwheels out there in the hay, my darling?

Ivanov Anna, you know the cold air is bad for you. Please go back in. (*Shouts.*) Uncle, can you close it? Please!

The window is closed.

Borkin We have only two days left to pay Lebedev his interest.

Ivanov (*looks at his watch*) That's why I have to go there tonight.

Borkin Of course, I'd forgotten, that's right, it's his daughter's birthday . . .

Ivanov I shall go and ask him to be patient.

Borkin Hey, it's Sasha's birthday. Why don't I come with you?

He sings and does a little dance.

'If you're coming, I'm going; if you're going, I'm coming . . .' (*Speaks.*) I'll have a quick swim. Chew a little blotting paper, then rinse my mouth out with meths and I can start drinking all over again. The sad thing is, you don't realise just how much I love you, my friend. You're always so moody, you find life so lowering. But you never look round and think: 'At least I've got a friend.' I'd do anything for you. I could even marry Marfusha Babakina. Yes. She's a dumb bitch but I'd do it. You could have half the dowry. Dammit, you could have the whole thing.

Ivanov You do talk such nonsense.

Borkin But that's where you wrong. (*Imitates him.*) 'You do talk such nonsense.' Why? Why is that nonsense? If that's what you wanted, that's what I'd do. I'm serious! It's a shame, you're such a bright man, so brilliant, but where is the whatsit? That little bit of extra? You know what I'm saying? Where is the drive? If you could only . . . I don't know . . . make the big gesture. If you were a normal person I could make you a million a year. Look, for example, say I was you – I'm you, all right? – if I had two thousand roubles today, then I swear within two weeks, I'd have twenty thousand. In the hand! There you go, look, your lips moving already: 'It's nonsense!' But it isn't nonsense, it's so! On the opposite river bank Ovsianov is selling his holding. If we bought that strip of land, then both of the banks would be ours. And then . . . well, you can imagine, we'd start saying we had plans for a mill. And for a mill we'd need to build a dam. And then we'd say to everyone who's living down river and who obviously would hate the idea: 'All right, if you don't want it, I'm sorry, *meine Damen und Herren*, but we're going to build it unless you pay up.' The Zarevsky factory would give us five thousand, Korolkov three thousand, the monastery would be good for six . . .

Ivanov Misha, please, I don't want an argument. But I cannot listen to this.

3 Count Shabyelski comes out of the house with Doctor Lvov, who is twenty-six.

Shabyelski Doctors and lawyers, there's really no difference except lawyers just rob you, doctors rob you and kill you as well.

Borkin (*sitting at the table*) Oh of course, it's not just that you won't do anything. But I'm not allowed to do anything either!

Shabyelski sits on the little bench.

Shabyelski Present company excepted, of course. Every one of them charlatans. Frauds. Perhaps in Utopia there exists an honest doctor. But as a man who has spent twenty thousand on medicine in his life, I can say: I've never met one who wasn't an obvious quack.

Borkin Enterprise, of course, that's vulgar. Not enough for *you* not to have any, but none of the rest of us must have any either.

Shabyelski Present company excepted, I have said. There may be other exceptions. But.

He yawns. Ivanov shuts his book and addresses Lvov.

Ivanov Well?

Lvov As I said this morning, she must go to the Crimea, and at once.

He has glanced at the window and is now pacing up and down. Shabyelski snorts.

Shabyelski The Crimea! Why, Misha, you and I must try this doctoring racket. As soon as some bubble-headed housewife starts to sneeze, then out with the scientific prescription: off to the Crimea! And then no doubt, when she gets there, the regular attentions of some virile young brute.

Ivanov In the name of God, Uncle, will you stop talking such tripe?

He turns back to Lvov.

She won't go. Even if I could raise the money – which I can't – she'll still refuse.

Lvov Yes. As things are.

There's a pause.

Borkin I mean, what are we saying here? Just how ill is she? Does she really have to go all that way?

Lvov (*glancing again at the window*) Yes. It's tuberculosis.

Borkin Ah, well then. I must say. Fair enough. Lately whenever I've looked at her, I have thought 'She's not with us long.'

Lvov Please. Quietly. She can hear you in there.

There's a pause.

Borkin That's life. What is it? A flower. It blossoms, it blooms. Then a goat comes along. Sk-lumph. And it's gone.

Shabyelski It's nonsense, she's fine. (*Yawns.*) Charlatans merely. And frauds.

There's a pause.

Borkin Now what I've been doing is trying to teach Nikolai here ways to make money. I had a brilliant idea. But Nikolai is not interested. Why not? Because Nikolai is gloomy. He's jaundiced. He's woebegone. He's forlorn. How is Nikolai? He's down in the dumps.

Shabyelski (*getting up and stretching*) Oh, you're such an entrepreneur. You're so full of advice for everyone, but you never have any for me.

Borkin I'm going for a swim.

Shabyelski Why don't you help me?

Borkin Goodbye to you all!

Shabyelski I mean it. Instruct me! Give me lessons: how to get ahead!

Borkin If you're really interested, you could be up twenty thousand by the end of the week.

Shabyelski Well then, show me!

Borkin I guarantee it.

Shabyelski Teach me!

Borkin Nikolai, by the way, lend me a rouble, will you?

Ivanov silently gives Borkin a rouble. Shabyelski has got up to pursue him.

Thank you. There's nothing to it. It's simple.

Shabyelski But what do I actually do?

Borkin I promise: twenty thousand, thirty thousand, how much do you want?

They go out. Ivanov and Lvov are silent for a moment.

Ivanov Needless words. Needless people. A perpetual drizzle of stupid questions. All this, Doctor, has exhausted me to the point of sickness. I am so angry I no longer know who I am. For whole days I'm driven mad by an unceasing noise in my head. I can't sleep and my ears buzz. But where can I put myself? Truly?

Lvov Nikolai Alekseyevich, we need a serious talk.

Ivanov By all means.

Lvov You say Anna will not go, but she will go if you accompany her.

Ivanov Yes. But it would cost twice as much. I've already had leave from work. I can't ask again.

Lvov Then listen. Whether she goes or not, what Anna needs above all is peace. She needs quiet. But every moment of the day Anna is in torment. The only thing she cares about is you, and your feelings towards her. Forgive me. But by your behaviour you are killing her.

There is a pause.

Ivanov, I want to think well of you. I want to believe in you.

Ivanov Yes, it's true, I know. I'm sure it's all my fault. You're right. But I'm confused, I'm . . . what? I'm *possessed*, is that right? Is that the right word? How do I put this? I lack strength. That's it. I lack the strength to lift myself up. The fact is, I've ceased to understand anyone, anything.

He glances at the window.

My friend, if you want, I can tell you the whole story, but . . . not here. We'll walk. I'll give you an inkling.

Yes? A sketch. Anna . . . now, if we start with Anna . . .
we agree, she's a wonderful woman. An extraordinary
woman. Any sacrifice I required, she was ready to make.
For my sake, she forsook her religion, she abandoned
her parents, she gave up all prospect of wealth. Whereas
I . . . as you know, I am in no sense wonderful. On my
side, I have sacrificed precisely nothing. I married her
because I loved her passionately and I swore to love her
for ever but . . . all right. Guess! Five years have gone by,
she is still in love, and I . . .

He spreads his hands to finish.

You tell me she's going to die, and I feel not love, nor
even pity, but just a terrible kind of emptiness. I'm sure
from the outside – I accept this – it must seem shocking.

*4 Ivanov and Lvov walk off towards the avenue, as
Shabyelski comes in, roaring with laughter.*

Shabyelski My God, this man isn't a fraud, he's a
genius . . .

Ivanov (*going out*) But I am past the stage where I can
make sense of it.

Shabyelski He's part-lawyer, part-accountant and part-
doctor. In other words, all the most poisonous modern
professions rolled into one.

He sits on the bottom step of the terrace.

Shame he never finished his studies. Give him a liberal
education, with just that little extra bit of culture, and
you'd have the perfect con man. 'No problem,' he says.
'You can make twenty thousand by the end of the week.
Just trade in your assets. Trade your title,' he says . . .

Shabyelski laughs. Anna opens the window.

Next question is, 'Why don't I fix you up with
Marfusha?' he asks. *Qui ça?* Marfusha Babakina, of
course. The one with a nose like a cab driver. Oh yes,
ideal Countess material.

Anna Is that you, Count?

Shabyelski Who's that?

Anna is laughing.

(*In a Jewish accent.*) What's so funny, my dear?

Anna Something you said at dinner once. How does it
go? A horse, a what, a Jew?

Shabyelski
'A horse you once saw limping
A thief who claims he's cured
A Jew who says he's Christian –
And you'd better be insured.'

Anna laughs again.

Anna The simplest joke and of course it has to be
malicious. No, I'm serious. I hadn't realised until recently
how much it affects me. It does. Living with you, just
being with you, Count, is depressing. Because in your
eyes everyone is a phoney or a crook. Tell me, in honesty,
do you have good word for anyone?

Shabyelski What a question!

Anna I mean it. You and I have lived under the same
roof for five years and not once have I heard you praise
a single human being. Why? What have they all done to
you? Do you think yourself so much better?

Shabyelski Far from it. If I'm hard on others, my God,
I'm hardest of all on myself. What have I become? A

parasite. Years ago, I was free, I was rich, I was happy, even. Now, what am I? I'm the licensed buffoon. Whatever I say, it makes no difference. I can be as rude as I like, they just think, 'The old man's off his head.' They pay no attention.

Anna (*quietly*) It's screeching again.

Shabyelski Screeching?

Anna The owl. Every night it screeches.

Shabyelski Let it screech. Things can't get worse than they are already.

He stretches himself.

Oh Anna, if I could just win that lottery, a small win, not even a big one, the things I could do! The places I'd take you! I'd be off your hands and not be back in this house till Judgement Day.

Anna Where would you go first?

Shabyelski Oh. Moscow. To hear the famous gypsy choir. Then on to Paris. I'd rent a flat, go to the Russian church.

Anna And what else?

Shabyelski I'd sit by my wife's grave for days. I'd sit, just thinking. And waiting for death. My wife is buried in Paris.

Anna Buried?

There's a pause.

How depressing! Can we play some more music?

Shabyelski Of course. Set it up.

5 Anna goes back indoors. Ivanov and Lvov reappear from their walk.

Ivanov My friend, you only graduated last year. You're young and full of life. I'm thirty-five. So I'm perfectly placed to offer you advice. It's this: don't marry a blue-stocking, a hysteric or a Jew. You think I'm joking, but I'm not. On the contrary. My advice would be: go for someone ordinary. The less stimulation the better. Get into a routine. I mean it. Finally it's safer. It's like, strong colours are fun, but ultimately it's cleverer to wear grey. What I'm saying is: don't take on the world. Don't tilt at windmills. Don't waste your time bashing your head against brick walls. What that means is, at least in my experience, at all costs stay away from progressive farming. Yes. And progressive education. And most of all, God help us! progressive rhetoric. It's a killer. Just pull your little shell up over your head, and get on with your life. Finally, it's the only way. I did the other thing, and it has destroyed me. I cannot tell you. My life? A story of unceasing error and absurdity!

He suddenly sees Shabyelski.

Oh Uncle, I cannot believe it!

Shabyelski What?

Ivanov Can I never get a moment to myself?

He has blurted this out and Shabyelski is hurt.

Shabyelski And can I . . . can *I*?

Ivanov Oh God!

Shabyelski I suppose I have nowhere.

Ivanov No! No, for God's sake!

Shabyelski I am always in the way, I am not to exist!

He jumps up and goes into the house. Ivanov at once shouts after him.

Ivanov Oh Lord, I'm sorry. Uncle, I'm sorry!

He turns back to Lvov.

What am I doing? What have I done?

Lvov Nikolai . . .

Ivanov How could I offend him like that? It's unforgivable. I must stop this. I must.

Lvov Nikolai, I have to speak you frankly.

Ivanov looks at him a moment.

Ivanov Very well.

Lvov I must tell you the truth.

Ivanov The truth? Go ahead.

Lvov I have listened, I have tried to listen as best I may. But it seems to me you cannot speak, no, you cannot even open your mouth without talking about yourself. Always. The subject is 'I'. It is 'I'! Just fifteen feet away – my God, the selfishness of it, the heartlessness – a woman is dying. She is dying from her very love for you. Her time on this earth is coming to an end. And yet you prance around like a pigeon boasting of your own . . . what do you call it? Despair! Words . . . the words are not in my gift, but I can only say: you are a man who is detestable.

Ivanov Perhaps. You see me from the outside. Probably you're right.

He listens a moment.

It sounds as if the horses are ready. I must go and change.

He stops on his way back into the house.

You do not hide your feelings, Doctor. You do not like me, and you say so. I admire you for that.

He goes inside. Lvov is alone.

Lvov I cannot believe it. What is it? What is it that stops me from speaking? I begin to tell him what he must do and my chest clamps. My tongue sticks to the roof of my mouth. How could I have let that moment go by? That was my moment. How I hate him. This imposter, this over-educated Tartuffe! He is going out! Going out, when his wife's only happiness is when he's close. He is her life. She begs him, implores him to stay just one evening at home. And he . . . cannot. Home? Not interesting enough. An evening at home and he'd have to shoot himself. Of course. This man needs space. He needs air. He needs room to think up new ways to betray her. I know why you go to visit the Lebedevs! I know!

6 Shabyelski comes out of the house with Anna and Ivanov, who is now wearing a coat and hat.

Shabyelski Nikolai, it's not right, it's completely unfair. You go out every night and we stay at home. We go to bed at eight from sheer boredom. Do you call this life? You're allowed out and we're not?

Anna Count, leave him alone. Let him go.

Ivanov Yes, but what about you, my dear sweet invalid? Ask the doctor. You shouldn't be out at this hour. You're not a child, Anna.

Anna No.

Ivanov You must think.

Anna Yes.

There is a moment's pause.

Of course.

Ivanov (*to Shabyelski*) Why are you so desperate to come with me?

Shabyelski To be anywhere! Not to be here! You make me stay at home, so that Anna will not be bored, you say, but it seems not to occur to you that you are leaving your wife in the company of the most boring person on earth.

Anna Leave him, Count. Let him go. He likes it there.

Ivanov Anna, I am hardly going because I 'like' it. I am not going because I like it. I am going because I have to discuss my debts.

Anna You don't have to justify yourself. Just go. Who is keeping you?

Ivanov Everyone, please let's . . . let's please be pleasant to one another.

Shabyelski Nikolai, I beg you. I haven't been out since Easter. I need people I can despise, I need entertainment.

Ivanov All right, very well. My God, how you bore me!

Shabyelski takes his arm to thank him.

Shabyelski Oh thank you, thank you. God in heaven be praised. But your hat, Nikolai, the straw one . . . may I borrow it?

Ivanov You can. Only quickly. Please!

Shabyelski runs into the house.

How did this happen? How did I reach this point?

He at once realises what he has said.

Oh Lord, I'm sorry, how can I say such things? Anna, I'm sorry. I am not myself, this is not how I speak. This is not me. And now goodbye, I'll be back about one.

Anna My darling, please.

Ivanov What? My sweet one, my darling.

There is a pause.

Anna Please stay.

Ivanov Anna, my sweet one, my own, I do have to ask you, please don't stop me. Don't stop me going out. I know it's selfish, but, forgive me, I need this selfishness. It must be allowed. As soon as the sun goes down, my own home begins to oppress me. I become consumed with anguish. Why? If only I knew! I feel terrible here, I go to the Lebedevs', I feel worse. I come home, I feel worse still. And so it goes. I am desperate.

Anna Nikolai, why not stay? We'll talk. We'll talk as we once talked. Let's eat together and read. Old Miseryguts and I have learnt all this music. We learnt it for you.

She puts her arms round him.

Stay!

There is a pause.

I don't understand. It's been a year now. What changed you?

Ivanov I don't know. I don't know.

Anna Then why can't I come? Why can't I come visiting with you?

Ivanov All right, let me say it. You ask me a question, I will tell you, since we value the truth. When I am in this

173

state, I begin not to love you. Yes. That's why I run. When I do not love you, I have to get out of the house.

Anna I understand. I understand this anguish. I understand it. Try, why not? Try to sing. Try to laugh. Anything. Get angry. I don't mind. Just stay. Have a drink. Laugh. Shout. We'll drive your anguish away. I'll sing for you. We'll lie in the hay. We'll sit in the study, in the dark, as we once sat in the dark, and you can talk about your unhappiness. Your eyes are so full of suffering. I shall look into them and cry, and we'll both feel better.

She begins to laugh and cry.

How does it go, that song? 'The flowers return in spring, but not the joy.' That's it, isn't it? Well then, go.

Ivanov Pray for me, Anna.

He starts to go out, then stops for a moment and thinks.

I can't stay! I can't!

He goes out. Anna sits at the table.

Anna Then go.

Lvov continues to pace.

Lvov Anna Petrovna, you must make a rule: on the dot of six you must go indoors and not come out till sunrise. The damp in the evening is bad for you.

Anna Whatever you wish, monsieur.

Lvov Why do you say that? Why do you talk like that? I'm serious.

Anna But I don't want to be serious.

She starts to cough.

Lvov There, I told you. You've begun to cough.

*7 Shabyelski comes out of the house in a hat and jacket.
He hurries across to kiss Anna's hand.*

Shabyelski Where's Nikolai? Are the horses waiting?
Goodnight to you, my beautiful. (*Pulling a face.*)
Mazeltov and eschkoozer me.

He goes out quickly.

Lvov Very funny.

*There is a pause. The sound of an accordion in the
distance.*

Anna It's so unfair. The cooks, the coachmen, they get to
dance. And I? I never dance. Yevgeni Konstantinovich,
why are you pacing about? Come and sit down.

Lvov I can't.

Anna They're playing 'The Starling' in the kitchen.
(*Sings.*)
    'Starling, starling, where have you been?
    Drinking vodka on the green . . .'

There is a pause.

Are your parents still alive, Doctor?

Lvov My father died. My mother's still living.

Anna Do you miss her?

Lvov Oh well, you know. I'm so busy.

Anna (*laughs*) 'The flowers return in spring, but not the
joy . . .' Who taught me that? I've forgotten. It must
have been him.

She listens.

The owl again.

Lvov Let it bloody well screech.

Anna I suppose I'm beginning to feel, Doctor, that life has somehow short-changed me. Most people, perhaps no more deserving than me, are happy. They pay nothing for their happiness. But I have paid. I am paying with my whole life. Why is such high interest demanded of me?

She looks at him a moment.

What did you say?

Lvov I didn't say anything.

Anna You are always so kind to me, so considerate. Do you think I haven't guessed what is wrong with me? I know perfectly well. It's boring to talk about. (*With a Jewish accent.*) Mazeltov and e-schkoozer me. How are you on funny stories?

Lvov Hopeless. I can't tell them.

Anna He does. Brilliantly. And also I begin to be shocked at the cruelty of people. Why is love not answered with love? Why is truth always answered with lies? Tell me, how long are my own mother and father going to go on hating me? From fifty miles away, day and night, even in my sleep, I can feel their hatred. How am I to deal with my husband? He says it's only in the evening, he stops loving me only in the evening, when the anguish is at its worst. I see that. But during the day . . . Say he stopped loving me entirely. Of course it's not possible. But if he did? If he has? No. Don't think about it. (*Sings.*) 'Starling, starling, where have you been . . .'

She shudders.

How frightened I am! You've never married, Doctor, you understand nothing.

He sits down beside her.

Lvov You say you are shocked, Anna. No, it is I who am shocked. You are so clever, so upright, so honest.

How did you end up in this place? What do you have in common with that unfeeling husband . . . All right, I'll leave him out of it . . . but why do you go on living in these depraved surroundings? That mad, mumbling, lunatic Count! And Borkin, that appalling plug-ugly little thug. Explain to me. What are you doing? Why on earth do you stay?

Anna You sound like him. It's funny. Him as he used to be. His eyes used to grow round. When he talked, they glowed like burning coals. He blazed with passion. Go on, talk to me more!

Lvov gets up, waving a hand.

Lvov Talk? Why? What's the point?

He suddenly shouts.

Just go indoors!

Anna You are so confident. My husband is this. My husband is that. But how can you tell? You haven't even known him six months. This man was remarkable. Two years ago. Or three. There was no man ever like him. I saw him once, *once* across a room. It's true. I saw him and the trap was sprung. I met him, I loved him at sight. He said, 'Follow me.' I followed. My life died behind me. It died, I killed it, quite consciously I killed it, and I never looked back.

There is a pause.

It's only now . . . only now when he goes to the Lebedevs' to be with other women. While I sit in the garden and the owl screeches.

A watchman is heard, knocking against the fences to drive away thieves.

And you don't have any brothers? Sisters?

Lvov None.

She cries.

Tell me. Tell me what's happening.

Anna (*stands*) I can't stand it. I am going there.

Lvov What do you mean?

Anna I shall follow him. I am going to find him. Order up the horses. Bring me the horses, quick!

She runs into the house.

Lvov No, this is not it. This is unprofessional. Not only do they fail to pay me, but they rip my heart out as well. Enough! I withdraw my services.

He goes into the house.

Act Two

A reception room at the Lebedevs' house. In the middle a door gives on to the garden, and there are doors to left and right. There is a great deal of expensive furniture, but the chandeliers, candelabra and pictures are under dust-sheets.

1 A game of cards is going on at the back of the stage. Among the players are Kosykh, the excise officer, and Avdotya Nazarovna, an old woman. Throughout the act guests are seen coming and going through the garden and the room. Gavrila, the servant, is in attendance. The young widow and heiress Marfusha Babakina comes in, and heads straight for Lebedev's wife, Zinaida Savishna, who is on the sofa. Around her young men are sitting on stiff-backed chairs.

Zinaida My darling Marfusha, how wonderful to see you.

Babakina Congratulations, my dear, on your daughter's birthday.

They kiss.

May God give her everything she desires.

Zinaida We thank you. We are simply so happy. And tell us, how have you been?

Babakina I've been well. Greetings, young friends.

The women sit together on the sofa. The men get up and bow.

First Guest Young? Come now, I suppose you're going to start claiming to be old.

Babakina I could hardly still hope to call myself young.

First Guest Please. It is only in name that you are a widow, Babakina. You are more attractive than any young girl.

> *There is a moment's pause. Gavrila has brought tea for Babakina.*

Zinaida Why on earth are you serving the tea without sweetening, Gavrila? Tea is nothing without jam. Some gooseberry, perhaps.

Babakina No. No thank you. No gooseberry.

Zinaida Are you sure?

Babakina Thanks but no thanks all the same.

> *There is another moment.*

First Guest So. Tell us, Marfusha Babakina. How did you get here?

Babakina How?

First Guest Yes. By what route?

Babakina Oh . . .

First Guest Did you come through Muschkino?

Babakina No. I took the Zaimischche road. It's quicker.

First Guest Good thinking.

Kosykh Two spades.

Second Guest Pass.

Fourth Guest Pass.

Avdotya Pass.

Babakina And what about the price of the lottery tickets?

Zinaida Oh don't tell us, we know!

Babakina Two-seventy roubles to enter the first draw. For the second, I do not exaggerate, already two-fifty. It's unprecedented.

Zinaida Just think, those fortunate souls who have already invested.

Babakina You say that, but the fact is, there's no guarantee.

Zinaida Yes, but what you're buying is hope. (*Sighs.*) Who knows? It's a ticket. God may be kind.

Third Guest You raise an interesting point. Is one well off with capital at this time? Look at interest rates. Dividends have gone through the floor. One is bound to ask is one better off with one's capital invested or with . . . or with . . . or with, well, its opposite . . .

Babakina Capital not invested?

Third Guest That's right.

The First Guest yawns.

Babakina And now one may yawn in front of ladies?

First Guest I'm sorry. I forgot myself.

Zinaida gets up and goes out of the room. A silence.

Fourth Guest Two diamonds.

Avdotya Pass.

Second Guest Pass.

Kosykh Pass.

Babakina Lord Jesus, the tedium. It is as if one had actually died.

2 *Now Zinaida is heard talking under her breath to her husband Lebedev as she leads him into the room.*

Zinaida What a prima donna! What on earth were you doing, sitting out here? These are your guests. You must mingle.

Lebedev Oh God, what an unendurable life we do lead.

> *Zinaida has resumed her place. Lebedev now sees Babakina.*

But look who's here. Radiance, beauty and laughter, sitting among us. (*Greeting her.*) How are you, you gorgeous piece of nougat?

Babakina Happy to be here.

Lebedev And we are happy to have you. Happy. Happy.

> *He sits down in an armchair.*

So. Very well. I could do with a vodka.

> *He drinks the vodka Gavrila serves him in one, then has a glass of water.*

First Guest Your good health, sir.

Lebedev Health? I'm alive, that's all one can say.

> *He turns to his wife.*

And where has the birthday girl got to, my love?

Kosykh (*tearful*) I just don't understand it. We haven't won anything. I simply . . . I cannot believe it. Not one. Not one single trick.

*He has jumped up in despair, and now Avdotya
Nazarovna gets up also, furious.*

Avdotya Whose fault is that? For goodness' sake you
went into their suits.

Kosykh I didn't!

Avdotya No wonder you were left with the ace.

Kosykh That is simply not true. Let me tell you . . .
everyone, I'll tell you my hand.

Lebedev Please!

Kosykh In diamonds, no, listen, I am holding, the king,
the queen and the jack. I also have the eight. I have the
ace of spades. Yet she – can you believe this? – she
refuses my slam.

Avdotya I didn't.

Kosykh I bid no trumps . . .

Avdotya What do you mean? I bid no trumps. It was
you who bid two!

Kosykh (*to Lebedev*) Dear friend, I implore you. I ask
you to judge this. Let me recap, my diamonds are as
follows . . .

Lebedev (*holding his ears*) Will somebody please get this
man to stop?

Avdotya It was me! As God is my witness. It was me
who bid the no trumps!

Kosykh For as long as I breathe on this planet, I will
never again play cards with this flabby old trout!

He runs into the garden.

Avdotya Trout! How dare he? The man has no conception
of manners.

Babakina My dear Avdotya, you seem to have mislaid your manners yourself.

Avdotya now sees Babakina and throws open her arms.

Avdotya Oh forgive me, my little plum, my angel, Babakina. Here I am, it's true, I'm talking like a fool. I didn't even see you, my lollipop.

She kisses her on the shoulder and sits down next to her.

Let me look at you, gorgeous. Perfection! But I mustn't praise you too highly, or it'll bring you bad luck.

Lebedev Praise her all you like, she still needs a husband.

Avdotya A husband? I promise you, my darling, finding you a husband will be my life's work.

She gestures across the room.

Though goodness knows where from, to judge by the present selection. Look at them, sitting there like hens in the rain.

Third Guest That hardly seems a suitable comparison. Have you thought, perhaps there's a good reason why men are choosing to stay single? Surely it says something about the society in which we now live?

Lebedev Oh please, anything but social theory. Spare us. Life is too short.

3 Sasha comes in and goes straight to her father.

Sasha Such a beautiful evening, and you're all sitting here in this fug!

Zinaida Sasha, did you not notice Marfusha Babakina is present?

Sasha I apologise. I didn't see you.

Babakina Really, Sasha, you've got so stand-offish, you no longer come and see me at all.

They kiss, then Sasha sits down next to her father.

Congratulations.

Sasha Well, thank you.

Lebedev No question you're right, Avdotya, there's a shortage of decent prospects. Forget would-be bridegrooms, you can't even find a best man. Young men today, they're all insipid. Cheerless. They don't know how to dance, they can't articulate, they can't even drink.

Avdotya I'd say drink is the one thing they can do.

Lebedev I don't mean drink like a horse drinks. I mean drink like we used to. After a hard day at lectures, at study, then out with the ladies, drinking and dancing till dawn. And talking! Talking like men kissed by the Almighty, talking with the eloquence of gods. But now . . .

He gestures dismissively.

You look, you see only dishmops. Men who are halfway to women, it seems. There's only one real man in the district. Needless to say he's already married. Oh yes, and one other small detail: he's also gone off his head.

Babakina Who can you mean?

Lebedev Well, naturally I'm talking about Ivanov.

Babakina Ah yes. A good man. But look at him: desperately unhappy.

Zinaida Well, is it any surprise?

Babakina (*sighs*) Ah well . . .

Zinaida It's his own fault. How could he? What an obvious disaster. Marrying a Jew. And as usual, it didn't pay off. All he wanted was to get his hands on little Sarah Abramson's fortune. But the parents were ahead of him. They cut her off the day she changed her religion. As soon as she changed her name. He should have foreseen it. Now the poor man's lumbered.

Sasha Mother, that is simply not true.

Babakina Oh my dear, I think one may say it's commonly accepted.

Sasha Is it?

Babakina It is fairly obvious. Why else would anyone marry a Jew? Are you telling me there aren't enough nice Russian girls?

She is becoming extremely animated.

The sad thing is, it's not him that suffers. She does. He tortures her because he knows he made a mistake. He comes home, he shouts, 'It's your fault, your parents have swindled me.' People have heard him. 'Get out of my house!' But where can she go? Her family won't have her. I suppose she could work as a maid. At a pinch. If she trained. Her life is unbearable. If the uncle weren't in the house, why, I believe Ivanov might well have murdered her by now.

Avdotya I've heard he did throw her in the cellar one time.

Babakina I've heard that.

Avdotya The best bit: he forced her to eat garlic.

186

Babakina It was garlic?

Avdotya I'm sure. It's a fact. He had her in there with twelve bulbs of the stuff. He forced them down her throat till she stank like a dog!

They all laugh.

Sasha Father, these are lies.

Lebedev No doubt, but at least they're amusing. More vodka!

Gavrila pours him another glass.

Zinaida All I know is that he's broke. If he didn't have Borkin to run the estate for him, then he and his Jewess would have nothing to eat. For us, it's been a real nightmare. For three years he's owed us this terrible debt. Nine thousand roubles!

Babakina (*horrified*) Nine thousand?

Zinaida All thanks to my brilliant husband, of course. Such a great judge of character. It's his choice where we lend. And, believe me, this is not a question of capital. We've not even started to get the interest returned.

Sasha Mother, you have said this over and over.

Zinaida Well . . .

Sasha You talk of nothing else.

Zinaida What business is it of yours?

Sasha How dare you . . . how dare you slander this man when he's done you no harm?

Third Guest If you will allow me, dear Sasha, I respect Ivanov as much as you do. He has welcomed me into his home. But you can hardly deny, through the whole region the man is known as a scoundrel.

Sasha I see.

She looks at him, furious.

And that's your idea of respect?

Third Guest I'm sorry, but there's evidence. We all know. The insurance swindle . . .

Sasha Oh really!

Zinaida It's true!

Third Guest Ivanov bought a herd of cows –

Sasha This is nonsense . . .

Zinaida He did!

Third Guest – during the cattle epidemic. And then, to make money, he infected them himself.

Sasha The scheme was obviously Borkin's. It has Borkin written all over it. When Ivanov found out, he was furious. All right, you can say he was weak. But he always wants to think well of people. He tries to help them. And how is he thanked? He's been swindled and plundered by every petty crook in the area. People exploit him. He gets exploited because he has a fine heart.

Lebedev Such passion, my God! And in a young girl . . .

Sasha But why? Why do we do this? Why do we talk this rubbish? Ivanov! Ivanov! We talk about nothing else. Do you never ask yourselves why? (*To the young men.*) Oh you lot, you love it. It's easy. So little effort. Let's all talk of one thing! Because of course it would be so much harder for you, you miserable sponges, to think of anything original to say . . .

Lebedev (*laughs*) That's right, you tell them, my dear . . .

Sasha No, that would involve you in actual mental activity. You'd have to try and be witty. You might have to find a new joke. And if you did, you'd risk being attractive to the women. For the moment, thank God, there's no danger of that! But why not? Why not just try it? As a favour? To me? Just once in your life? Think of something brilliant, think of something outrageous, on one single occasion, do something, *do* something even, which would make women sit up? Isn't that what you want? That young women should admire you? Desire you? Because as things stand, I tell you, you don't have a chance.

Zinaida Well, really!

Sasha has gone to the door.

Sasha Until you all change I will never stop saying it: this is a town of dismal young men!

4 *Shabyelski comes in with Ivanov through the right-hand door.*

Shabyelski Ah, the noble sound of oratory! Marvellous! Speechmaking, always the perfect birthday activity . . .

He takes Sasha's hand and kisses it.

May you live a long life, and never have to come back.

Zinaida (*to Ivanov*) Nikolai Alekseyevich, what a pleasure to see you!

Lebedev But who's this? Lord God, it's the Count himself!

Shabyelski reaches his hand towards Babakina and Zinaida.

Shabyelski Ah, the entire banking community on one sofa! What a treat! (*To Zinaida.*) Greetings to you,

Zuzu. (*To Babakina.*) And to you, my little lemon sherbet.

Zinaida Count, this is such a rare privilege. (*Shouts.*) Gavrila! Do sit down please, everyone.

She goes anxiously to the door but comes back immediately. Ivanov greets everyone silently. Sasha returns to her place, as Lebedev embraces and kisses Shabyelski.

Lebedev So where have you popped up from? My God, he's slobbering all over me.

He leads him aside.

Why do we never see you? Are you angry with us or what?

Shabyelski I don't have any horses. What am I meant to do? Come on a bloody broomstick? Nikolai refuses to bring me, because he wants me to sit all evening entertaining Anna. Send me your horses, I'll be over like a shot.

Lebedev You're joking. Zinaida'll do anything rather than lend horses. Oh my dear boy, it's such a pleasure to see you. You're all I have left. The only friend I have left from the old days.
  'The days we knew of youth and laughter,
  Love came first, then grief came after . . .'

He hugs him.

Joking apart, I could almost cry.

Shabyelski Hey, let go of me, you stink like a brewery.

Lebedev My dear boy, I cannot tell you how much I miss my friends. Some days I could slit my wrists with the boredom. (*Quietly.*) Thanks to her banking activities,

Zinaida has driven away every decent person we know, and we are left with this lot. Every one a Zulu. A bunch of Wearies and Drearies. That's about it. Have some tea.

Gavrila has arrived to serve Shabyelski.

Zinaida How many times must I say? With tea you serve jam. Gooseberry jam.

Shabyelski laughs out loud, then turns back to Lebedev.

Shabyelski What did I tell you? I had a bet with him on the way that as soon as we got here the gooseberry jam offensive would begin.

Zinaida Thank you, Count. You still love a joke, I see.

Lebedev She did make twenty barrels of the stuff. What the hell are we to do with it?

Shabyelski sits by the table.

Shabyelski Going well, is it? The moneylending? Made a million yet?

Zinaida Oh yes, I know, people think we're rich. But it's all rumour.

Shabyelski Of course. We all know you've no gift for that sort of thing. (*To Lebedev.*) Come on, swear on the Bible. Have you reached the million?

Lebedev No use asking me. Ask her.

Shabyelski (*to Babakina*) And you must be pretty close to a million as well. Wealth suits you, I must say. Your little pigeon feathers get fluffier by the day.

Babakina Thank you, Your Excellency, but I don't care to be mocked like this.

Shabyelski I assure you, madam, there's not a trace of mockery. It's a cry from the heart. I look at you two wealthy women, and I am moved to the bottom of my soul. I cannot see either of you without being filled with love.

Zinaida Oh Count, I see you don't change.

She nods to Gavrila.

Gavrila, the candles, please. If they've finished playing, there's no point in wasting the light.

Gavrila obediently starts blowing out the candles. Zinaida turns to Ivanov.

So tell us, how is your dear wife?

Ivanov Not well, I'm afraid. Today the diagnosis was confirmed. Tuberculosis.

Zinaida What a tragedy. We were just saying. Everyone here loves her so much.

Shabyelski Oh come on, this is crazy! This is a doctor who will say anything just to be close to a female patient. It's a game, for God's sake. Just be grateful her husband doesn't suffer from jealousy.

Ivanov gestures dismissively.

Even Anna herself, I don't believe a word she says on the subject. Not a word. It's a good rule. Never trust doctors, lawyers or women. Quackery and lies, that's their stock in trade.

Lebedev You really are extraordinary, you know.

Shabyelski Why?

Lebedev It's like misanthropy actually seizes hold of you. Once you start, you talk as if it were lodged in your throat, like a cancer. You speak with the voice of the cancer.

Shabyelski Well, that's charming. What are you suggesting? I'm meant to stay silent?

Lebedev No!

Shabyelski I'm meant to tolerate fools and imposters and liars?

Lebedev Be specific. Which fools? Which imposters?

Shabyelski Well . . .

Lebedev Which liars?

Shabyelski Ah well . . .

Lebedev Well?

Shabyelski hesitates.

Shabyelski I don't mean anyone here. Naturally . . .

Lebedev Ah naturally . . .

Shabyelski But present company excepted . . .

Lebedev Oh come on, you know full well this is all posturing.

Shabyelski You think so? Huh. What do you know? How fortunate you are, my friend, to have no philosophy of life!

Lebedev I will sit here in this room, and one day I will die. *That's* my philosophy. (*Shouts.*) Gavrila! Forget philosophy, my friend, we're too old for all that stuff.

Shabyelski I'd say you've Gavrilaed enough already. Your nose looks like a squashed blueberry.

Lebedev drinks again.

Lebedev Who cares? It's not as if I'm going anywhere.

Zinaida Why do we never see the doctor? He seems to have forgotten us altogether.

Sasha I can hardly say I missed him. The embodiment of virtue! He can't light a cigarette without sending out the message: 'I'm an honest man.'

Shabyelski I couldn't agree more. What an utter phoney! The scourge of society! 'Make way for the working man!' Squawking like a parrot! And what original views! Any peasant who's making a reasonable living must by definition be doing so at his brothers' expense. And as for the rest of us, if we own more than one jacket, or have a servant to help us get dressed in the morning, then we must all be exploiters. The man is practically exploding with honesty. It's bursting to get out of him. It's like a physical threat. He's aching to punch you in the face with his honesty.

Ivanov I know. He's exhausting. But I like him. He's sincere.

Shabyelski *Sincere?* Oh yes, he's *sincere*. He's throbbing with sincerity. Yesterday, he came up to me. I thought the vein would burst in his neck. I saw it, pulsing away there. 'Count, you repel me,' he said. Oh, thanks very much. I mean, I don't disagree with him. I'm a worthless old fool, I know that. But do I really need to be told? My hair is white. It'll grow white regardless. Do I really need someone to remind me? What sort of honesty is that?

Lebedev Oh come on, you were young once yourself.

Shabyelski Yes, I was young. And I was foolish too. I stood around like a prig, denouncing the world. But I had a little tact. I never went up to a thief and said, 'You're a thief.' There are things you don't do. You don't go into the condemned man's cell and show him the noose. It's not . . . it's not needed. Whereas this man . . . his idea of complete very heaven would be to punch me in the face – not because he wants to, oh God no – but as always in his case, for some bloody principle. He's a man who'd shoot you because he thought it was *right*!

Lebedev That's youth, isn't it?

Shabyelski Not entirely.

Lebedev I had an uncle once, a disciple of Hegel. He used to invite his friends to the house. Then he'd climb on a chair and denounce them. 'You're the forces of darkness!' he'd say. 'A new life is dawning at last. Blah-di-blah.' He'd lay into them for hours.

Shabyelski And how did they react?

Lebedev How would you react? They carried on drinking. Being denounced? They loved it. They couldn't get enough of it.

5 There is a sudden stir of excitement from outside as Borkin arrives, carrying a parcel, and dressed up to the nines. He is skipping and singing as he arrives, and surrounded by excited Young Ladies.

Shabyelski Ah, good news!

Lebedev My goodness me, Borkin is here.

Young Ladies Mikhail Mikhailovich!

Shabyelski It's Borkin. The life and soul of the party.

Borkin Your humble servant, and here in person, my friends.

He goes straight to Sasha and offers her the parcel.

Bella signora, the universe was honoured the day you were born. As a mark of my own enslavement, may I present you with this small parcel of fireworks of my own manufacture? May they lighten up the night, just as your beauty lightens the gloomy lives we all lead.

He bows theatrically.

Sasha Thank you.

Lebedev (*laughing, to Ivanov*) Really, you know, you should sack this ridiculous Judas.

Borkin (*to Lebedev*) My host! (*To Ivanov.*) My patron! (*Sings.*) Nick-a-dick-a-dang-dang, Nick's my man. (*Walking round.*) The rest of you, so many, so beautiful. Bella Zinaida! Bella Marfusha! Bella Avdotya! Bella, bella, bella, the whole lot of you! (*Finally.*) And no less a person than the Count.

Shabyelski You see! The party cheers up the moment he arrives.

Borkin Have I missed anyone? I'm exhausted already. So what's going on? What's the news? (*At once to Zinaida.*) Just listen, Mumsy, on the way over I couldn't help noticing . . . (*To Gavrila.*) Tea, yes, Gavrila, but spare us the gooseberry muck. (*To Zinaida.*) Peasants were stripping the bark off your trees. Why don't you rent those trees out?

Lebedev (*to Ivanov*) Just sack the little bugger.

Zinaida (*alarmed*) But you're right. It had never even occurred to me.

Borkin has started doing aerobics.

Borkin I can't live without exercise. I'm full of energy. Marfusha Babakina, you are looking at a man at the peak of his game. (*Sings.*) 'I see your eyes, and I's your servant, I see your lips and I's your slave . . .'

Zinaida Oh, please, yes, do entertain us. Everyone's so bored.

Borkin Come on, there's no need for these drooping heads, gentlemen. Shall we dance, you luscious yam?

Babakina I can hardly dance tonight. It's the anniversary of my husband's death.

Borkin Then party games, charades, fireworks, what shall it be?

All Fireworks, fireworks.

People begin to follow him out into the garden in a buzz of excitement.

Sasha Why are you so quiet?

Ivanov I've a headache. Your mother said it. We're bored.

Zinaida turns down the big lamp as she and Lebedev follow.

Zinaida If everyone's in the garden, there's no point in wasting candles. Isn't he wonderful? No sooner he's come than we're all feeling more cheerful.

Lebedev I really think we should give them something to eat, my love.

Zinaida Candles everywhere. No wonder people get the idea we're rich.

She is putting more out.

Lebedev My darling, these people are young, they have healthy appetites, they can't survive on nothing . . .

Zinaida The Count never finished his tea. What a waste of sugar.

She goes out.

Lebedev I wish to God you'd just die.

6 Lebedev follows her out. Sasha and Ivanov alone.

Ivanov It's an extraordinary irony. I used to think and work all the time and I never felt tired. Now I do nothing and I'm completely exhausted. And all because of my conscience. Hour after hour, eating away at me. All the time I feel guilty. But of what? What am I guilty of? I look round, I have no money, my wife is ill, my day goes by in constant, meaningless gossiping and squabbling, I talk gibberish all day with idiots like Borkin. The result is I have come to hate my own home. You are a friend, Sasha, and between friends I hope there is honesty. Is there? I cannot stand the company of a wife who loves me. Tonight I came here purely for distraction, but already I am aching to go home. Forgive me. I'm going. Forgive me.

Sasha Nikolai, I understand you. You are unhappy because you are lonely. Only love . . . love alone can help you.

Ivanov Love? Does love help? Does it? Really? I do mean 'really'. Aren't I a little old? What sort of love? Romance? Oh my God. Hardly. No, it's not romance I need. Anything but. And what goes with it . . . all that unhappiness. God, no! I promise you, I could endure it all, everything I'm experiencing, the poverty, the depression, the loss of my wife, the loneliness, my own useless decay, but the one thing I cannot endure – I *cannot*! – is the contempt I now feel for myself. That above all. I'm half dead with the shame of it. There are men, I've met them, men who long to be Hamlet, it's all they want, to play the outsider, the superfluous man. To them it's glamorous. Not to me. To me, it's failure. Deep shaming failure. For me – strong, healthy, in my right mind – to be reduced to this state. To me, it's disgrace.

Sasha (*laughing, through tears*) Oh let's just go, let's run away to America . . .

Ivanov I'm so spent, I couldn't reach that door, let alone America . . .

They head for the garden.

And what about you? What will you do? When I look at this place, when I look at these men you might have to marry, what a fate! Unless some soldier passes through town, or a student . . .

7 Zinaida Savishna comes from the left-hand door with a pot of jam.

Ivanov Excuse me, Sasha, I'll be with you in a moment.

Sasha goes out to the garden.

Zinaida Savishna, forgive me, if I may ask a question?

Zinaida Please. Ask away.

Ivanov Well . . . to be frank, as you may recall, the interest on my loan falls due in – what? Is it two days? Yes. Two days. It would mean a great deal to me if it could be deferred. As I have no money. In fact.

Zinaida Nikolai Alekseyevich, I am scandalised. Are you out of your mind? I am a respectable woman . . .

Ivanov Of course . . .

Zinaida To make such an obscene suggestion . . .

Ivanov I know.

Zinaida In private.

Ivanov I'm sorry . . .

Zinaida To take advantage. When you've lured me, trapped me alone. To suggest such a thing.

Ivanov I apologise.

Zinaida The deferment of a loan!

Ivanov My fault. My fault. I apologise.

He goes out quickly into the garden.

Zinaida I'm starting to palpitate. My heart!

8 *As she goes out by the right-hand door Kosykh crosses the stage from left to right.*

Kosykh I was holding the ace, the king, the queen, the jack of diamonds, the ace of spades, and one, just *one* small heart, and she – the ditsy slut – didn't even know to bid a small slam.

9 *Kosykh goes out by the right-hand door. Avdotya comes in with the First Guest from the garden.*

Avdotya It's actually some sort of world record. We've been here since five o'clock and we haven't seen so much as a stinking kipper.

First Guest I'd eat the carpet, I'd eat the paintings on the wall . . .

Avdotya What a house! What a way to run a house!

First Guest I'd drop to my knees, like a wolf. I'd savage her. If she came in now, I'd sink my teeth in her thigh . . .

Avdotya Me too. I'd happily rip the flesh from her bones.

First Guest It'd be food! Supper at last! Raw, bloody hunks of our hostess. I'm so hungry I could actually eat a whole leg.

Avdotya There's not even a drink.

First Guest They push these young women at you. How can you think about women when you haven't even had a drink?

Avdotya Come on, let's go and look . . .

First Guest There's schnapps in the dining room. I know for a fact. Come on, we'll at least get a drink.

10 As they go out by the left-hand door, Anna and Doctor Lvov arrive.

Anna It's fine. They must all be in the garden. They'll be so glad to see us.

Lvov Why have you brought me to this house of reptiles? This is not a place where honest people should be seen.

Anna Would you mind, Doctor, can I give you a social tip? It's bad manners to take a lady out and keep on about how honest you are. Perhaps it's true, but nobody wants to know. I promise you, it's good advice. Don't draw attention to your virtues, let women discover them for themselves. When Nikolai was your age, then he did nothing but sing songs and tell stories. And there wasn't one woman alive who couldn't sense what a fine man he was.

Lvov Please. Don't compare me with Nikolai. I know everything about him.

Anna No. You don't. You're a good man but you know nothing. Let's go into the garden. Nikolai never used to rail against the menagerie. You never heard Nikolai call people reptiles. Or boast about his own superiority. He left people alone to live their own lives. If he spoke at all it was to blame himself for his own impatience, or to

express his pity for some poor soul. That's how he was.
Forgiving. Not like you . . .

*11 As they go out the First Guest and Avdotya return
from the left.*

First Guest Well if it's not in the dining room, it must be
in the larder. This way.

Avdotya I would happily tear her limb from limb.

*12 Babakina and Borkin come running in laughing from
the garden. Shabyelski comes in, aping the manner of the
guests.*

Babakina Oh my God, what a bore! What a bore it all is!
A lot of mummies, all stiff as pokers, standing around
like a bunch of stuck pigs.

She begins to jump around.

Oh Lord, my bones have all gone rigid. I have to move!
I have to live!

*Borkin grabs her by the waist and kisses her on the
cheek. Shabyelski laughs and snaps his fingers.*

Shabyelski Ladies! Gentlemen! Please, some decorum . . .

Babakina Take your hands off me, you brazen seducer,
or goodness knows what the Count will think.

Borkin Angel of loveliness, light of my life. (*Kisses her.*)
Lend me two thousand three hundred, will you?

Babakina No, absolutely not. No, no no! Do with me
what you will. Me, yes. My money, no.

Shabyelski half dances around them.

Shabyelski Look at her, the little pit pony. I have to admit she has her good points . . .

Borkin (*serious*) All right, enough. Now. Let's talk business. Let's level, as they say. Answer me: no prevarication. Yes or no? Which is it?

He points to the Count.

On my left, a man in need of a fortune. On my right, a woman in need of a title.

Shabyelski That is putting it a little bit brutally, Misha.

Borkin He needs a minimum of three thousand a year. Tell me, do you want to be a Countess or not?

Babakina Please, Misha, this is not . . .

Borkin This is not what?

Babakina This is not the correct way of proceeding. Surely the Count . . . the Count can speak for himself.

Borkin Why?

Babakina I haven't yet discerned the Count's feelings . . .

Borkin His feelings? I don't think his feelings need bother us. His feelings are hardly the point.

Shabyelski is rubbing his hands and laughing.

Shabyelski Well I must say, the odd thing is I find this way of doing things rather erotic. My precious . . . (*Kisses her.*) My sweetheart . . . my little gherkin . . .

Babakina Please, no, this isn't right. Leave me. Go away. No, don't go away. Not yet.

Borkin So come on, tell us, are we in business? Yes or no?

Babakina Could we . . . I mean, I'm just wondering . . . if the Count came to stay with me, say in three days.

Then we'd have time. I suppose what I'm asking: is this serious?

Borkin (*angry*) Of course it's serious. What do you think the whole thing's about?

Babakina Oh please, I can't believe it. I feel quite dizzy. A Countess! The idea of it. It's impossible. I'm feeling quite ill . . .

13 Borkin and Shabyelski, laughing, take Babakina by the arm, kiss her and lead her through the right-hand door. Ivanov and Sasha run in from the garden. Ivanov is clutching his head in despair.

Ivanov No, you mustn't. Please. Really, you mustn't. Sasha, I implore you. You have to stop.

Sasha I love you. I love you more than I can tell you. Without you, life has no meaning. To me you are everything on earth.

Ivanov Why? Why me? Please. I understand nothing. Sasha, you mustn't say one word more.

Sasha Since I was a child, it's only been you. I loved you, body and soul from the moment I saw you. I love you, Nikolai Alekseyevich. I'll follow you anywhere, to the end of the earth, wherever, to the grave. Only soon, only now, or else I'm going to die.

Ivanov suddenly laughs.

Ivanov I can't believe it. To hear those words. To start again. Is there hope again, Sasha? Is there happiness?

He draws her to him.

Oh my sweet youth, my sweet lost youth . . .

Anna comes in from the garden and stands quite still, watching them.

Yes? We live again. Yes? We start work again. Yes?

They kiss. Then they turn round and both see Anna.

(*Horrified.*) Anna!

Act Three

*Ivanov's study. It is midday. His writing desk is covered
with letters, papers, official envelopes and odds and
ends, including revolvers. On the walls are maps of the
area, paintings, shotguns, pistols, sickles and whips. And
beside the papers, next to the lamp, is the detritus of a
serious drinking session: a carafe of vodka, a plate of
herrings, pieces of bread with pickled gherkins. Pyotr
stands by the door.*

Lebedev I like the French. They're good people.

Shabyelski Are they?

Lebedev Of course! French politics are simple. They're
not like the Germans. The French at least know what
they want. What they want is to rip the Germans' guts
out. Who can argue with that?

Shabyelski If only it were true.

Lebedev Get hold of the sausage-eaters and de-sausage
them.

Shabyelski French, Germans! There's no difference.
They're all cowards. You wait! They're like little
schoolkids, making rude gestures. Take my word for it.
When it comes to it, they're not going to fight.

Borkin He's right. What's the point of fighting anyway?
Wasting good money on weapons and guns? You know
what I'd do? I'd get hold of that Louis Pasteur. He could
round up every dog in the country, inject them with rabies,
and send them raging into enemy territory.

Lebedev He's brilliant, eh?

Borkin The Germans'd be foaming at the mouth within days.

Shabyelski The great military strategist!

Lebedev The brain may be small but it's swarming with ideas.

They all laugh. Lebedev turns back to the vodka and pours three glasses.

There we are. We've fought their war for them, but we haven't had a drink.

Shabyelski Let's have a drink.

Lebedev Good idea. Everyone, good health! Death to the Hun!

They all drink and then eat the zakuski.

No question, the salted herring's the best.

Shabyelski I don't think so. With vodka? No. The gherkin is better. Man struggles up the lonely rockface of evolution, but for all his ingenuity he invents nothing finer than the pickled cucumber. (*To Pyotr.*) Pyotr, more gherkins, and some onion pasties to go with them. Hot, mind, hot!

Pyotr goes.

Lebedev Caviar's good with vodka. But it's all down to how you prepare it. A quarter of pressed caviar, two lengths of spring onion, a few drops of olive oil and a squeeze of lemon. Mix them together. The smell alone will drive you insane.

Borkin No, for me, the best thing with vodka is gudgeon.

Shabyelski (*contemptuous*) Gudgeon! Gudgeon!

Borkin No, but wait. I'm saying fried. Rolled in breadcrumbs, and fried. So they're dry. Outside, clean and dry. Inside, piping hot and moist. So they crunch between your teeth. Crunch, crunch. Crackle, crackle.

Shabyelski Yesterday at Babakina's she served something good. White mushrooms . . .

Lebedev Ah well, yes, white mushrooms . . .

Shabyelski But listen. Steamed with onion and bay leaf and – I don't know – some kind of herbs.

Lebedev Not bad?

Shabyelski When they opened the saucepan, I thought I would faint.

Lebedev Let's drink again.

Shabyelski Very good.

Lebedev One more it is.

All Death to the Hun!

They drink. Lebedev looks at his watch.

Lebedev So. No Nikolai. I have to go soon. You say you had mushrooms at Babakina's, but there's not a whiff of them at my place. Perhaps you might tell us why on earth you're frequenting Babakina's.

Shabyelski nods at Borkin.

Shabyelski It's his fault. He wants me to marry her.

Lebedev Marry? Uh-huh. How old are you?

Shabyelski Sixty-two.

Lebedev Perfect. The perfect age for it. And the bride – ideal.

Borkin We're not interested in the bride, it's the bride's money we're after.

Lebedev Her money? You're joking. Dream on, Shabyelski.

Borkin All right, you're laughing now but when they're living together, then you'll be sorry.

Shabyelski He's serious, you know. Our great military strategist. He's convinced I'm going to do it.

Borkin Of course you are. What are you saying? Are you getting cold feet?

Shabyelski My dear friend, come on, they've never even been warm.

Borkin You mean I've been wasting my time?

Shabyelski Oh really! Misha!

Borkin What is this? 'One day I will, next day I won't'? Where does that leave me? Perhaps I might remind you, I gave this woman my word.

Shabyelski Astonishing! The man really does mean it . . .

Borkin (*furious*) How can you think of betraying a perfectly decent and honest woman? Her whole day spent dreaming of social advancement. She can't eat, she can't sleep. You do have some responsibilities, you know. You can't just walk away.

Shabyelski (*snaps his fingers*) All right, very well. Shall I do it? Out of sheer devilment. Is that what we want? Mark it up as a joke?

2 *Doctor Lvov comes in, and at once Lebedev takes his hand and sings to him.*

Lebedev Ah the great doctor in person! (*Sings.*) 'I'm scared to death of dying, I'm scared to death of death . . .'

Lvov No sign of Ivanov?

Lebedev No. I've been waiting over an hour.

Lvov strides impatiently up and down.

So how is Anna today?

Lvov Not good.

Lebedev May I pay my respects?

Lvov I'd rather you didn't. She's sleeping.

Lebedev She's a good person. Truly. The night she fainted at our house, I looked into her face. I saw death written all over it. I don't know what happened. I came in, she was on the floor, Nikolai kneeling beside her, Sasha in tears. For a full week after, Sasha and I couldn't get over it.

Shabyelski (*to Lvov*) Yes, now tell me something, Doctor, that I've always wanted to know. Which genius of science was it who first discovered that the closer one puts one's ear to a lady's chest the more fully one may comprehend her sickness? Which branch of medicine takes credit for this discovery? Homeopathy? Allopathy?

Lvov looks at him with contempt and walks out.

My God, what a look!

Lebedev Why do you do that? Why do you insult him like that?

Shabyelski Because he's a liar, that's why! He loves it, all that 'grave situation' and 'I am sorry to have to inform you'. He's lying. I can't stand it.

Lebedev But *why*? Why would he lie?

Shabyelski gets up and walks around.

Shabyelski I cannot accept it. That a human being is alive one moment and drops dead the next. It makes no sense. Please, let's change the subject.

3 Kosykh comes running in, out of breath, and quickly shakes everyone's hand.

Kosykh Hello. Good morning. Is Nikolai home?

Borkin Not yet.

Kosykh In that case, goodbye. I'm so busy. I can't tell you, I'm completely worn out.

He has sat down and got up again. Now he has a vodka and a zakuska.

Lebedev Where've you blown in from?

Kosykh I had a night at Barabonov's. We've only just finished. We were playing the whole night. Right through the night. I lost every penny. Barabonov is useless at cards.

He turns, tearful, to Borkin, who moves away at once.

I'll tell you . . .

Borkin Thanks, but if it's all the same to you . . .

Kosykh I'll describe the situation, so you really understand it: I'm holding hearts and he plays a diamond . . .

Borkin Oh please!

Kosykh I play another heart. He plays another diamond. So, inevitably, I don't have to tell you, I don't take a trick. (*To Lebedev.*) All right, so we start playing four clubs. I am holding the ace, the queen, six in all, ten, three of spades . . .

Lebedev (*blocking his ears*) I literally cannot endure this!

Kosykh (*to Shabyelski*) No really, it's interesting . . .

Shabyelski Go away, I don't want to know.

Kosykh It's textbook. I have the ace, the queen, six others, and suddenly disaster! No, listen –

Shabyelski takes a revolver from the desk.

Shabyelski If you don't shut up, I will shoot.

Kosykh (*waves a hand*) Ah yes, I see, this is how things are going. This is how things are now. Suddenly we are all living in Australia. Live your own life, follow your interest, damn the other man and no common culture at all.

He lifts his hat.

However. I have to go. It's time. Time is precious.

He shakes Lebedev's hand.

I pass!

4 *They all laugh as Kosykh goes out and bumps into Avdotya Nazarovna at the door. She lets out a shriek.*

Avdotya Watch where you're going, for goodness' sake.

All Ah here she is, she's back.

Lebedev The ubiquitous Avdotya Nazarovna.

Avdotya I've found you, my beauties. I've been looking everywhere. Greetings to every one of you.

She shakes all their hands.

Lebedev What are you doing here?

Avdotya Business, sir, business. Matters concerning the Count.

She bows.

The young woman in question sends her regards and tells you that if you do not visit tonight, she will cry her little peepers out. She did ask me to take you aside and whisper this news for your ears only. But as we're all in on this – there are no secrets here – it's not as if we're robbing a bank, this is love, it's out in the open and all above board, so, well . . . I don't usually drink but I must admit on this occasion, perhaps a small one. Just to celebrate.

Lebedev I'll join you.

He pours.

I must say, Avdotya, you're in not in bad shape yourself. Given that you seem to have been an old bat for about thirty years now.

Avdotya Thirty? You think? I've lost count. I can't even remember how old I am. I've buried two husbands. I'd be up for a third, but I have no dowry. I've had eight children. No one'll take me without cash.

She takes her glass.

So, here we are, in at the start of something wonderful. May they live to finish what we have begun. Love and happiness to them for the rest of their lives.

She drinks.

Ah now, that is good vodka.

Shabyelski (*laughing, to Lebedev*) It's incredible, people do actually think I'm going to do it.

He gets up.

So maybe I will. Why not? Go through with it? Why not?

Lebedev It's too late, my friend.

Shabyelski What would you call it? One last crime? One final, glorious act of madness?

Lebedev You long since missed your chance to be rich. The grave, not the wedding bed for us. We've seen the best of our days.

Shabyelski I'm going to do it. Yes, I mean it! As God is my witness, I shall!

5 Ivanov and Lvov come in. At once Lebedev gets up to greet Ivanov and kiss him.

Lvov I am only asking for five minutes.

Lebedev Ah Nikolai! At last, good morning.

Avdotya (*bows*) Ah, good morning, sir.

Lebedev I've been waiting a full hour.

Ivanov (*bitterly*) Again! I cannot believe it. Once more you have turned my study into a taproom. I have begged you a thousand times.

He goes to the desk.

Look! There's vodka all over my papers. Crumbs. Gherkins. It's disgusting.

Lebedev My fault entirely, dear friend, I apologise. But I have serious things to discuss.

Borkin I was here first.

Lvov I have asked you repeatedly.

Ivanov Please, gentlemen, please. I cannot listen to everyone. Pasha comes first.

Lebedev I'm afraid my business is private. I'm sorry, gentlemen.

Shabyelski and Avdotya go out. Borkin follows, and Lvov last.

Ivanov I have to ask you, Pasha, drink all you like, that's your problem, but don't infect my uncle. He never used to be a drinker.

Lebedev (*alarmed*) I'm sorry, I didn't know . . .

Ivanov It's bad for him.

Lebedev I'd never noticed . . .

Ivanov Yes, and if the drink kills him, it will be me that suffers, not you. What did you want?

There is a pause.

Lebedev Oh Lord, I have to put this carefully, so it doesn't sound callous. You must understand, I'm ashamed before I've even said it. I'm blushing in advance. But please – put yourself in my place. Just imagine the life I lead. What am I? Effectively a serf. Not even a serf. A footcloth, a Negro.

Ivanov Well?

Lebedev I've been dispatched by my wife. Like a parcel. Pay her the interest. Just pay it. I beg you. For the sake of our marriage. I implore you. I can do no other. I'm exhausted. She's bullied me to death.

Ivanov Pasha, I cannot.

Lebedev Please!

Ivanov I have no money at all.

Lebedev I know, I know. But what can I do? She cannot wait. She cannot. If she takes you to court, just imagine. How will Sasha and I ever look you in the eye?

Ivanov I am ashamed as well. I wish the earth would swallow me up. But where can I find money? Where? My only hope is the harvest.

Lebedev (*shouts*) She can't wait!

There is a pause.

Ivanov Yes, your situation is tricky but mine is far worse. I've racked my brains, but there's nothing.

Lebedev Go to Milkbakh. He owes you sixteen thousand.

Ivanov Oh . . .

He makes a gesture of despair.

Lebedev Look, I know you won't like this, but just humour an old drunkard for once. Here we are. Both graduates of Moscow University. Both students. Both liberals. With ideas and values in common. And, what's more, friends, I would hope.

He takes money from his wallet and puts it on the table.

This is money I've stashed away for myself. It can't be traced. Think of it as a loan. Yes? Swallow your pride. I promise you, if our positions were reversed, I would take what you gave me, and without a second thought.

There is a pause.

There it is. Go over to the house, put it in her hand and say to her, 'Zinaida Savishna, here is your money, now drop dead.' But for God's sake don't tell her where you got it, or she'll choke me to death with gooseberry jam.

*He looks Ivanov in the face. Then he takes back the
money and quickly puts it in his pocket.*

I'm sorry, a joke. I meant it as a joke. A joke in bad
taste. Forgive me.

There is a pause.

Have you given up hope?

Ivanov gestures again.

I understand. It's . . . existence. The nature of it, I mean.
Calm times, then troubled. Man? I'd say almost like a
samovar. That's right. He cannot sit cold on the shelf for
ever. The moment will come when the burning charcoal
arrives. All right, it's a rotten analogy, but it's the best
I can do. (*Sighs.*) Bad times are good for you. If you see
what I mean. That's why I'm not worried for you.
Though I am disturbed when . . . when I hear people
talking. Why are there so many rumours? Why are they
all about you, Nikolai? What started it? One day you're
a murderer, the next day you're a thief, the next the
police are coming to arrest you . . .

Ivanov It means nothing. My head hurts.

Lebedev Try not thinking.

Ivanov I don't think.

Lebedev Oh, let it all go to hell. Why not? Why don't
you visit us any more? Sasha's fond of you. She
understands you. She's a decent person. She's loyal and
sincere. I can't think where she gets it from. Certainly
not her mother, still less from me. There must have been
some sort of illicit union I never heard about. I look at
her and can't believe that this drunk with a luminous
nose could have such a jewel for a daughter. Why don't
you come over, do all your brilliant talking together?
Really. Sasha'll cheer you up.

There is a pause.

Ivanov My friend, please leave me alone.

Lebedev All right, I understand. Truly.

He looks quickly, then kisses Ivanov.

I understand. Farewell. New school, opening today. Have to be there.

He moves to the door, then stops.

I've always said my daughter was clever. Yesterday we were discussing all these rumours about you and she said, 'Papa, glow-worms shine at night to make it easier for birds to see them and eat them. So good people only exist so that gossip and rumour may have somewhere to feed.' Not bad, eh? I told you. A genius. Watch out, George Sand.

Ivanov Pasha!

He stops him.

What is wrong with me?

Lebedev Ah, yes. Good question. I've not wanted to ask. I thought perhaps your troubles had got the better of you. But you're not the type. Usually you overcome misfortune. So, well . . . it's something else. But I don't know what.

Ivanov Me neither. Though sometimes . . . oh Lord, no. No it's not that.

There is a pause.

The nearest I can get: I used to have a workman. Semion, he was called, you remember? At harvest time he wanted to show off in front of the girls, so he loaded two sacks of rye at once. He strained his back. And he died soon after. That's how I feel. As if my back has been broken.

School, university, agriculture, village education, civic
projects . . . From the start I was set on doing everything
differently. I married differently, I lived differently, took
more risks, used my own money, threw it away. I was
happier and unhappier than anyone else in the region.
But these things were like sacks. I loaded them on my
back. And now it's snapped, it's literally given way. At
twenty we're all heroes, we can do anything, can't we?
By thirty, we're already exhausted. How do you . . .
I ask, how do you explain it? We're so tired. It's as if . . .
I don't know . . . What can I say to you? Go, Pasha, go.
Leave me. You must be so tired of me.

Lebedev You know what it is?

He gestures round.

This place. These surroundings. They are what's killing
you.

Ivanov (*smiles*) No. That's the usual excuse. It's stupid.

Lebedev Yes. Well, no doubt yes, you're right, it's stupid.
I said it. And it's stupid. I'll get out of your way.

6 Lebedev leaves. Ivanov is alone.

Ivanov How spent I am, how I despise myself. It's only
a drunk like Pasha who can still respect me. I hear my
own voice and I hate it. I look at my own hands, my
clothes, my feet even and I seem to know them too well.
Just a year ago! That's what's so crazy, I was healthy and
strong. I was cheerful, I worked. I could make sentences.
When I talked, strong men wept and even idiots were
inspired. When I saw unhappiness, I cried. When I saw
evil, I raged. The inspiration was there. I sat alone every
night at my desk, I felt the poetry of the evening, from
the sun's going down to the sun's rising. I worked

through the night in the quiet and I dreamed. I looked into the future like a child looking into its mother's eyes. But now . . . I search for faith, I spend days and nights in idleness, in doing-nothingness, my mind, my body in permanent revolt. I look out of the window: my estate is in ruins and my forests are under the axe.

He weeps.

It needs me. The land needs me. And I have no hope, no expectation. My sense of tomorrow is gone. I swore to love Anna for ever. Eternal love, that's what I promised. I opened her eyes, I offered her a future of which she'd never even dreamed. Yet these last five years I've watched her fading, growing weaker every day, sapped by the struggle, but never once turning to me, never uttering a single word of reproach. And how have I rewarded her? By ceasing to love her. Why? To what end? Somebody explain! My own wife is dying, her days are numbered and all I can do is run from her awful pleading eyes, from her face, from her cough. The shame, the shame of it . . .

There is a pause.

And this child, Sasha, touched by my unhappiness. She declares her love to this ludicrous old man, and he is charmed, as if by music. He shudders back into life and stands there, shaking, spellbound, crying out, 'A new life! Happiness!' Then wakes the next day, like a cheap drunk in a brothel. What is it? Why am I heading for the cliff? Why am I drawn to it? What's happened to my strength? A gun goes off, a servant drops a dish, my wife says the wrong thing, and suddenly my nerves are tattered and my temper screams out.

There is a pause.

Do it. Do it, Nikolai. Put a bullet in your brain. I don't understand.

Lvov comes in.

Lvov Nikolai Alekseyevich, it is essential we talk.

Ivanov We talk every day, Doctor, there must be some sort of human limit.

Lvov Will you just let me speak?

Ivanov You speak every day, sometimes three times a day, and I still have no idea what you're trying to say.

Lvov I speak plainly and to the point. Only a man without a heart could misunderstand me.

Ivanov Usually you make three points. One, my wife is dying. Two, it's my fault. Three, you are an honest man. So, tell me, which order do you wish to put these points in today?

Lvov I need to speak out because I cannot endure cruelty. It is the cruelty of things that dismays me. In the next room, a woman is dying. The least she deserves is to see her own parents. They know full well that she loves them, that she needs to see them, but because of their pride – the stubbornness of their religion – they refuse to relent. Still they condemn her! And you are the man for whom she sacrificed everything, even her own family. Yet without apology and with no sense of shame you go tripping over to Lebedev's, for purposes which are clear to us all.

Ivanov You're wrong, actually. I haven't been there for weeks.

Lvov (*not listening*) People tell me I'm young, but I have learnt one thing in life. One must be straight with people. One must be blunt. I have watched you, Ivanov. I have seen you. And I have seen through you. You are longing for her death. Yes, I know what I'm saying. You will welcome her death because it will give you the chance to move on. But I have come today in the name of humanity to ask you to wait. If nothing else, just wait. Give Anna her time, let her die in the goodness of time. Don't drive this woman to the grave. Is there really such a rush? Would you lose this new girl if you slowed down? You are so accomplished, so proficient, so adept . . . Surely the seduction of any woman will not detain you for long. Why do you need your present wife to die straight away?

Ivanov Doctor! What sort of doctor are you?

Lvov Oh please! Who are you trying to fool?

Ivanov How little you understand if you expect me to control myself while you say these things to me.

Lvov Ivanov, the mask is off! It's been off for months. Your whole life is a fake.

Ivanov You're such a clever man, Doctor. A clever doctor. For you, things are easy. They are what they seem to be. I married Anna to get her fortune. I didn't get it. I made a mistake, so now I'm trying to dispose of her, so I can fix on somebody else and get their money instead. Yes? Isn't that what you think? How simple human beings are to you. What uncomplicated machines! Well no, actually, Doctor. Look a little closer. There are so many cogs in us, so many wheels, so many valves that we judge each other at our own peril. I don't understand you. You don't understand me. And least of all do we understand ourselves. Least of all. You may be a great doctor, but about humanity you know nothing. Don't be so absurdly self-confident. Listen and learn.

Lvov What a convenient philosophy! No such words as 'good' or 'bad'? No 'right', no 'wrong'. Everything 'complicated'. 'Complex'. Is that right?

Ivanov Look. You come to see me all the time. Not a day goes by. Plainly it's not for a meeting of minds. So then why? You're obsessed with me. Have you ever looked inside yourself? Have you ever asked yourself why? Examined your own behaviour? Asked what you want from me?

He is suddenly furious.

Just who am I speaking to? My wife's doctor or the counsel for the prosecution?

Lvov I'm a doctor. It's a clinical judgement. I am instructing you: change your ways, you are killing your wife.

Ivanov Ways? My ways? Please, you understand me better than I do myself. Tell me what changing my ways would entail.

Lvov You know full well.

Ivanov No. Tell me. How would you wish me to change?

Lvov I would wish you . . . to be more discreet.

Ivanov Oh my God, out! Out of here!

He drinks some water.

How dare you? How *dare* you? Yes, I shall answer to God, I know that, for everything I am, for everything I have done. But I do not have to answer to you. You have no right no torment me.

Lvov I? You say I torment *you*? Do you have any idea? Do you have any idea of what you have done to me? Before I came to this godforsaken region, I believed in humanity. I knew people were stupid. I made allowances. But never once did I dream that people could be criminal, that they could be deliberately evil. I loved people. I respected them. I had faith. Until I saw you.

Ivanov I've heard this before.

Lvov And that makes it not true?

He looks and sees Sasha come in, wearing a riding dress.

Ah. Well then. My point is made for me. At least now things are clear.

7 *Lvov shrugs his shoulders and goes out. Ivanov is taken aback by Sasha's appearance.*

Ivanov Sasha . . .

Sasha Yes. What's wrong?

Ivanov What are you doing here? Why have you come?

Sasha You never visit, you no longer visit us . . .

Ivanov For goodness' sake, this is madness. Didn't you think? Did you never consider the effect on my wife?

Sasha I thought of it. I came round the back.

Ivanov Sasha, I cannot believe it. My wife is already in torment. She's at death's door. And you choose to come here . . .

Sasha What else could I do? You don't answer my letters. All day I think about you. I imagine you suffering. I've not slept. Not one single night.

She looks at him a moment.

All right, I'll go. Just tell me: are you all right?

Ivanov All right? How can I be all right? I'm completely exhausted. The whole world is beating a path to my door. Now you! I'm almost insane with guilt.

Sasha Ah yes, guilt . . .

Ivanov Yes!

Sasha Guilt! How you love it. What's your crime, then?
Name it. Go on.

Ivanov says nothing.

Sinners surely can name their own sin. What's yours?
Forgery?

Ivanov (*turning away*) Sasha . . .

Sasha What have you been doing? Printing up
banknotes?

Ivanov That isn't funny!

Sasha Isn't it? You feel guilty because you've stopped
loving a woman. Isn't that right?

Ivanov I don't know. I don't know.

Sasha So why is that a sin? Are you not allowed
feelings? It was hardly at your wish. Or is the sin that
she happened to walk into a room? Again, it's hardly –

Ivanov I know. And so on. These words we all use!
'Allowed our own feelings!' 'It isn't at my wish.' These
tawdry, exhausted little phrases that human beings love
to fool themselves with.

Sasha Whatever I say, you tear it apart.

She looks at a painting.

This dog is good isn't it? Was this done from life?

Ivanov Yes, from life. And this so-called romance we are
having, also a cliché. It's out of a book. 'He had lost his
way, he had stumbled. Then she reached out a hand to
save him.' That's how it happens in novels.

Sasha It also happens in life.

Ivanov Life! Goodness, life . . .

Sasha Yes!

Ivanov Which you understand so instinctively. Oh and how you relish it when I'm unhappy!

Sasha Do I?

Ivanov Yes. The unhappier the better! Because it means you're in love with Hamlet. But to me, you see, Hamlet's an idiot. He's a figure of fun. Healthy people laugh at their own weaknesses. They mock self-indulgence. But naturally that holds no appeal for you. Insufficiently romantic! You, you're only happy in the Ambulance Corps. Here come the nurses! All in freshly starched linen, riding in like the cavalry to bandage the wounds! Oh Lord, I'm sorry. Something must break today . . . the truth is, I'm longing for violence . . .

Sasha Good. Let it out. You're angry. Smash some china. Why not? You're entitled to shout. After all, it's my fault. I've done something stupid. I should never have come. So yell at me. Please.

There's a pause.

Well?

Ivanov It's funny.

Sasha Good then, it's funny. It's *something*, thank goodness. Anything. Just as long as you manage to smile once again.

Ivanov (*laughs*) I look at you when you're doing your cavalry acting. There's this wonderful look on your face. Pure innocence. As if you were watching a comet. Your pupils get bigger. Wait, there's some dust on your coat.

He brushes some dirt off her shoulder.

Why is it attractive for a woman to be innocent when it's so ridiculous in a man? Why are you all drawn to despair?

Sasha Are we?

Ivanov When a man is strong and happy you ignore him completely, but the moment he slides downhill, whoosh, you're off after him like a shot.

He presses his face to her shoulder.

Let me rest and forget, if only for a moment.

There is a silence, the two of them still.

Sasha There's so much you don't understand. For men, love is just how-are-you-darling? It's just a stroll in the garden. One day, it will be a few tears at the graveside. But for us? No, it has to be life itself. If you climb a mountain, I'll climb with you. Jump over the cliff: I'll jump. I never told you, there was a day about three years ago when you came to our door, sunburned, tired, covered in dust. You were fresh from harvesting. You asked for a drink. When I brought you the glass, you were laid out on the sofa, dead to the world. You slept in our house and I stood at the door, guarding you, keeping people away. I stood for a full twelve hours. I've never been happier in my life. The more effort you have to make, the better love is.

Pyotr appears silently with a plate of hot pasties.

Pyotr Pasties.

Ivanov What? What did you say?

Pyotr Hot pasties. The Count ordered them.

Ivanov Go away.

*Pyotr turns and goes out. Ivanov shrugs, suddenly
cheerful.*

My dear girl, how wonderful you are. And how stupid
I've been, playing at tragedy. Boo-hoo. Upsetting people
wherever I go. *Épatant les bourgeois . . .*

He laughs and moves quickly away.

You have to go, Sasha. We're forgetting ourselves.

Sasha I know. I'm off. I fear the honest doctor may feel
it's his duty to tell Anna Petrovna I was here. So, please,
go to her and stay by her bed. Sit. If you need to, sit for
a year. If you need to stay ten years, stay ten. But do
your duty. Grieve with her and ask her forgiveness.
Weep. It's right. And above all don't neglect your estate.

Ivanov Oh God, I'm under Matron's orders again.

Sasha God bless you, Nikolai. You may now put me out
of your mind altogether. It's fine. As long as you write
me a letter. Say, in two weeks. I'd be grateful. And I shall
write to you.

8 *Borkin looks in the door and then sees Sasha.*

Borkin Nikolai, is it my turn? Oh Good Lord, I'm sorry,
I didn't see you there. *Bonjour, mam'selle.*

He bows. Sasha is embarrassed.

Sasha How do you do?

Borkin My goodness, look at you! Prettier than ever,
and if I may say so, you've filled out.

Sasha (*to Ivanov*) So, I must go, Nikolai Alekseyevich.
I must go.

She goes out.

228

Borkin What a vision! Extraordinary! I came for prose and stumbled across poetry. (*Sings.*) 'A bird in flight, a streak of light . . .'

Ivanov walks up and down, upset. Borkin sits down.

She really does have something, doesn't she? Something none of the others have. She's almost like a fantasy. Financially, she's actually the best prospect in the district, but her mother's such a skunk nobody wants to go near the daughter. Who can blame them? I mean, Sasha'll get the lot when her mother dies, but until then she's bumbling along on ten thousand a year and the odd toffee apple, and even for *that* she's expected to say thank you all day.

He searches through his pockets and finds his cigar case.

Cigars. Fancy one? They're not bad. They're quite smokeable.

Ivanov approaches Borkin, furious.

Ivanov Get out! Get out of this house for ever!

Borkin half rises, dropping his cigar.

Now! This very minute!

Borkin Hold on. What is this? What have I done?

Ivanov Where did you get those cigars? Do you think I don't know?

Borkin Cigars? Is this about the cigars?

Ivanov And where you take that old man every day, and what you're up to with him?

Borkin What's that got to do with you?

Ivanov Everyone in the district knows what you're doing. You're a low, dishonest scoundrel. You bring disgrace on this household. We have nothing in common, and I insist you leave my house this instant.

Borkin Oy-oy-oy! *Quel mauvais humeur!* Well, I refuse to rise to it. Please, insult me as much you like.

He picks up his cigar.

As for these depressions of yours, can I just say they're a thundering bore? You're not an adolescent any more.

Ivanov Did you not hear me? Out! Out! You think you can play with me?

9 *Ivanov is now shaking with rage. Anna Petrovna comes in.*

Borkin Ah well, if Anna Petrovna is here . . . then fine. No problem.

Borkin goes out. Ivanov stops by the desk and stands, his head bowed.

Anna What was she doing here?

A pause.

I need to know. Why did she come here?

Ivanov Don't ask.

Anna What was she doing here?

Ivanov I am profoundly guilty. Punish me any way you choose. But please, don't ask any more. I've no strength to tell you.

Anna Now I see. Now I begin to see you. At last I see the kind of person you are. A man without honour.

Ivanov No!

Anna You came to me, and lied. I gave up my religion, my family. I even gave up my name. You talked to me about goodness and truth. You told me you loved me. But the words were dirt. And I believed every word.

Ivanov Anna, I have never lied to you.

Anna I have lived here five years, I've suffered and grown ill, but I did not stop loving you for one moment. You were my god. And all that time you have been deceiving me . . .

Ivanov Anna, accuse me of anything but not of dishonesty. I have never once lied in my life. Accuse me of anything, but not of dishonesty.

Anna Everything now makes sense to me. You married me because you thought my parents would give in . . .

Ivanov No!

Anna You thought I'd inherit.

Ivanov Oh my God, Anna, no, please don't torment me.

Ivanov cries.

Anna Be quiet! And now you've a fresh plan. Now everything is clear to me. I understand everything.

She cries.

You have never loved me. You have never been faithful. Never.

Ivanov Anna, these are lies. Say what you feel, but don't degrade me with lies.

Anna Crooked and dishonest! You owe money to Lebedev, so now you want to seduce his daughter. You want to trick her just as you tricked me. It's the truth.

Ivanov (*gasping*) Please, Anna, be quiet.

Anna I will not be quiet!

Ivanov I beg you, say nothing else. The anger is killing me. I am going to insult you.

Anna All the time you've pleaded innocence. You've manipulated us all. You've put schemes in Borkin's head, then blamed them on him.

Ivanov Be silent. I beg you, be silent. I cannot stop myself. The words will burst out of me.

He shouts.

You dirty Jew.

Anna I will never be quiet. Never again. Not after what you've said to me, not after what you've done.

Ivanov You refuse? You refuse to be silent?

He struggles with himself.

In the name of God . . .

Anna Now go off and start swindling Lebedev.

Ivanov You are going to die. I have spoken to the doctor. You are going to die very soon.

Anna sits down. Her voice fades.

Anna When did he say that?

There is a pause. Ivanov clutches his head with hands.

Ivanov Oh my God, the evil! How evil I am!

Act Four

*A full year has passed. One of the drawing rooms in
Lebedev's house. At the front is an arch, dividing it from
the ballroom. There are doors left and right. There are
old bronzes and family portraits. There are decorations
for a party. There is a piano, with violin and cello
nearby. Throughout the act visitors pass to and fro
through the ballroom, all in evening dress.*

1 Doctor Lvov comes in and looks at his watch.

Lvov Past four already. Soon the blessing, and in no time
at all, the wedding itself. So there we are. A triumph for
the forces of good! One wife dead, and now another
lined up, waiting to be fleeced. Turn her upside down,
shake her pockets out, and then throw her in the same
grave as the last one. All while pretending you're a man
of integrity.

There is a pause.

He thinks he's in seventh heaven and will live to a ripe
old age and die with a clear conscience. No! I'm here to
tell him he won't. I shall wrench the mask from the
hypocrite. I shall seize him in his hiding place, and throw
him burning into the deepest pit in hell! Citizens have
duties. It's the duty of the honest man. But how? Talk to
Lebedev? Hardly. A waste of breath. Start a row? Provoke
a duel? Create a scandal? Oh, God, I'm nervous now.
My stomach. I'm not thinking clearly. Think clearly.
What's best? A duel?

2 Kosykh comes in and at once addresses Lvov cheerfully.

Kosykh Ah, so listen, this is interesting: yesterday I bid a small slam in clubs and won a big one instead. I was playing with Barabonov . . .

Lvov I'm sorry, I'm afraid I don't play cards myself, so I can't share your enthusiasm. Has the blessing happened?

Kosykh Not yet. They're trying to calm Zinaida down. She's screaming like a fishwife. Can't face losing the dowry.

Lvov What about losing her daughter?

Kosykh No, not the daughter, the dowry. It means writing off a debt. Don't think she hasn't thought of it, but when it comes to it not even she can sue her own son-in-law.

3 Babakina walks by, dressed to the nines, and Kosykh at once starts giggling behind her back. But she catches him.

Babakina Philistine!

Kosykh touches her waist with his finger and laughs loudly.

Peasant!

She goes out. Kosykh goes on laughing.

Kosykh The woman's gone mad. She was all right until she started dreaming of elevation. Now you can't go near her.

He imitates her.

'Philistine!'

Lvov Kosykh, I have a question to ask you. Tell me honestly. What do you think of Ivanov?

Kosykh Truthfully?

Lvov Yes.

Kosykh Very little. He bids trumps almost regardless of what's in his hand.

Lvov No, I mean, is he a good man?

Kosykh A good man? Ivanov? What do you think? He's a strategist. Surely you can see that. He and the Count are two of a kind. It's all a game. Ivanov is a consummate games-player. That's what he is. He lost out to the Jewess, so now it's double or quits. He'll take Zinaida's money, the Count'll take Babakina's. And the two women'll be out on the street within a year. That's the way of it, that's the game. You watch, I'm expecting a perfectly played hand. Doctor, you're looking pale. Are you all right?

Lvov I'm fine. Perhaps I've been drinking too much.

4 *Lebedev comes in with Sasha, sending Lvov and Kosykh away.*

Lebedev We can talk in here. You two hooligans, join the ladies, please. I need privacy.

Kosykh snaps his fingers as he passes Sasha.

Kosykh Natty as the queen of trumps, and just as welcome.

Lebedev Come on, caveman, out!

Kosykh and Lvov go.

Sit down, Sasha, that's right.

He sits himself.

Now. I want you to listen in the appropriate manner. With the appropriate deference. All right? I'm here at your mother's bidding. You understand? Although I shall be speaking, it will only be as her representative. Her mouthpiece.

Sasha For goodness' sake, Papa, get on with it.

Lebedev Your dowry. Will be fifteen thousand roubles in silver. Hold on, let me finish. There's more to come. The round figure, the official figure is fifteen. However. Since Nikolai Alekseyevich happens to owe your mother nine thousand, she has decided that the figure which will actually be surrendered, will be nearer . . . well . . . as you might say . . . six.

Sasha Why are you telling me this?

Lebedev Because your mother has asked me to.

Sasha For what possible purpose? If you had the slightest respect for me, you wouldn't dream of telling me. I don't want your dowry . . .

Lebedev Oh now Sasha, please . . .

Sasha I didn't ask for it and I certainly have no intention of taking it.

Lebedev Why take it out on me? You're meant to listen, you are at least meant to *listen* to the offer. It's only good manners. Give it a sniff. But you're so desperate to appear progressive, you can't even wait two minutes to turn it down.

Sasha I find this kind of talk about money demeaning.

Lebedev Demeaning! Oh please. I'm the intermediary, that's all. On one side I have a wife who thinks of nothing else, all day she sits there counting her kopecks as if her life depended on it, and on the other, here before me – the spirit of emancipation! Despises her own father for even daring to mention the subject. Well forgive me! I'm just the poor idiot who gets mashed between the two of you.

He goes to the door.

Do you not see? Can you not even tell? I hate this. I hate it.

Sasha What do you hate?

Lebedev I hate the whole thing.

Sasha What whole thing?

Lebedev Do you really want me to say? Should I spoil your wedding day? Should I say 'When you marry, I shall not be able to look'?

He goes up to Sasha, suddenly tender.

Forgive me, Sasha, maybe there is something here, something in this marriage which is passing me by. Since you're involved, then I've no doubt it's something pure, something noble, something high-minded. But to this bulbous old nose, it smells wrong. How do I say this to you? Look at you. You're beautiful, you're young. And he? An exhausted widower who has already worn himself out. Worse, a man whom nobody understands.

He kisses her.

Sasha, I'm sorry. There is something not wholesome. People are talking, and, as it happens, with good reason. I'll say it. I'll say it one time only. His wife dies and at once he marries you.

He changes his tone to briskness at once.

Now. I sound like an old woman. Forgive me. I'm becoming absurd. I'm like some ghastly old maid. Take no notice. Follow your own heart.

Sasha My heart?

Lebedev Yes.

There is a pause.

Sasha Then tell me. Tell me it's right. Help me. In my own heart . . . I don't know. It's unbearable. If you had any idea of what I've been through. Cheer me up, Papa. Cheer me up, my darling, tell me what to do.

Lebedev What to do?

Sasha I am frightened to death.

She looks round.

Sometimes I think I don't understand him and I am terrified I never will. All the time we've been engaged he hasn't smiled once. Nor once looked me in the eye. All I hear is endless complaint, guilt, hints, rambling allusions. Talk of unnamed crimes. He shakes. Shakes. There are times when it seems to me I don't love him as I should. As I need to. When he comes here, he begins to talk, and I feel . . . impatient. What does that say? Tell me, Papa, tell me what that says.

Lebedev My dear child, my dear sweet child, I beg you, let him go.

Sasha (*terrified*) What do you mean? Let him go?

Lebedev Just do it. Why not?

Sasha How can I? I can't!

Lebedev We'll ride through it. A year's scandal, my God, two years maybe –

Sasha How can I?

Lebedev – but better that, better ride out the gossip than ruin your whole life.

Sasha No. You mustn't say that. We have to fight, Father, it's our duty. We have a duty to fight. It's true. This is a fine upstanding man and my job in life is to understand him. That's my calling. I'll set him on his feet and he'll start again.

Lebedev That's not a calling, that's a prison sentence.

Sasha Father, I have to ask you: today I said things to you I would say to no one else. Now you must forget them. Tell no one.

Lebedev What's happening? Has the whole world got too clever for me? Or has it just got too stupid?

5 Shabyelski appears.

Shabyelski Oh damn and blast everyone. Myself included. Me most of all. May we all go to hell!

Lebedev What's going on?

Shabyelski I am preparing myself, my dear friend, to do something contemptible, for which everyone will despise me. And rightly. I am going through with it. I've instructed Borkin to announce my engagement. Yes! Today.

He laughs.

The world is a whorehouse, I shall simply be one more whore.

Lebedev Oh come on, pull yourself together, man. Whorehouse? Madhouse!

Shabyelski What difference does it make? Take me to either. Take me to both. Take me to both at once! How

239

can it be worse than living among these trivial, tenth-rate, talentless people? I'm glutted with self-disgust. I hear myself speak and I don't even believe my own words.

Lebedev There's meant to be a wedding. Shall I tell you what's best? Stuff an oily rag in your mouth and set light to it. Go breathe fire over everyone. Or better still, go home. We're meant to be cheerful, and here you are, squawking like a demented raven. I mean it.

Shabyelski leans over the piano and starts to cry.

Oh Lord, look, I'm sorry. My dear friend! Matyusha, have I offended you? Please! Forgive an old drunkard. Have a glass of water.

Shabyelski I don't want it.

He lifts his head.

Lebedev Why are you crying?

Shabyelski I shouldn't say.

Lebedev Come on, my dear fellow, tell me. What's the reason?

Shabyelski Just for a moment, I looked across at the cello over there and it reminded me. I remembered the little Jew, I remembered Anna.

Lebedev What great timing! My God. All respect to her, may she rest in peace, but this is hardly the moment.

Shabyelski We played duets. She was remarkable. Truly. A truly remarkable woman.

Sasha starts to cry as well.

Lebedev Oh Lord, now it's both of them. Can we just . . . Does anyone mind if we don't actually cry in sight of the guests?

Shabyelski Pasha, we can all be happy, as long as we have hope. But I am a man without hope.

Lebedev I do see that, my friend. Believe me, I see it. No children, no money, no future. I understand. But what can I do?

He turns to Sasha.

What started you off?

Shabyelski Pasha, just give me some money. Give me some. I'll pay you back. Not in this world, admittedly. But in the next. I'll go to Paris and sit by my wife's grave. I've been generous, you know that, in my lifetime I have given away half my fortune. I have the right to ask. I'm asking a friend. Please.

Lebedev Look . . . actual money. I don't have any. Not of my own. But all right . . . if I can, I will. It's not a promise but . . . I will find you some. (*Aside.*) They get to you. Eventually they wear you down.

6 *Babakina heads for Shabyelski, whom she hits on the arm with her fan.*

Babakina Now well really! Where's my handsome hero? How can you have left me by myself?

Shabyelski (*with loathing*) All too easily.

Babakina What?

Shabyelski Go away. I hate you.

Babakina What are you saying?

Shabyelski What I have long dreamed of saying. Leave me, leave me alone for ever!

Babakina falls into an armchair and starts crying.

Babakina Oh no! No, no, no . . .

Zinaida appears in a new dress, with a wet towel round her head, also crying.

Zinaida Someone's coming. It must be the best man . . .

Lebedev Oh, for God's sake . . .

Sasha (*imploring*) Oh, Mother . . .

Zinaida It must be time for the ceremony.

Lebedev Ah, wonderful! Now we have a full house. A full quartet! This is marvellous. We shall all be washed away. I might as well join in myself.

He starts to cry, as Sasha takes her mother in her arms.

Oh God!

Zinaida If he had one ounce . . . one *ounce* of self-respect he would have paid his debt before proposing.

7 *Ivanov comes in, wearing a tail coat and gloves.*

Lebedev Now this is the limit! What on earth is this?

Sasha Nikolai, why are you here?

Ivanov I am sorry, ladies and gentlemen, but I must speak with Sasha alone.

Lebedev It's impossible. It can't be done, for the groom to speak to the bride. You should meet in the church.

Ivanov Pasha, I'm sorry. I have no choice.

8 Lebedev shrugs his shoulders, then he, Zinaida,
Babakina and Shabyelski all go out. Sasha is defiant
when they are left alone.

Sasha What do you want from me?

Ivanov Sasha, as I dressed for my wedding, I looked in
the mirror. And as I looked, I saw grey hair. This must
be the end of it. I feel this rage. Your whole life stretches
before you.

Sasha I know. You've told me. You've told me repeatedly.
Get over to the church, and don't hold people up.

Ivanov I'm not going to the church. I'm going back to
my house. You must take your family to one side and
simply inform them: the wedding is off. We've been
acting. I've been playing Hamlet and you've been playing
the missionary. Shall I tell you? Performance over!

Sasha (*exploding*) What is this? How dare you? I simply
won't listen.

Ivanov Perhaps you won't listen, but I shall still talk.

Sasha What are you doing here? It's a joke.

Ivanov A joke? Well, that would be welcome. I'd love
that.

Sasha This is our wedding day!

Ivanov A joke is exactly what I'd most like it to be. Let
the whole world laugh at me, please!

He laughs.

Do you know what it feels like? To watch yourself
wither? To know you have gone on living too long? To
look up at the sun and see it still shining? It shines
regardless. To look at an ant, carrying its burden. Even
an ant can be happy with its lot. To look round, to see

243

people's faces – this person thinks I'm a phoney. Another one pities me. Another one thinks I need help! And worst of all, to catch people listening respectfully, as if by listening they could actually learn! People think there's something deep about despair. But there isn't. As if I could found a new religion, and impart some earth-shattering truth. I still have some pride. As I came here, laughing at my own absurdity, it seemed to me the birds and the trees were beginning to laugh at me too.

Sasha This isn't rage. This is madness.

Ivanov Madness? This is cold sanity. Yes, the rage is speaking. But the rage tells the truth. You and I . . . we're in love, but we cannot marry. I have a perfect right to destroy my own life, but I have no right to destroy other people's. Yes. And that's what I did to my first wife. By my endless complaining. And now it's the same with you. Since we met, you've stopped laughing. You've aged. You look five years older. Your father who once was at peace with the world now stands round in confusion. Lost. The only thing I have ever wanted: to try to be honest. To try to tell the truth. And the effect has been only to spread dissatisfaction around me wherever I go. I'm contagion. Everywhere I spread my contempt. As if I was doing life a favour by consenting to be alive! Oh, let me be damned in hell.

Sasha Do you not see? This is the moment I've longed for.

Ivanov Why?

Sasha This is the step you've been waiting to take. At last, here, today, before this wedding, you see your condition clearly. You see it and you resolve to start a new life.

Ivanov A new life?

Sasha Yes.

Ivanov How? How can I? I am at the end.

Sasha You're nowhere near the end.

Ivanov I've done it! I'm finished!

Sasha Keep your voice down! The guests . . .

Ivanov Finished!

Sasha We have to go to the church.

Ivanov The road I am on leads one way, and one way only. When a man who is educated, who is healthy – I am by no means stupid – when a man like me starts on this path, then he's like a child wrapped in a blanket, who finds himself rolling downhill. What can stop me? What? Wine gives me a headache, I can't drink. Write rotten poetry? I can't. I won't. I'm not willing to take my condition and somehow elevate it into something poetic. I refuse. Because I've always known the value of things. I call laziness laziness. The word for weakness is weakness. Oh, you say I'm not finished. I'm more finished than any man on earth.

He looks round.

We may be interrupted any moment. If you love me, do me one favour. Disown me. Disown me right now.

Sasha Oh Nikolai, if you had any idea how hard you make things.

Ivanov Analyse! Try to understand!

Sasha You're a kind man, a decent man. But every day you invent some terrible new task.

Ivanov You're not in love with me. You're in love with an idea. You set yourself the task of saving me. The idea of resurrection, that's what you love.

Sasha No!

Ivanov Every nerve in your body tells you to abandon me. Your body is screaming: let go of him. But it's your pride that prevents you.

Sasha It isn't true.

Ivanov How can you love me? Nobody could love me. It isn't love, it's stubbornness.

Sasha The logic . . . your logic is crazy. How can I walk away and leave you alone? How can I leave a man who has nothing? No family, no friends. Your estate is ruined, your money is gone. Everyone slanders you.

Ivanov I should never have come here. I should have stuck to my plan.

9 Lebedev comes in, and at once Sasha runs over to him.

Sasha Oh, Father, help us, please help! Nikolai rushed in, screaming like a lunatic, begging me to be kind and to call the wedding off.

Ivanov There will be no wedding.

Sasha There will. Papa, tell him I know what I'm doing.

Lebedev Hold on, wait a moment. Why do you not want the wedding?

Ivanov I've explained to Sasha. She refuses to see.

Lebedev Don't tell her. Tell me. And do it in a way which people like me can understand. Really, Nikolai Alekseyevich, may God forgive you. You have brought more confusion into our lives than I ever dreamed possible. I feel I'm living in the skull of a demented skunk. What's the point? What do you want from me? That I challenge you to a duel?

Ivanov There's no need for a duel. I have said what I have to say, and in simple sentences.

Sasha is walking up and down, distressed.

Sasha This is terrible. He's become like a child!

Lebedev Listen, Nikolai, no doubt to you, with all your new-fangled psychology, what you're saying makes perfect sense. But to me it seems much the same as bad behaviour. Because life is actually quite simple. It is. The ceiling is white. Shoes are black. Sugar is sweet. You are in love with Sasha. She is in love with you. If you are still in love, stay. If you no longer love her, go. We won't hold it against you. You are both healthy, you are both intelligent, you have reasonable morals, a roof over your head and clothes on your back. What more do you need? Perhaps you need money. Of course. Money isn't everything, but on the other hand it's something. Your estate is mortgaged, I know that, and you have nothing to pay interest with. But I'm a father. I understand. Just for a moment leave your mother out of this, damn her. If she won't give you any more, so be it. Sasha says she doesn't want a dowry, fair enough. Principles, feminism, Schopenhauer – all that stuff. But I have ten thousand in the bank.

He looks around.

There's not a human being alive who knows this. Up till now. It belonged to your grandmother. Take it. It's for both of you. Only, if you could do me one small favour, can you give Shabyelski, I don't know, two thousand, say?

The Guests are now gathering in the ballroom.

Ivanov Pasha, this is not about money. This is about conscience.

Sasha And I have a conscience too. You may talk all you wish but nothing will change. I am going to marry you. I refuse to let you go.

10 Sasha goes out.

Lebedev Nothing makes sense to me.

Ivanov Oh my poor friend, if only I could explain. If only I could say who I am. Honest, dishonest. Healthy, sick. Courageous, cowardly. I don't think I could ever put it into words. I was young, that's all. That's the only way to put it. I was full of faith, I believed. So few people bother. I worked and loved and tried and hoped and gave, all in full measure, without even measuring, never stopping to think: am I giving too much? Oh my dear Pasha, there are so few of us, so very few. So few of us and so much work to be done! And for this . . . arrogance, life has broken me. I am in my thirties, and already I am spending my days in a dressing gown. With a heavy head and a sluggish soul. Exhausted, broken, cracked. Without belief, without love, without hope. Like a ghost I stagger among people, without knowing who I am or why I'm alive. In love I find no tenderness. In work I find no relief. In song I hear no music, in speeches I hear nothing new. Everywhere I go I feel revulsion for life. Inside I have died. Before you stands a man beaten at thirty-five, crushed by his own weakness and burnt out with his shame. All I have left, the thing that burns, that never stops burning, is the shame, the shame that turns now to anger.

He begins to sway.

Get Shabyelski. I have to go home.

11 From the drawing room, voices are heard saying, 'The best man's arrived.' Shabyelski comes in.

Shabyelski I'm coming. Dressed in an old tail coat, of course. And without gloves. So all the sniggering has started, all the spiteful little jokes. What vermin they all are!

Borkin comes in quickly with a bouquet. He is wearing tails and has a best man's buttonhole.

Borkin Ay-ay-ay-ay! Where is the foolish fellow? Everyone's been waiting at the church for hours and here you are, philosophising as usual, by the look of it. The man is a card. What a card he is! You're not meant to travel with the bride, remember? It's against the rules. You travel with me. Is that really too hard to grasp? The man is an irrepressible comedian.

Lvov comes in and addresses Ivanov.

Lvov Ah, you are here.

He speaks deliberately loudly.

Nikolai Alekseyevich, I am here to declare publicly that you are a scoundrel and a rogue.

Ivanov (*cold*) I thank you. From the bottom of my heart.

Now there is general astonishment. People are pouring into the room.

Borkin I have to say to you, sir, that you have insulted my friend. I challenge you to a duel.

Lvov Monsieur Borkin, I would find it degrading even to speak to you, let alone fight you. But your friend may have satisfaction whenever he likes.

Shabyelski I will fight you, sir. Yes, Count Shabyelski will fight!

Sasha (*to Lvov*) What is this? What happened? Did you insult him? What on earth for?

Lvov I promise you, Alexandra Pavlovna, I did not insult him without good reason. It is why I am here. I came today as an honest man to open your eyes. I ask you to listen to what I have to say.

Sasha What can you say? What is your news? That you are an honest man? That will hardly come as a revelation. On the contrary, Doctor Lvov, you have hounded us all with your so-called honesty. For weeks now, for months, you have pursued Ivanov, you have followed him like a shadow, you have interfered in his private life, you have slandered and judged him, and at every turn you have bombarded me and all his friends with anonymous letters. Yes! And all this in the guise of an honest man. Honest? Honest, was it, not even to spare his wife, never to let her rest, constantly to feed her suspicions, when she was dying. To feed her worst fears? And no doubt, it's clear, whatever you do in the future – be it murder or cruelty or just another act of downright mean-mindedness – they will all be excused. Why? Because you are an honest and enlightened young man.

Ivanov (*laughing*) Bravo! Not a wedding, a parliament! Bravo, bravo!

Sasha (*to Lvov*) Just think it over. Do you have any idea what you've done? Do you? You stupid, heartless people!

She takes Ivanov by the hand.

Let's get out of here, Nikolai. Come with us, Papa.

Ivanov Where can we go? Tell me. Where on earth can we go? I begin to see now, I begin hear my young voice. My youth! The old Ivanov is stirring again.

He takes out a revolver.

Sasha I know what he's going to do. Stop him! Nikolai, for God's sake.

Ivanov I've gone down far enough. It's enough. Time to get out of here, yes. Thank you, Sasha. Time to go.

Sasha Nikolai, for God's sake! Stop him! Stop him!

Ivanov Let me free!

He runs to one side and shoots himself.

THE SEAGULL

adapted by David Hare
from a literal translation by Helen Rappaport

Note

Everything went wrong with the first performance of
The Seagull, which took place on 17 October 1896 at the
Alexandrinsky Theatre in St Petersburg, nine years after
the unhappy premiere of *Ivanov*. There were only a few
hurried rehearsals, the original Nina was aged forty-two,
and the leading actress who had requested the play for
her benefit performance then withdrew from playing
Masha. The result was that her many admirers who had
paid top dollar to pack the theatre were furious at her
absence. The jeering and laughter began during Nina's
monologue in Act Two, and by the time Konstantin
appeared with his head bandaged in Act Three the
audience were so noisy the actors couldn't hear each
other speak. Chekhov had left the theatre by then to
walk the streets. 'If I live seven hundred years,' he said,
'I'll never give a theatre another play.'

In fact, even in St Petersburg, the play's five subsequent
performances were far better received, and its reputation
was fixed for all time by the Moscow Art Theatre's
production of December 1898. It was first performed on
a British stage in November 1909 by the Glasgow
Repertory Company, directed by George Calderon.

The play is in part based on the experience of an ex-
girlfriend of Chekhov's, Lika Mizinova, who failed as
an opera singer, was seduced and then left pregnant by
the writer Ignaty Potapenko. She wrote to the dramatist,
'Yes, everyone here says *The Seagull* is taken from my
life, and that you have called a certain person to account.'

There are at least twenty-five English versions of the play in print. There are many pitfalls, not least the title. The first English translator Constance Garnett wrote to Philip Ridgeway, who directed her version at the Barnes Theatre in 1925 with John Gielgud as Konstantin:

You know, it isn't a Seagull, but a Lake Gull – and what ought it to be called? The names of water birds sound very unromantic. Puffin, for instance. You can't have a heroine drawing tears from the audience by saying 'I am a Puffin! No, that's wrong.' Seagull's bad enough. Gull alone is impossible. Imagine a girl saying 'I am a Gull etc. . . .'

It was Michael Frayn, unlike the rest of us a Russian speaker, who changed the rendering of Nina's most famous line from 'I am a Seagull' to 'I am the Seagull', making her not a generic bird, but the particular bird in Trigorin's story. There are very few permanent advances in adaptation, most especially in this most adapted of plays. But this surely was one.

The Seagull in this version was first performed at the Festival Theatre, Chichester, on 28 September 2015. The cast, in order of appearance, was as follows:

Medvedenko Pip Carter
Masha Jade Williams
Sorin Peter Egan
Konstantin Joshua James
Yakov Nebli Basani
Nina Olivia Vinall
Evgeny Dorn Adrian Lukis
Polina Lucy Briers
Arkadina Anna Chancellor
Trigorin Samuel West
Shamraev Des McAleer
The Maid Sarah Twomey
Ensemble Mark Donald

Director Jonathan Kent
Set Designer Tom Pye
Lighting Designer Mark Henderson
Music Jonathan Dove

Characters

Irina Nikolaevna Arkadina
an actress, forty-three

Konstantin
her son, twenty-five

Sorin
her brother, sixty

Nina Zarechnaya

Shamraev
estate manager

Polina
his wife

Masha
his daughter, twenty-two

Boris Alexeyevich Trigorin
novelist

Evgeny Dorn
doctor, fifty-five

Medvedenko
teacher

Yakov
workman

Cook

Maid

The action takes place on Sorin's country estate.
Two years pass between Acts Three and Four.

Act One

A corner of the park on Sorin's estate. A line of trees
leads away towards a lake, which is obscured by a stage
which been hastily put together for amateur dramatics.
Shrubbery on either side. A few chairs and a table.
  The sun has just gone down. Construction noise.
Yakov and other workmen are onstage behind the
lowered curtain. Coughs and banging audible. Masha
and Medvedenko come in from the left, on their way
back from a walk. She is dressed in black.

Medvedenko Who died?

Masha Me, since you ask. I'm unhappy.

Medvedenko I can't think why. You have your health.
Your father's no plutocrat but he's doing all right. Try
living on a schoolteacher's pay. See how you like that.
Twenty-three roubles a month, minus deductions, minus
pension contributions. But even so I don't feel I have to
go around dressed in black.

  They sit down.

Masha It's not about money. Lots of poor people are
happy.

Medvedenko Happy in theory. But in practice what
actually happens: there's me, there's my two sisters,
there's my mother, there's my little brother, and we've all
got to live on my twenty-three roubles. So it comes down
to: do we have to have tea? Do we have to have sugar?
Can we go without cigarettes?

Masha looks at the stage.

Masha Not long till the play starts.

Medvedenko Well that's it, isn't it? Konstantin writes the play, Nina Zarechnaya acts in it, and so their love finds concrete expression. In art. Their souls mingle. They're lucky because our souls do no mingling at all. None whatsoever. I love you so much I can't stand being at home. I walk four miles here and four miles back, always to be totally blanked. Which I understand. A large family and no money. I'm hardly a prospect, am I?

Masha That's not the reason.

She takes snuff.

Your love for me is actually very touching, but it's not reciprocated, so what can I say? Have some.

Medvedenko No thank you.

A silence.

Masha It's close tonight, there must be a storm on the way. You talk about money all the time, as though it defined you. Nothing worse, you say, than being poor. But in my opinion it's a thousand times easier to be a beggar on the street than to – oh look, with you, there's no point in even trying to explain.

Sorin arrives with Konstantin. Sorin leans on his stick.

Sorin I've never got used to the country, and I never shall. It's too late now. I went to bed at ten last night, and I woke up at nine feeling as if my brain were somehow stuck to my skull. I sleep all the time. After lunch, I found myself fast asleep yet again. I woke, I thought, 'This is hell on earth.'

Konstantin You're better off in town, it's true.

He sees Masha and Medvedenko.

Sorry, but you two need to get out of here. I'll call you when we're ready but we're not ready yet.

Sorin Masha, one thing: can you please ask your father not to keep his dog on the leash? It barks all night. My sister got no sleep at all.

Masha Talk to him yourself. It's nothing to do with me. (*To Medvedenko.*) Come on, let's get out of here.

Medvedenko (*to Konstantin*) Don't forget. We don't want to miss it whatever happens.

Masha and Medvedenko go.

Sorin Wonderful. So we're condemned to another night's barking. The thing about the country: it's never how you want it to be. I used to come here for four weeks' annual leave but the moment I arrived they'd bombard me with the whole year's problems and I just wanted to make a quick exit as soon as I got here.

He laughs.

I've never been happier than when leaving this place. But sadly now I'm retired I don't really have anywhere to go. I'm stuck here whether I like it or not.

Yakov speaks to Konstantin.

Yakov We're going to take a swim if that's all right, sir.

Konstantin Fine, but ten minutes at most. You'll need to be in position.

Yakov Understood, sir.

Konstantin Back in ten.

Yakov goes, Konstantin gestures to the stage.

Konstantin Now that's what I call a theatre. A curtain, a wing, a back wing, and beyond, an empty space. No scenery. Just the lake and the horizon. The curtain will rise at 8.30, for when the moon comes up.

Sorin Sounds marvellous.

Konstantin That's why I'm jumpy. If Nina is late, the whole effect will be lost. Her father and stepmother virtually keep her under lock and key. Almost impossible for her to escape.

He straightens his uncle's tie.

You don't think you should do something about your hair?

Sorin runs his fingers through his beard.

Sorin Tragedy of my life. Even when I was young I looked like an old drunk, and that's it. That's why I never had any luck with girls.

He sits down. Konstantin joins him.

And tell me why my sister's in such a bad mood.

Konstantin Partly she's bored. But she's also jealous. A play being performed that she's not in? And Nina is? Mama hasn't even seen it but she knows she hates it.

Sorin (*laughs*) You do have the most ridiculous idea of her.

Konstantin Do I? She's furious. Right here, on this little stage, Nina's going to be acclaimed and she's not. Her idea of a nightmare. She's a very complicated woman, my mother. Oh, gifted, yes, beyond question, intelligent, wonderful feeling for literature, can recite swathes of poetry by heart, never happier than when ministering like an angel to the sick, but just try mentioning the

word Duse. Wow! Stand back! If you praise Duse. No.
Only *she* must be praised. Only *she* must be reviewed.
It's not happening if it's not about her: her fabulous
performance in *The Lady of the Camellias*, or some
other dreary old play. And because out here in the
country, there's no one to praise her, she gets antsy. 'Get
me some praise, I'm starved, I'm desperate.' And it must
be our fault, it must be us that's to blame, suddenly
we're the enemy. Add to which she's superstitious – God
forbid anything adds up to the number thirteen. And
purse-proud. I know for a fact she has seventy thousand
in a bank in Odessa. But ask her for a loan and she'll
treat you to one of her greatest performances.

Sorin For goodness' sake. You're having the reaction
before you have the event. We call it 'discounting'. It's
nonsense. Your mother adores you.

Konstantin pulls the petals from a flower.

Konstantin She loves me, she loves me not. There you
are! Not!

He laughs at the proof.

My greatest crime is that I remind her how old she is.
Because she wants to go on dressing like a girl and, let's
face it, having affairs like a girl. That's what it's about.
But she can't get round the fact that I'm twenty-five
years old. When I'm not here, she can play thirty-two,
but unfortunately when I'm standing anywhere near she
has to own up. Let's say it: forty-three. She's forty-three!
No wonder she hates me. And she knows that I'm not
what they call a theatre-lover. For her, theatre is this
sacred calling, it's there to serve humanity, but in my
opinion the theatre you see today is just boring. It's stuck
in the past. Up goes the curtain, and then always the
same thing. The exaggerated lighting, the three walls,

these priests of art wandering around doing their little imitations of how real people eat and drink and love and walk and wear their clothes. Then two-thirds of the way through, here it comes, the message! You can see it a mile off. Some poker-work moral, carefully embroidered, so everyone can take it home. One size fits all! The minute they give me the message, I want to run screaming from the theatre, like Maupassant aghast at the Eiffel Tower. If I haven't already.

Sorin People can't live without theatre.

Konstantin Maybe. But we need new forms. And if we can't get a theatre that's new, that's genuinely new, then sorry, it's better to have none at all.

For a second time he checks his watch.

I love my mother, I love her very much, but she lives a meaningless life. She's always swanning around with that so-called man of letters. You can't open a newspaper without reading about her. All right, you may just think I'm being selfish, but, oh my God, I do sometimes wish that my mother were anonymous like everyone else. It puts me in such a hideous position. She has parties: every single person is a celebrity – they're an artist or they're a writer or an actor – and I'm standing there for no other reason but that I'm her son. So no wonder, Uncle, I find myself asking: who am I? What am I? I was sent down from university in my third year, for failures of discipline, as they say. I have no particular gift, I have absolutely no money, not a penny, and on my passport it says I'm petty bourgeois from Kiev. Again, all right, my father was petty bourgeois from Kiev, but at least he was an actor, and what's more, rather a famous one. So every time one of the celebrities looks at me, all they're thinking is: what the hell is he doing here? It's just utterly humiliating.

Sorin Yes. About that so-called man of letters . . .

Konstantin What about him?

Sorin I mean, just a question, but does he speak? I've never heard him say anything.

Konstantin He's all right. Nothing wrong with him. He's decent enough. Maybe a bit sad. He isn't yet forty, fame came too easily and basically he's blasé. As for his work, well, how do I say this? It's not nothing, but on the other hand if you've been reading Tolstoy or Zola, you're not going to feel an urgent need to read Trigorin.

Sorin I like literary folk. Always have. Time was, I longed for two things: to get married and to be a novelist. I didn't achieve either. I can't think of anything nicer than being even a minor novelist.

Konstantin Listen, she's coming.

He hugs his uncle.

Just the sound of her feet, I can't believe it. I can't live without her. I'm so incredibly happy.

Nina Zerechnaya comes in as Konstantin goes quickly to greet her.

Nina I'm not late. Don't tell me I'm late.

Konstantin No, you're not late. You're not late.

He is kissing her hands.

Nina I've spent the whole day worrying. I was terrified my father wouldn't let me out. But a great stroke of luck: he's just gone out with my stepmother. I was in such a panic. The sky was red, the moon was on its way and I was yelling at the horse to speed up. I'm so happy I made it.

Nina squeezes Sorin's hand tightly. He laughs.

Sorin Are those tears in your eyes? That's not good.

Nina It's nothing, only I'm out of breath, that's all. And I can stay exactly thirty minutes, so we have to start right away. I can't be late, whatever happens. My father doesn't even know I'm here.

Konstantin That's fine, we're ready. Let's get everyone seated.

Sorin Let me, I'll round them up.

He heads off, singing.

'In France there were once two soldiers
In Russia they had been taken . . .'

He turns back.

Funny, I was once singing this very song when a friend, the public prosecutor, said 'Your Excellency, you have a powerful voice.' Slight pause. 'Powerful but off-putting.'

He laughs and goes out.

Nina My father and his wife forbid me to come here. They say you're a bunch of bohemians, and I'll end up wanting to be an actress. But it's as if I'm drawn across the lake, like a seagull. Oh, my heart's so full of you.

She looks round nervously.

Konstantin It's all right, we're alone.

Nina I don't think so.

Konstantin We're alone.

They kiss.

Nina What tree is that?

Konstantin An elm.

Nina Why is it so dark?

Konstantin It's not the trees, it's the light. In this light, everything looks dark. Don't go straight back after the play.

Nina I have to.

Konstantin Perhaps I'll follow. I'm going to follow you all the way home. Stand in your garden, looking up at your window.

Nina I don't think our guard dog'll be too happy. You have to get to know Trésor first.

Konstantin I love you.

Nina Shh . . .

Konstantin hears a noise behind the stage.

Konstantin Yakov, is that you?

Yakov (*behind the stage*) It's me.

Konstantin Then please get ready, it's time to start. Any sign of the moon?

Yakov It's coming up now, sir.

Konstantin You have the methylated spirits? And the sulphur? Remember, the smell of sulphur to go with the red eyes. (*To Nina.*) Here we go. Are you nervous?

Nina Incredibly. Not because of your mother, she doesn't bother me at all, but Trigorin. When I think I'm going to act in front of Trigorin, the famous novelist. He's still young?

Konstantin Yes.

Nina I love his work.

Konstantin (*cool*) Do you? I haven't read it.

Nina You know, it's not easy acting in your play. There are no real people in it.

Konstantin People! The job is not to show life as it is, or as it should be, but to create a world. A new world which is as real and as powerful as a dream.

Nina Nothing really happens in your play, it's just talk. I think, to be effective, a play has to have love in it.

They go behind the stage. Dorn and Polina arrive.

Polina Go back and get your galoshes. It's wet underfoot.

Dorn I'm hot.

Polina It's so typical. You deliberately refuse to look after yourself. Out of sheer stubbornness. You're the doctor, you know full well that damp air is bad for you, but you love getting me worried. Yesterday you sat outside on the terrace all evening.

Dorn (*hums*) 'Do not say that youth is ruined . . .'

Polina But of course so wrapped up in your conversation with Irina Nikolaevna that you didn't even notice the cold. You like her, don't you?

Dorn I'm fifty-five.

Polina What's that to do with it? You haven't lost your looks. You're still attractive to women.

Dorn So what do you want me to do about it?

Polina I never met a man who didn't fall over and grovel as soon as they came across an actress.

Dorn (*hums*) 'Here I am before you . . .' That's as it should be. If artists are treated differently from shopkeepers, that's fine. It's a very proper form of idealism.

Polina And for as long as I can remember women have been throwing themselves at you. Is that a form of idealism too?

Dorn (*shrugs*) It's because I'm a doctor. And what's more a good doctor. That's what they love. What's wrong with that? Remember, ten or fifteen years ago I was the only male obstetrician in the entire region. They knew they could trust me. They were right.

Polina (*taking his hand*) My dear.

Dorn Hush. Everyone's coming.

Arkadina arrives on Sorin's arm, with Trigorin, Shamraev, Medvedenko and Masha.

Shamraev Yes, I remember it must have been 1873. In Poltava it was, at the fair, she was absolutely extraordinary. As great an actress as we ever had. And do you know what happened to Pavel Semenych Chadin? He was the best Rasplyuev I ever saw. Far better than Sadovsky, whatever anyone tells you. Where is Chadin now?

Arkadina How on earth should I know? This is prehistory.

Shamraev It's thinking about actors like Chadin which makes you realise how poor the theatre is nowadays. Once there were mighty oaks, now just little stumps.

Dorn It's true there are fewer outstanding talents, but the overall standard is higher, I think.

Shamraev I'm not even sure about that. But then what do they say? *De gustibus . . . de gustibus*, something, they say, you know what they say.

Konstantin comes out from behind.

Arkadina Darling, how much longer do we have to wait?

Konstantin Forgive me, we're about to start.

Arkadina (*quoting from* Hamlet)
'Oh Hamlet, speak no more,
Thou turn'st mine eyes into my very soul . . .'

Konstantin (*completing it*)
'And there I see such black and grained spots
As will not leave their tinct.'

A horn sounds.

Ladies and gentlemen, please take your seats. The play is about to begin.

There's a pause.

We begin.

He raps with a stick and intones.

Two hundred thousand years. We dream of how things will be in two hundred thousand years' time.

Sorin There won't be anything in two hundred thousand years.

Konstantin Then I call on the shadows of the night, the shadows of the lake, drift across, show us the nothingness, the non-being. Lull us to sleep.

Arkadina Oh good, permission to sleep. Thank goodness for that.

The curtain goes up. The lake beyond, the moon on the horizon reflected in the water. Nina is all in white, sitting on a large stone.

Nina Humans, lions, eagles, partridges, deer, geese, spiders, the fish swimming silent at the bottom of the sea, micro-organisms too small to detect – in a word, everything that lives, everything that has life, everything that is – everything has lived out its cycle and died. In its place, nothing. For thousands of years, the moon has shone down useless on an empty world. The cranes no longer wake and call to each other in the meadows. In the lime groves, the May beetles are silent. Everything is cold. Everything is empty. Terror. Terror. Terror.

There's a pause.

Nothing draws breath. Everything is dust. Everything that was body is stone. Is water. Is cloud. And the soul of everything that ever lived has become one soul. I am that soul, the universal soul, the soul of the world. The soul of Alexander and the soul of Caesar, the soul of Shakespeare and the soul of Napoleon, the soul of the lowest slug that ever crawled along the ground. The fine reasoning of man has merged with the dazzling instincts of the animal, and everything that ever was is contained in me, and lives again in me.

The marsh lights appear. Arkadina speaks quietly.

Arkadina Avant-garde or what?

Konstantin Mama!

Nina I am alone. Only once every hundred years do I open my lips to speak, and when I speak there is nobody to hear. Even the lights around me that come from the marsh and wander until daybreak, even they do not listen. The devil changes everything lest it come to life. Ceaselessly, he plays with the atoms. The devil, the father of matter, changes the stones into water, the water into stones. One thing alone remains true. One thing remains constant. The soul, the spirit itself.

There's a pause.

Like a prisoner thrown deep down into an empty well,
I do not know where I am or what is waiting for me.
The only thing I know is that I must fight with the devil.
The soul must fight matter, and it must win. I am
destined to win. One day matter and soul will merge in
perfect harmony, and the will of the world will begin its
reign. But this day will only arrive after thousands more
years, when the moon is dust, the stars are dust, the
earth is dust. Until then, terror. Terror. Terror.

Two red spots appear, hovering over the lake.

Now my powerful enemy, the devil, approaches. I see his
fierce red eyes.

Arkadina I can smell sulphur. Is that to do with the play?

Konstantin Of course it's the play.

Arkadina (*laughs*) I should have guessed. Special effects!

Konstantin Mama!

Nina The devil is bored without human company.

Polina (*to Dorn*) You've taken your hat off. Put it back
on or you'll catch cold.

Arkadina He's taken it off out of respect for the devil,
the father of eternal matter.

Konstantin loses it.

Konstantin Right, that's it. That's enough. Enough!
Curtain.

Arkadina What's happening?

Konstantin I said, curtain! Curtain, I said. Bring it
down. The play is over. It's enough.

He is stamping his foot. The curtain is lowered.

Stupid of me, of course. Stupid. Foolish. How stupid.
Not to realise that only an elite can make theatre. Only
a precious elite. The theatre elite. How vulgar of me to
crash the circle! How . . . how . . .

But he can't finish. He waves a hand and runs off.

Arkadina I don't understand. What's upset him?

Sorin Irina, he's young. You've hurt his feelings.

Arkadina How have I hurt his feelings?

Sorin You know perfectly well. You offended him.

Arkadina He said to me beforehand it was just a skit,
just a little sketch, so I assumed that's what he meant.
A sketch.

Sorin Even so.

Arkadina Now you're telling me he's written a great
masterpiece. Please! He got this performance together,
did he, and choked us all to death with sulphur, and it's
all because it's not a sketch, it's a manifesto. He wants to
teach us all a lesson in how to write and how to act. It's
getting to be too much. Whatever you say, it's not easy
for me to sit here and endure all these stupid jibes and
attacks. The boy is hopelessly wilful and self-centred.

Sorin He wanted to please you, he wanted to give you
pleasure.

Arkadina Then why not write a proper play? Not this
ridiculous avant-garde provocation. I mean, I don't mind
cutting edge. I don't mind provocation, I like it, it makes
me laugh, but don't come to me and tell me it's all about
a new form, a new dawn in the history of art. I don't
think so. There's no new dawn, just bad faith.

Trigorin Everyone writes what they must. We write what
we can.

Arkadina Fine. Let him write whatever he likes, as long as he doesn't drag me into it.

Dorn Ah, the anger of Jupiter.

Arkadina I'm not Jupiter and I'm not even angry. I'm just irritated. How can any young man waste his time in such a boring and predictable way? I didn't set out to upset him.

She has lit a cigarette.

Medvedenko In my view, the play's based on a misunderstanding, because it's impossible to separate soul from matter. It's a false dichotomy. Soul *is* matter, that's the problem. (*To Trigorin.*) I think it would be much more worthwhile and interesting to put on a play about real life. I'm just suggesting, for instance about how hard a schoolmaster's life is nowadays. That's an interesting subject.

Arkadina Yes, fascinating, I'm sure, but can we all take a break from theatre and soul and matter? It's such a beautiful evening. Listen, can you hear someone singing? Gorgeous.

Polina It's from the other side of the lake.

Arkadina turns to Trigorin.

Arkadina Come and sit next to me. Not so long ago – ten, fifteen years – you could hear music from the lake almost every night. In those days there were six houses on this side alone. There was always laughter, there was always music, shots going off, and oh, love affairs, so many love affairs. And the leading man in all six houses – may I present to you our very own Doctor Dorn?

She nods at Dorn.

Arkadina Today the doctor is merely enchanting, but in those days I can assure you he was irresistible. Oh God, I'm starting to feel guilty now, I can't put it out of my head. Why did I upset my little boy like that? Kostya! Where are you? Kostya!

Masha I'll go and find him.

Arkadina Bless you, please do.

Masha Where are you? Konstantin? Where are you?

She goes out. Nina appears from behind the stage.

Nina It doesn't seem like we're going to resume, so I might as well say hello.

She kisses Arkadina and Polina.

Sorin Bravo! Bravo!

Arkadina Bravo indeed! Bravo! You were wonderful. With your looks and your voice, it's unimaginable you're going to spend your life here. It would be a sin. Wasting away in the countryside. You have talent. When you have talent, you have a solemn duty to put it to use.

Nina Oh, that's what I want most in the world. But it's never going to happen.

Arkadina Don't be so sure. Allow me to introduce you: Boris Alexeyevich Trigorin.

Nina I can't believe it. Really. I've read every word you've written. Truly.

Arkadina sits beside her.

Arkadina Don't blush, my dear. Yes, he's very famous, but he's still a normal person. Look, he's as embarrassed as you are.

Dorn Am I the only person who finds it spooky with the curtain down?

Shamraev Yakov, can you oblige, would you mind pulling the curtain up?

The curtain goes up. Nina speaks to Trigorin.

Nina It's a strange play, isn't it?

Trigorin I don't pretend to have understood it. But that doesn't mean I didn't enjoy it. Your acting is so truthful. And the setting was beautiful.

There's a pause.

The lake must be full of fish.

Nina Yes.

Trigorin I love fishing. I don't think there's anything I love more in the world than watching evening come down on a riverbank, the float in the water.

Nina But surely there can't be any pleasure to compare with the pleasure of creativity?

Arkadina (*laughs*) Oh, don't say things like that. Really. It makes him squirm when anyone says nice things.

Shamraev Best theatre story ever. We were at the Opera in Moscow, and the famous Silva was attempting bottom C. So, imagine, the bass from our church choir, all the way up in the gallery, to everyone's amazement, yells out, 'Bravo, Silva!' Only, guess what, he's an octave lower. (*Imitates.*) 'Bravo, Silva!' Whole audience, silent.

There's a pause.

Dorn An angel flying over.

Nina I have to get back. I'm sorry.

278

Arkadina Impossible, no, you mustn't. I insist. We won't let you.

Nina Papa's waiting for me.

Arkadina How you put up with him. Really.

They kiss.

Well there it is, what can you do? Such a shame to see you go.

Nina If you knew how little I want to go.

Arkadina Someone should accompany you.

Nina (*alarmed*) Absolutely not.

Sorin Please. Stay. Just for an hour.

Nina I can't, Petr Nikolayevich.

Sorin Give us the pleasure of your company one more hour. Surely.

Nina hesitates, tears in her eyes.

Nina I can't.

She squeezes Sorin's hand and runs out.

Arkadina That poor girl. Apparently her mother left the whole enormous family fortune to the father, every single kopeck, and he's already signed a will giving it all to the second wife. The daughter's left with nothing. It's a scandal.

Dorn Rare you can say of any human being that they're a complete pig but you can say it of her father.

Sorin (*rubbing his hands*) Come on, it's getting damp. We should move inside. My legs have started to ache.

Arkadina Your legs look more like wooden pegs, you can barely walk.

She offers him an arm.

Come on, you poor lost soul.

Shamraev (*offering Polina an arm*) Madame?

Sorin And there's that damned dog again. Could you do me a favour, Ilya Afanasevich, and set the wretched animal free?

Shamraev Can't do it, sir. There are thieves around, and I've got millet in the barn.

He walks out beside Medvedenko.

I'm not exaggerating. One whole octave lower. 'Bravo, Silva!' And we're not talking about a professional singer, this is just a regular church chorister.

Medvedenko So tell me, how much exactly does a church chorister earn?

They've gone. Dorn is alone.

Dorn I don't know, perhaps I'm wrong, perhaps I'm losing my judgement, but I liked the play. There's something about it. He deserves encouragement. When that girl was talking about being alone, and you saw the red eyes of the devil, I found that my hands were shaking. There's something authentic, a bit gauche.

Konstantin has appeared.

Konstantin All gone.

Dorn Yes. Except me.

Konstantin Masha's screaming her way round the park, yelling for me. She's an unbearable woman.

Dorn Konstantin Gavrilovich, I want to say this: your play meant a lot to me. It's an unusual work, and unfortunately it was cut short, but even so, in the time it lasted, it made a strong impression. You have talent and you should keep writing.

Konstantin squeezes his hand tightly and hugs him.

Goodness, you're over-sensitive. And I see tears in your eyes. I want to be clear about this: you've taken a subject from the realm of abstract ideas. And I like that, because art surely has to be charged with a big idea. But it also has to be serious. An art work is only good if it's serious. You're going pale.

Konstantin What you're saying is: keep at it.

Dorn Yes. And aim only for what is timeless and enduring. Myself, I've lived, as you know, what they call an interesting life and a rewarding one. I'm at peace. But if by chance it had been *my* lot in life to experience what an artist experiences – that epiphany – then it seems to me I would have despised the physical, and everything that goes with it. I would have left the earth behind. I would have risen above.

Konstantin You don't happen to know where Nina is, do you?

Dorn And I'll tell you something else: too few artists have an objective. There's no such thing as good art without purpose. You have to know why you are writing – to what end – because if you don't, the artistic life will destroy you.

Konstantin It's Nina I'm concerned about.

Dorn Nina? Oh –

Konstantin She went home? I don't believe it. What on earth do I do? I have to see her. I have to. I'm going to go after her.

Masha comes in.

Dorn Come on, calm down, it's not that bad.

Konstantin But I still have to go. I do. I have to.

Masha You need to go and see your mother, Konstantin Gavrilovich. She's back in the house and she's extremely concerned.

Konstantin Tell her I've gone out. Tell everyone. And tell everyone to leave me alone. Don't go screaming round the park.

Dorn Honestly, this is not a good idea. This is . . . this is not good.

Konstantin is crying now.

Konstantin Doctor, thank you. And goodbye.

He goes.

Dorn Youth! Youth!

Masha Yes, that's what people say when there's nothing to say. Youth! Youth!

She takes snuff, but Dorn grabs the snuff box and throws it violently into the bushes.

Dorn Disgusting habit.

Pause.

I'm sure there's a card game. I'll go in and join in.

Masha Wait.

Dorn What is it?

Masha I need to talk to you. I can't talk to my father, I've never been close to him. Somehow I'm closer to you. All my life I've felt that. For some reason. I need help or else I really do think I'm going to do something desperate.

I'm going to make a total mess of my life. The greatest mess of all time.

Dorn You ask me to help, but I have no idea how.

Masha I'm in agony. Nobody can begin to understand the agony I'm in.

She puts her head on his chest.

I'm in love with Konstantin.

Dorn It's the lake. The magical lake, which is casting its spell on you all. You're all so dramatic, all of you. But what can I do, my little child? What? What can I do?

Act Two

A croquet lawn. In the background, to the right, a house with a large terrace. To the left, the lake, the sun reflected on the water. Flower beds. Noon. Heat. Arkadina, Dorn and Masha are sitting on a bench at the side of the lawn, in the shade of an old lime. Dorn has an open book on his knee. Arkadina speaks to Masha.

Arkadina Come on, let's do an experiment. Stand up.

They stand.

Here, next to me. Now. You're twenty-two, and I'm nearly, well almost twice that. And which of us looks younger?

Dorn There's no contest.

Arkadina There you are.

Dorn You!

Arkadina And why? Simple. Because I work, I keep busy, I live life to the full. But you just sit there. You don't live. That's why. I have some simple rules. Never think about the future. Never think about old age. Never think about death. Because there's nothing you can do about any of them.

Masha I feel as if I was born such a long time ago, and now I have to drag the years round behind me, like the train of a dress. And at times I even lose the will to live. Of course I know it's all nonsense, of course I do. I should cheer up.

Dorn (*hums*) 'Tell her, my flowers . . .'

284

Arkadina Another reason: I'm properly presented, like the English. I'm well turned out. My clothes – just so. My coiffure – impeccable. Am I ever seen outside the house, in the garden, say, in a housecoat or with my hair down? No, I am not. The reason I'm in such good shape is because I stay sharp and I don't let myself go.

She walks round the lawn, arms akimbo.

You see – like a little bird. If they said to me 'You have to play a fifteen-year-old', I'd get away with it.

Dorn Yes, well, be that as it may. Nevertheless. Shall we continue? We'd got as far as the rats and the corn merchant . . .

Arkadina Right, the rats. Good. Read on. Or better still, give it to me. It's my turn. I'll read.

She has sat and taken the book from Dorn. Now she searches for her place.

Where are we? Ah yes. 'It's as dangerous for people of good breeding to invite novelists into their houses as it is for corn merchants to invite rats into their stores. When a woman sets out to seduce a writer, she lays careful siege to him by means of strategically praising his work.' Well, in France maybe, but not here. In my experience it's the other way round. First of all the woman falls desperately in love and it's only later she gets round to strategy. To take the obvious example, if you look at me and Trigorin . . .

Sorin comes in, using his stick. Nina is beside him. Behind, Medvedenko pushes a wheelchair. Sorin talks to Nina as though to a child.

Sorin So something tells me you must be happy at last, am I right? (*To Arkadina.*) Such good news! Her father and stepmother have gone to Tyver, and she's allowed out for three whole days.

Nina sits next to Arkadina and hugs her.

Nina I'm so pleased. At last I get to spend time among you.

Sorin (*getting into his wheelchair*) Such a beautiful creature, isn't she?

Arkadina She's chic, she's intriguing, she's clever as can be. But let's stop there because too much praise brings bad luck. Where's Boris Alexeyevich?

Nina He's fishing, down by the bathing area.

Arkadina And seemingly never bored, heaven knows why.

She is about to resume her book.

Nina What is it you're reading?

Arkadina Maupassant. 'On the Water'. Reluctantly. It isn't working for me.

She closes the book.

I can't concentrate. I'm worried about my boy. Why is he so depressed? Why is he so down on the rest of us? He spends the whole day at the lake, I hardly see him at all.

Masha He's pining. (*To Nina.*) Why don't you read us something from one of his plays?

Nina I don't think so. Not really. They're so dull.

Masha When he reads his own dialogue, it's like his whole body catches fire. His eyes blaze, you can see the blood draining from his face. The voice, the gestures, everything about him says poet.

Sorin snores.

Dorn And goodnight.

Arkadina Petrusha!

Sorin What? What?

Arkadina You're not falling asleep, are you?

Sorin Certainly not.

Arkadina I wish you'd take something for it. You need to take something.

Sorin I'd be happy to, but the doctor here refuses to treat me.

Dorn Why would you need treatment at sixty?

Sorin Even at sixty, you still want to live. If you don't mind.

Dorn (*dismissive*) If you insist on taking something, take valerian drops.

Arkadina Better, he should spend time at a spa. That really would do him good.

Dorn Going to a spa could be good. Not going to a spa could also be good.

Arkadina And what on earth does that mean?

Dorn It means exactly what it says. It's a perfect diagnosis.

There's a pause.

Medvedenko Best thing you could do is give up smoking.

Sorin Rubbish.

Dorn No, not rubbish at all. It's wine and tobacco which destroy your sense of yourself. After a few vodkas you're no longer Petr Nikolayevich, but Petr Nikolayevich plus someone else. A second person appears. Your own core being splits in two and you have to start handling the new arrival.

Sorin (*laughs*) I know what you're saying, that's a wonderful way of putting it. But it's different for you. You've had a good life. Me? Twenty-eight years in the Justice Department, and at the end of it all, it's not just that I haven't had a good life, truthfully I haven't had *any* life. You're fine, and because you've lived you now get satisfaction from philosophising. But I haven't, so I need alcohol. And I need cigars. And that's just how things are. It's how they are.

Dorn Life is serious. It's serious! And heading off to spas at the age of sixty, and endlessly complaining about the life you haven't lived, sorry, but that's the very opposite of serious.

Masha It must be lunchtime. My leg's gone to sleep.

She walks out, limping.

Dorn You can be sure she'll be knocking back a couple of vodkas before lunch.

Sorin Poor thing, she's so unhappy.

Dorn Your Excellency, you do talk the most ridiculous rubbish.

Sorin And you always talk as if somehow you're above it all.

Arkadina Oh, please, gentlemen. This is everything I hate about the countryside. People sitting around in unbearable heat telling each other how to live. Believe me, I love your company, my friends, I really do, and you're a joy to listen to, but on the other hand set me down in a hotel room with a wonderful leading role to learn!

Nina That must be so fulfilling. I can't imagine.

Sorin Obviously, it goes without saying, town's better than country. Obviously. You sit in your study, the servants don't let anyone in without warning, no horrible surprises, you have the telephone, there are taxis outside. Where's the contest?

Dorn (*hums*) 'Tell her my flowers . . .'

Shamraev comes in with Polina. He kisses the hands of Arkadina, then Nina.

Shamraev And the very people we're looking for. Good morning. Wonderful to see you in such good health. I'm just a little concerned, my dear lady, because my wife is telling me that you'd like to go into town with her today. Is that right?

Arkadina We're going, yes.

Shamraev I know you'd like to go, but tell me, ma'am, how exactly are you planning to get there? We're transporting the rye all day, and every man jack of us on the job. So where on earth do you imagine you can find horses?

Arkadina I would have thought that was your business, not mine.

Sorin We own carriage horses.

Shamraev Yes we do. Yes we do own carriage horses.

Sorin So?

Shamraev And where do you suggest I find harnesses for carriage horses? What, I conjure up harnesses which I don't have? There is actually a point at which I just fail to understand how anyone – my dear lady, forgive me, as you know I revere your talent, I have given you ten years of my life but today – horses? – no, I cannot give you.

Arkadina And if I *have* to go? This is ridiculous.

Shamraev With the greatest respect, you know nothing whatsoever about farming.

Arkadina (*losing her temper*) It always comes down to that, doesn't it? It's always the same charge. Know nothing about farming! All right, very well, in that case, I shall go back to Moscow where obviously you think I belong. Straight away. Get me horses from the village, and if that's too difficult for you, I'll walk!

Shamraev (*losing his*) If that's what you want, then I resign. Find yourself another estate manager!

He stomps off.

Arkadina Every summer this happens, every summer they insult me. It's the last time I ever come to this place.

She goes off to collect Trigorin, and a few minutes later they can be seen going into the house, he with his fishing rods and a bucket.

Sorin This is insubordination and no other word for it. I simply won't put up with it. All the horses are to be rounded up immediately. This instant!

Nina (*to Polina*) She's a great actress, how can anyone deny her what she needs? Surely every desire of hers, every whim, is far more important than farming.

Polina (*in despair*) What can I do?

Nina I find it unbelievable. I really do.

Polina Imagine being me! It's impossible.

Sorin (*to Nina*) Come with me, we'll persuade my sister to stay. Isn't that the best thing to do?

He shouts in the direction of Shamraev.

You impossible man! You tyrant!

Nina stops him from getting up.

Nina Please, sit down, leave it to us, sit down, we'll wheel you there. This is all so upsetting.

Sorin Yes, it's agony. But he mustn't resign. I'll talk to him now.

Nina and Medvedenko wheel Sorin out. Polina and Dorn are left alone.

Dorn People are so predictable, aren't they? They really are. They should have sacked your husband years ago. Instead of which that craven old woman Sorin and his sister will go grovelling to him on their knees. You wait. I'm right.

Polina And what he doesn't say: there are no carriage horses because they're all working in the fields! Every day there's this sort of foul-up. It makes me ill. I'm actually trembling, because I'm so nervous of what the latest mistake is going to be. And the way he talks to people. Oh Evgeny, my love, my own, please can't you take me away, take me to live with you. Time's going so fast, we're not young any more. And wouldn't it be wonderful, at the end of our lives, finally to be honest, finally to stop telling lies?

Pause.

Dorn I'm fifty-five. It's difficult.

Polina For goodness' sake, I'm not stupid, I know there are other women. I know that. Other women who are close to you. But you can't live with all of them. You're tired of me, aren't you?

Dorn No. I'm never tired of you.

Nina can be seen near the house picking flowers.

Polina And I'm jealous. I admit it. You're a doctor, in your job you deal with women all day. I understand.

Dorn speaks to Nina.

Dorn What's the latest development?

Nina Irina Nikolaevna is in tears, and her brother has asthma.

Dorn (*getting up*) Sounds like valerian drops to me. For both parties.

Nina hands him the flowers.

Nina These are for you.

Dorn *Merci bien.*

Polina goes with Dorn.

Polina What beautiful flowers.

But as they approach the house, she is heard in an urgent whisper.

Give them here, give them to me.

She is seen to tear them to pieces and scatter them on the ground. They go indoors. Nina is alone.

Nina You don't expect to see a famous actress cry, and over something as trivial as that. And it's strange, isn't it, that a famous writer, adored by the public, profiled in the newspapers, whose portrait you can buy in the street, who's translated into goodness knows how many languages, spends the whole day fishing. He's in heaven because he's caught a couple of chub. I had everything wrong. I thought fame and brilliance were a sort of revenge. You would use them to get your own back on people who were born to wealth and power. You'd make yourself proud and unapproachable, you'd look down on ordinary people. Far from it. Here they are, going

fishing, playing cards, joking around and having rows –
just like everyone else.

*Konstantin comes in, bareheaded, holding a rifle and a
dead seagull.*

Konstantin You're alone?

Nina Yes. Alone.

He puts the dead bird at her feet.

Tell me what this means.

Konstantin I did a terrible thing today. I killed a bird.
And I'm bringing it to lay at your feet.

Nina What's wrong with you?

There's a silence.

Konstantin And soon I shall kill myself in the same way.

Nina You've changed. I don't know you any more.

Konstantin I've changed because you have. But you
changed first, remember? You stepped back. Now you
behave as if I'm an embarrassment.

Nina You've become so difficult.

Konstantin Have I?

Nina You keep speaking in a way no one can understand.
It's all symbols, everything's a symbol. This gull? Symbol.
Or you want it to be, but a symbol of what precisely I
have no idea.

*She has picked up the bird and now she lays it on the
bench.*

Clearly I'm too stupid for you.

Konstantin Everything started to go wrong on the night
of my play. The one thing women can never forgive is

failure. Well, I burnt the text, every word of it destroyed, down to the last comma. And now I'm more unhappy than you can believe. Because I can feel you moving away from me, and it's like I've woken up and suddenly the lake has gone. There's a drought. There's no water in the world. You said just now you're too stupid to understand me, but honestly what is there to understand? My play was a flop, you don't think I'm talented, as far as you're concerned, you agree with the others, I'm one writer among a thousand. I'm ordinary.

Konstantin stamps his foot.

Oh God, this thing in my brain. Like a nail. This rusty nail is killing me. Damn it. And it's all like my own stupid vanity is sucking my blood, it's sucking it like a snake.

He sees Trigorin coming, reading his notebook.

And hallelujah, here's a real writer. Got the walk. Got the book. Hamlet to a T. 'Words, words, words.' This burst of sunshine has not even reached you yet, but already you're smiling. Your eyes have melted in the heat. Please. I won't get in your way.

He goes quickly out. Trigorin stops to make a note.

Trigorin Takes snuff and drinks vodka. Always in black. A schoolteacher who's in love with her.

Nina Boris Alexeyevich.

Trigorin Well. Sudden change of plan, and it turns out we're leaving right away. Which means you and I are unlikely to see each other again. Which is a shame. Because I don't often come across young women, women who are young and interesting. I have no memory of being eighteen or nineteen, so it's hard for me to think myself back. That's why the young women in my novels and stories are often so unconvincing. The thing I'd like most: to spend one hour being you. It would only take an hour. So I can find out how you think and what sort of sweet little creature you are.

Nina And in return, can I be you?

Trigorin Why?

Nina Oh. To know what it's like to be talented and famous.

Trigorin Famous?

Nina What fame really feels like. And how do you know? How does it come across to you, the actual knowledge that you're famous?

Trigorin How? I'm not sure it does. I've never thought about it. Anyway, am I famous? As famous as you make me sound? Maybe that's the problem.

Nina But when you read about yourself?

She waits.

Well?

Trigorin A good review and I feel good. A bad review and I feel – not so good. And the not-so-good feeling lasts for a couple of days.

Nina It's just such a special kind of life. You have no idea how much I envy you. It's the difference between what different people are allocated. Most of us live lives of routine, of absolute insignificance, nothing to distinguish one day from another. Every day unhappy. But others – and you're among them – are handed a destiny. An interesting, brilliant existence, charged with significance. You're happy.

Trigorin I'm happy? Honestly, the words you're using – fame, happiness, brilliance – to me these words are like pastry, and, forgive me, I don't eat pastry. I'll just say: you're very young and you're very kind.

Nina You're not denying your life is wonderful?

Trigorin Wonderful? My life is wonderful? Anyway, I must go and write. I don't have time to take you on.

He has checked his watch.

Look, I think you realise you've struck a particularly painful nerve and now I'm getting tetchy. Because, you know, if we *do* actually talk about this, about my brilliant life . . . well how do I put this? How do I start? The Headline: What Being A Writer Is Like. There are certain obsessions, people think about them all the time, say they think about the moon, all right? Well I have a moon, and my moon is that at every hour of the clock I am consumed by one overriding need. I must write. I must write. I must. I don't even stop long enough to put 'The End' on the last story when for some reason I feel compelled to begin the next. Then a third, and then after the third, a fourth. Incessantly, without a break. I write. That's what I do. And I can't do anything else. So in what way exactly is that life beautiful and brilliant? Cruel, more like. Here I am getting exercised talking to you, and all the time I'm conscious that there's an unfinished story waiting for me in there, waiting for my attention. Look, that cloud up there, it looks like a grand piano. So what do I think immediately? Put it in a story. Cloud goes over looking like grand piano. Smell: heliotrope. Are you getting it?

Nina Yes.

Trigorin Make a mental note. Remember to put sickly smell of heliotrope in next description of purple summer

evening. It's as if I'm fishing every minute of the day,
hoping to pull in words and phrases, then throw them
on ice for when I need them. When I'm finished, either
I rush off to the theatre or I go and fish. As if doing
something else might bring relief. But it doesn't. Nothing
does. Because all the time, the next story, like a great big
cannonball is rolling around in my empty skull. And I
can feel the pull of the writing table, all the time. And
it's always like this, there's no respite, I have no peace,
even from myself. I feel I'm consuming my own life, and
all for the sake of this honey I'm making for someone
out there whom I don't even know. I'm out gathering
pollen from my own flowers, then I pick the flowers and
trample them underfoot. Am I mad? After all, my friends
and family hardly treat me as if I'm sane. On the contrary.
'What are you writing at the moment?' 'What are you
giving us next?' Over and over and over and over, and it
seems to me from the way they treat me, giving me their
opinion and their praise and their admiration – really,
underneath, they're just humouring me, as you would
humour a sick man. When what they're planning is to
steal up behind me, grab me and throw me in the
madhouse. As in Gogol. *Diary of a Madman.* And back
in the early days, when I was just starting out – and they
ought to be the best years, believe me, when you're a
young writer – far from it, it was a special kind of
misery. If you're not established, if you're not in any way
successful, then I can't tell you how clumsy you feel, how
awkward, how downright superfluous. Your nerves are
in tatters, you become hysterical. You can't help hanging
around with other writers, with other artists. But they
take no notice of you – why should they? They don't
know who you are – and in return you can't look them
in the eye, you keep your eyes on the floor, because it's
like you're in the casino, only nobody's given you any
chips. And as for readers – I never got to meet my readers,

but when I even thought about them they just all seemed so resentful and mistrustful. I was scared of the public. They terrified me. I wrote a play and I would look at the audience, and when I looked it seemed to me that the dark-haired ones were actively hostile, whereas the fair-haired ones were simply indifferent. Oh my God! I can't begin to tell you what agony it is.

Nina Maybe you don't enjoy the way of life, but the actual moment of creation, the inspiration, that must be extraordinary. That must make you happy.

Trigorin You're right. The moment it's happening, yes. The writing, yes. And reading the proofs. But then no sooner it's in print and you look at it, and all you can see is the book you didn't write, and this mistake and that mistake, and once more you feel stupid and angry.

He laughs.

And then the public get hold of it, and suddenly it's 'Yes, it's nice, it's charming but it's not exactly Tolstoy, is it?' Or 'A fine piece of work, but Turgenev's not going to be threatened, is he?' And so to my dying day, everything will be talented and charming, and charming and talented. Never more than that. And when I'm underground, my friends will walk past my grave and say 'Trigorin's down there. He was a good writer but not as good as Turgenev.'

Nina It's an act, isn't it? It's all an act. And you get away with it because success has spoiled you.

Trigorin Success? Not in my book. I don't read myself and think, 'This is good.' The truth is, I don't like my own writing. The worst of all is that I write in some kind of daze and I'm not sure I even understand what I write. I love nature. Look at it. This lake, the trees, the sky. It's looking at this which fills me with such profound emotion and makes me want to write. But sadly, I can't

298

just stick to landscape. After all I live in Russia, I'm a citizen. I love my country and I love its people and if I'm a writer, then I have a simple obligation to write about the people who live here, about their suffering, why they suffer, where their future may take them. And science, too. Human rights. These are vital and important subjects, and so I dash about all over the place, like a fox being chased by hounds. Life advances, science advances, I'm frantically trying to keep up, but without success, so that I fall further and further behind, like a peasant running for a train. And in the end, really, all I know about or care about is landscape, and when I stray from landscape, everything I write is false. False to the marrow of my bones.

Nina How can you know? How can you know the stature of your own achievement? It's too early. You're exhausted, that's all. With overwork. And it's not you who'll make the decision. It's others, and others consider you great and wonderful. If I were a great writer like you, then I would sacrifice my whole life to the people, I'd know that their happiness depended on them coming up to my level. And in return they would pull me along in their chariot.

Trigorin A chariot? You mean I'm Agamemnon?

Nina You're Agamemnon.

They both smile.

I'd do anything. For the joy of being a writer or an actress. I wouldn't mind going without. Going without love, going without food, going without hope. I'd live in a garret and eat rye bread, I'd live with all my own inadequacies, with the knowledge of my own shortcomings, but in return I would demand glory. Real, overwhelming glory.

She covers her face with her hands.

Oh Lord, my head, my head is spinning.

Arkadina calls from the house: 'Boris Alexeyevich'.

Trigorin They're looking for me. Probably to pack. But now the last thing I want to do is leave. Just look at the lake. Look, look how splendid it is.

Nina Can you see the house on the other side?

Trigorin Yes.

Nina My mother's. I was born on that estate. I've spent my whole life on this lake, and there's not an inch of it I don't know.

Trigorin Born into paradise.

Then he sees the seagull.

What's this doing here?

Nina Oh, it's a seagull. Konstantin Gavrilovich shot it.

Trigorin It's a beautiful bird. Do you think you could work on Irina Nikolaevna and get her to stay?

Nina What are you writing?

Trigorin Just a note to myself. I had an idea. An idea for a short story. A young girl lives on the shore of a lake since childhood. A girl like you. She loves the lake, like a seagull. And she's free, like a seagull. But a man happens to come along, catches sight of her, and for no other reason but that he can, he destroys her. Just like this seagull.

Arkadina appears at the window.

Arkadina Boris Alexeyevich, what are up to?

Trigorin I'm coming.

He heads away, then looks back at Nina. Then he calls to Arkadina.

What's the plan?

Arkadina We're going to stay.

Trigorin goes into the house. Nina comes forward towards the audience, ecstatic.

Nina It's a dream.

Act Three

Inside Sorin's house. The dining room. Doors on right and left. A sideboard. A medicine cabinet. A table in the middle of the room. A trunk and cardboard boxes suggest preparation for departure. Trigorin is eating a late breakfast. Masha is standing near the table.

Masha I'm talking to you as a writer. You can use what I'm telling you. If he'd done himself serious damage, then I don't think I'd have been able to carry on. It would have been the end. But, in the circumstances, I found my courage and I made a resolution. 'Right, I'm going to rip this love from my heart, tear it up by the roots.'

Trigorin How are you planning to do that?

Masha By getting married. To Medvedenko.

Trigorin Is he the schoolteacher?

Masha Yes.

Trigorin I can't see much future in that.

Masha What's the alternative? Living without hope, waiting years for something that's never going to happen. When I get married, then I can forget about love, there'll be other things to worry about. And besides, it'll be a change of scenery. Let's have another drink.

Trigorin Is that a good idea?

She pours two vodkas.

Masha Oh come on, don't look at me like that. Women drink far more than you realise. Agreed, only a few of us do it openly, but all of us do it. And always vodka or brandy.

They clink glasses.

Here's to you. You're unaffected, I like that. It's a shame you're leaving.

Trigorin Believe me, I don't want to leave.

Masha Then talk her into staying.

Trigorin I can't. She's determined to go. Her son's behaviour is impossible. First trying to shoot himself and now they say he wants to challenge me to a duel. A duel about what exactly? He's always muttering furiously, pontificating about how art needs new forms. Well of course it does. But it needs old forms too. And surely the point is, the two can perfectly well co-exist side by side.

Masha It's not about art. Not that it's any business of mine.

Yakov crosses left to right with a suitcase. Nina comes in and stops by the window.

My schoolteacher is not a brilliant man, but he's a good person, he's poor and he loves me with all his heart. I feel pity for him. And for his poor mother. Now, let me wish you godspeed. Think kindly of me.

She shakes his hand warmly.

I'll always be grateful for how good you were to me By all means send me your books, but I'll want a dedication. And not the usual 'To my dear friend'. No, put this: 'To Masha, unclear how she was born, unclear why she was alive.' Goodbye.

She goes out. Nina holds out a hand to Trigorin, fist tight.

Nina Odd or even?

Trigorin Even.

Nina opens her palm. One pea only.

Nina (*sighs*) No. You're wrong. I wanted a sign. Should I become an actress or not? If only someone would tell me.

Trigorin I'm not sure anyone *can* tell you.

Nina Since you're leaving, and it's possible this is the last time we'll ever meet, I want you to accept this small medallion to remember me by. I had your initials engraved on one side, and on the other, the title of your novel *Days and Nights*.

Trigorin That's generous! What a wonderful present.

He kisses the medallion.

Nina I hope you will think of me sometimes.

Trigorin I certainly will. The image is fixed in my head. A week ago, the sun shining, you in a light dress, we were talking, and on the bench beside you, a white seagull.

Nina A seagull, yes.

She is thoughtful a moment.

I'd love to say more but someone's coming. Please try and give me two minutes before you go. It's important.

As Nina goes out left, in comes Arkadina from the right with Sorin in a dress coat with a medal, and then Yakov organising luggage.

Arkadina Why do you insist on going round paying respects to all the neighbours? With your rheumatism, it would be far more intelligent to stay at home. Who was that, just left? Nina?

Trigorin It was Nina.

Arkadina Oh well then, pardon me, of course.

She sits. Trigorin looks at his medallion.

I think we've remembered everything. I'm utterly exhausted.

Trigorin *Days and Nights*, page 121, lines 11 and 12.

Yakov Am I meant to be packing the fishing rods, sir?

Trigorin Yes, please. I want them with me. But you can give my books away to whoever wants them.

Yakov As you wish, sir.

Trigorin (*to himself*) Page 121, lines 11 and 12. What on earth are they about? (*To Arkadina.*) Do you have any of my books in the house?

Arkadina In my brother's study, in that bookcase in the corner.

Trigorin Page 121.

Trigorin goes out.

Arkadina Really, Petrusha, home's where you belong.

Sorin With you gone, it's not going to be fascinating, is it?

Arkadina Yes, but what would you do in town?

Sorin Not much. Nevertheless.

He laughs.

I do have an invitation to the laying of the foundation stone for the new local government building. That's my life. Even if it's just for an hour or two, I've got to find some way of enlivening my existence, because I'm sitting around like some old cigarette holder. I've ordered my horses at one, we can all leave together.

Arkadina All right, let's make a deal: you go on living here, you don't get bored and you don't get the flu. Most of all, keep an eye on my son. Take care of him. And if necessary, keep him in line.

There's a pause.

Shame is, I'm leaving and that means I'll never know why Konstantin took a shot at himself, but my best guess is jealousy. Which is why the sooner I get Trigorin out of here the better.

Sorin I'm not sure. I think the causes may run deeper. Consider his situation: an obviously intelligent young man living miles from anywhere with no money, no status and no prospects. He has absolutely nothing to do all day, and he's both ashamed of that and frightened by it. I'm extremely fond of him, and I think he feels the same about me, but all the same, in the final analysis he feels he has no role in this house. He's a dependent. A hanger-on. He has some pride, credit him with that.

Arkadina I worry about him all day, every day. Maybe we should find him a job in the civil service.

Sorin whistles for a moment.

Sorin Oh for goodness' sake, it's obvious, just give the boy some money. That's what he needs. First up, get him dressed like a normal human being. He's been wearing the same jacket for three years, and he doesn't even have a coat to go out in. Get him out. Get him out and about.

That's what'll turn his life round. Travel, go abroad. It doesn't cost that much.

Arkadina A suit, certainly, I can get him a suit, but as for travelling abroad . . . And when I think about it, I'm not sure I can even do the suit. Not right now. Not at this moment. I simply can't afford it.

Sorin laughs.

I can't!

Sorin whistles again.

Sorin Well then, there we are. There's no need to lose your temper, I'm not doubting you for an instant. I know you to be a kind and generous woman.

Arkadina (*through tears*) I have no money!

Sorin If I had any, I'd give him some, but I'm flat-out broke. I don't have five kopecks. My whole pension is whipped away by my estate manager the moment it arrives. Everything goes into the farm, into the cattle, into the bees. I might as well tear my pension into pieces and throw it to the wind. The bees die, the cows keel over, and just try getting hold of a horse when you need one!

Arkadina Of course I have *some* money. Some. But I'm an artist. You won't believe the cost of a single costume nowadays.

Sorin It's all right, honestly, you don't have to defend . . . Oh my God, no, I'm having one of my moments, it's . . . Oh God, its . . .

He staggers and holds on to the table.

It's happening again. I'm not at all well.

Arkadina rushes across to support him, yelling out at the same time.

Arkadina Petrusha, Petrusha, quick, come and help. Help. He's not well.

Konstantin comes in with a bandage round his head. Medvedenko follows. Sorin smiles and drinks some water.

Sorin No, I think, hold on, it's passing. It's beginning to get better. There we are, there it is.

Konstantin Don't panic, Mama, it happens all the time. It's nothing serious. (*To Sorin.*) You should go and lie down.

Sorin Yes, a short lie-down, maybe. But I'm still going into town. Whatever happens. I'll have a lie-down and then I'll go. That's fair. That's a plan.

Medvedenko tries to take his arm as he walks with his stick.

Medvedenko Do you remember this one? In the morning on four, at midday on two, and in the evening on three.

Sorin (*laughs*) Of course, Oedipus! The riddle of the Sphinx! And at night on his back. Thank you, I shall walk unassisted.

Medvedenko Somehow I feel it's not the moment to argue.

They go out.

Arkadina He gave me a scare.

Konstantin It's living in the country. It gets him down. You know, I'll tell what would be best for him, if you could just reach into your pocket and lend him a couple of thousand, he could live in town year round.

Arkadina I have no money. I'm an actress, not a banker.

There's a pause.

Konstantin Mama, do you think you could change my bandage? I love it when you do it.

Arkadina gets an antiseptic and bandage from the medicine cabinet.

Arkadina I don't know why the doctor's so late.

Konstantin He said ten, and it's already midday.

Arkadina Sit down.

Arkadina unpeels the old bandage.

It looks more like a turban. Someone passing through yesterday in the kitchen asked what nationality you were. Look, it's almost healed. Just a few tiny scars.

She kisses the top of his head, then makes a gunshot noise.

So promise me, no more pyooo-pyooo while I'm not here to look after you.

Konstantin I promise. It won't happen again. It was a moment of madness, I lost control.

He kisses her hand.

Your hands are so wonderful. I remember a long time ago, I was still a child, you were working at the state theatre, there was a fight outside our apartment, there was a washerwoman who lived in our building who got beaten up outside. Do you remember? They left her unconscious. And you kept on going to look after her, you took her medicine, you bathed her children for her. Surely you remember?

Arkadina No.

She starts putting on the new bandage.

Konstantin There were two ballet dancers, lived in the same block as us. They used to come round for a coffee.

Arkadina That I remember.

Konstantin They were believers. Incredibly devout.

There's a pause.

I've been reminded these last few days. Because I've loved you these last few days in the way I used to love you when I was child. Tender, easy. Face it, you're all I have left. That's why I don't understand. Why on earth do you let that awful man walk all over you?

Arkadina You don't understand him, Konstantin. He's a man of the very finest character.

Konstantin Oh very fine, yes.

Arkadina He is.

Konstantin And when he heard I was about to challenge him to a duel, he became rather less fine and more what you might call cowardly. Suddenly he's leaving. Off! Gone! How fine, exactly, is that?

Arkadina He's leaving specifically because I asked him to, and for no other reason.

Konstantin Yes, and no doubt while you and I quarrel because of him, he'll all the time be lounging in the garden or in the drawing room, having a good laugh at our expense. While introducing Nina to the extraordinary breadth of his genius.

Arkadina It seems to give you some sort of special pleasure, upsetting me. This is a man I respect and I forbid you to run him down in my presence.

Konstantin But you see the difference is, I don't respect him. That's the difference. You want me to call him a genius, but he isn't. His work repels me.

Arkadina And you don't think there might be a reason for that? People who have nothing but pretension and no talent have nothing better in their lives than to denigrate real talent. There's not much comfort in jealousy, you know, not much consolation. Attacking other people's work won't make your own better.

Konstantin Real talent! What the hell does that mean? I'm more talented than any of you.

He grabs the bandage from his head.

It isn't even art you make, it's imitation. It's just copying – the same old stuff. And of course the only things you consider real and legitimate are the things you yourselves do, and everything else you want to make sure it's killed at birth. Well, I don't buy into it. I don't buy into you. And I'm most certainly not buying into him.

Arkadina The sheer complacency of the avant-garde!

Konstantin Well you don't have to deal with it, do you? Run back to your theatre bunker and perform in those pathetic third-rate plays.

Arkadina I have never done third-rate plays. How dare you? You couldn't even write a miserable little sketch. The petty bourgeois from Kiev! Parasite!

Konstantin I'd rather be a parasite than a miser.

Arkadina Scarecrow! Total nobody!

Konstantin sits down and cries. Arkadina walks up and down in distress.

Please don't. Please don't cry. Please don't.

She begins to cry herself. She kisses him on his forehead, his cheek, his head.

My darling, forgive me. Forgive your wicked mother. Really. Forgive a wretchedly unhappy woman.

Konstantin embraces her.

Konstantin If only you knew! I've lost everything I ever wanted. She doesn't love me any more. I can't write. I've lost all hope.

Arkadina Don't despair. Everything will be fine. He's leaving soon. And when he leaves, she'll come back to you.

She wipes away his tears.

Come on, it's enough. We're friends again.

Konstantin (*kissing her hands*) We're friends, Mama, we're friends.

Arkadina Now please, make your peace with him. No more talk of duels. We don't need duels, do we?

Konstantin All right, but please don't make me talk to him. I can't. I don't have the strength.

Trigorin comes in.

He's here, I don't want to see him. The doctor can bandage me later.

He puts the medicine away, picks the bandage up from the floor and heads for the door.

Trigorin Page 121, lines 11 and 12. Here. 'If you ever have need of my life, please, come and take it.'

Konstantin goes. Arkadina looks at her watch.

Arkadina They're due to bring the horses round any minute now.

Trigorin (*to himself*) 'If you ever have need of my life, please, come and take it.'

Arkadina I hope you're all packed.

Trigorin (*irritable*) Yes, of course. I'm packed. (*Lost in thought.*) Why do I detect such sadness when a pure soul pleads with me? And why does my own heart break?

He turns to Arkadina.

One more day. Yes? Shall we stay one more day? Please.

Arkadina You think I don't know why? Of course I know why. You need to take control of yourself. You're drunk, and you need to sober up.

Trigorin But you could be sober too. Be objective. Be reasonable. Why not? Look at it in the way a true friend would look at it.

He takes her hand, squeezes it.

You're capable of the sacrifice. Be loyal to me. Let me go.

Arkadina (*agitated*) You really are as desperate as that?

Trigorin It's as if I'm drawn to her. It's as if she's what I've always needed.

Arkadina Oh yes, desperately, of course! The love of a small-town provincial girl? How little you know yourself.

Trigorin It's like being a sleepwalker. I'm awake, I'm moving around, I'm talking to you, but in my dreams I see only her. And it's the dream that possesses me. This sweet, wonderful dream. Oh please let me go.

Arkadina (*shaking*) No. How can you talk to me like that? I'm a normal woman, like any other. No different. Don't do this, Boris, it's agony. I'm scared.

Trigorin You don't need to be normal, you could be extraordinary. Because love – youthful love, beguiling, poetic, can transport you into a world of dream. For me,

she's the only one who can do this, give me this happiness.
The sort of love I've never known. When I was young,
I was far too preoccupied, running round editors' offices,
struggling to make a living. But now. I'm ready. At last
love has arrived, and it's calling to me. What possible
reason can there be for running away?

Arkadina (*furious*) You've lost your mind.

Trigorin It's possible.

Arkadina Everyone got up this morning determined to
upset me.

She starts to cry. Trigorin holds his head.

Trigorin It's wilful. She doesn't want to understand. She
refuses to understand.

Arkadina Am I really so old, so ugly, so *invisible* that
you think you can talk to me about other women? Am I
not a woman? Do I not exist?

She starts to kiss him and hug him.

Oh my beloved, my beautiful, you've lost your head. Do
you have any idea? You are the last page of my life.

She goes down on her knees.

My joy, my pride, my happiness!

She embraces his knees.

If you leave me, even for an hour, I shan't survive. I
shan't. I shall go mad, my amazing, magnificent lord in
all things. My liege.

Trigorin Someone may come in.

He helps her to her feet.

Arkadina I don't care. I love you, I've nothing to be
ashamed of.

She kisses his hands.

I know how badly you want to go crazy, I understand that, but I won't let you. My treasure, my desperate, desperate man.

She laughs.

You belong to me. You're mine. This forehead, these eyes, this beautiful silky hair, all mine. It's my luck in life to be with the most intelligent man, the best writer alive, Russia's only remaining hope. And he's mine. You have such sincerity, such simplicity, such wonderful freshness, such good spirit. Sometimes I read, and just in a word, there it is, distilled, captured, in a phrase, the very heart, the very essence of a human being or of a landscape. It's as if your characters were really alive. They live. The only way to read you is with a full heart. I mean it. You think I'm exaggerating? You think I'm lying? Very well then, look me in the eye and tell me I'm a liar. Do I look like a liar? What do you see? The only woman in the world who knows your value. The only one. And the only one who tells you the truth. My darling, wonderful man. You'll come with me? Yes? You won't abandon me?

Trigorin No will. Never had any willpower. Never had *any*. Is this really what women want? A man who's feeble and submissive and acquiescent? Is that what they want? How can that be so? All right, take me, take me with you, only don't let me stray one step away from your side.

Arkadina (*to herself*) He's mine.

Suddenly it's as if nothing had happened.

Honestly, if you want to stay please do. I can go and you can follow in a week. If that's what you'd prefer. There's no rush.

Trigorin No. I think we should go together.

Arkadina It's up to you. Together, then.

Trigorin makes a note in his notebook.

Tell me.

Trigorin No, it's just . . . a nice phrase from this morning. 'The virgin forest'. Might be useful.

He stretches.

So, back on the road. More railway carriages, more stations, more buffets, more railway catering, more greasy cutlets. More conversation.

Shamraev comes in.

Shamraev Madam, sadly I have to announce that the horses are ready. The moment has come to leave for the station. If I can remind you, the train is due at five minutes past two. And when you get there I'm hoping you won't forget to enquire what happened to the actor Suzdaltsev. I'd love to know if he's alive. There was a time when he and I used to drink together. He was absolutely superb in *The Mail Robbery*. He was in the same theatre company as the tragic actor Izmailov, they often appeared together in Elisavetgrad. Another remarkable actor. Please, dear lady, I wasn't trying to rush you, we're comfortable, you have five minutes. There was a famous evening when they were playing conspirators who've suddenly been discovered and Izmailov was meant to say 'We're caught like rats in a trap,' only he said 'We're caught like taps in a trat.' Well you can imagine. Taps in a trat!

> *While he is speaking, Yakov attends to the luggage and the Maid brings Arkadina her hat, umbrella and gloves. Everyone helps her put them on. The Cook*

*looks through the door, then enters hesitantly. Then
Polina comes in, then Sorin and Medvedenko.*

Polina I've brought you plums for the journey. They're
very sweet. I thought you'd like to have something nice
to eat.

Arkadina You're so kind to me, Polina.

Polina Goodbye, my dear. And if things haven't always
been as they should be, please forgive me.

She is crying. Arkadina hugs her.

Arkadina Everything was perfect. Just perfect. So I
promise you, no need to cry.

Polina But our lives are running out.

Arkadina And what do you suggest we do about it?

*Sorin comes in and crosses in a coat with a cape
attached, a hat and a stick.*

Sorin Sister, it's time to get going, because otherwise the
simple truth is that you are going to be late. And that's
the truth. I'm going to get in.

Medvedenko And I am going to walk to the station to
see you off. So I'd better get a move on.

They go out.

Arkadina So, dear friends, goodbye. All being well, if we
are spared, then we shall see each other next year.

*The Cook, Yakov and the Maid all kiss her hand. She
gives the Cook a rouble.*

Please don't forget me. Here's a rouble to share between
you.

Cook Thank you very much, madam. We're very grateful.
Have a safe trip.

Yakov All the luck in the world to you, madam.

Shamraev Oh, and if you have a moment, a letter wouldn't go amiss. Goodbye, Boris Alexeyevich.

Arkadina Where's Konstantin? Does he know we're leaving? I have to say goodbye to him. And when you think of me, think kindly. (*To Yakov.*) Cook has the rouble, divide it three ways.

> *Everyone goes off. The stage is empty. The noise of the travellers saying goodbye and getting into the coaches offstage. The Maid comes out, collects the forgotten plums and takes the basket out. Then Trigorin returns.*

Trigorin My stick, it must be on the veranda.

> *Nina comes in, excited.*

It's you. We're just leaving.

Nina I had a feeling we'd see each other once more. Boris Alexeyevich, I've made my decision. Irrevocably. Once and for all. I'm going on the stage. Tomorrow I shan't be here. I shall leave my father, abandon everything, take up a new life. I'm going away, just as you are. I shall be in Moscow. We can see each other there.

Trigorin Stay at the Slavyansky Bazaar. Let me know as soon as you arrive. Molchanova, Grokholsky's House. I have to hurry.

> *Shamraev calls from outside.*

Shamraev Come on, everyone, we're leaving.

Nina Stay one minute more.

Trigorin You look so beautiful. What joy to know that we shall see each other so soon!

She lays her head on his chest.

So soon, and I shall be looking into these wonderful eyes, basking in that inexpressibly lovely smile. These gentle features, the look of pure innocence. Like an angel. My love.

They kiss.

Act Four

Two years later. Konstantin has turned one of Sorin's drawing rooms into his study. Doors left and right lead to inner rooms. A glass door, centre, opens on to the veranda. In the right-hand corner, a writing table. Next to the left-hand door, a Turkish divan, and a bookcase. The whole room is overflowing with books. Otherwise, the usual living-room furniture.

Evening. A single lamp under a shade. Shadow. The trees rustling, the wind howling and outside the watchman is turning his rattle to ward off strangers. Medvedenko and Masha come in.

Masha He doesn't seem to be here. (*Calls.*) Konstantin Gavrilovich! Konstantin! No luck. The old man never stops asking 'Where's Kostya?' 'Where's Kostya?' He can't bear to be without him.

Medvedenko He's frightened of being alone. What terrible weather. It's been like this for two days.

Masha turns up the flame of the lamp.

Masha Have you seen the waves on the lake? Enormous waves.

Medvedenko It's dark outside. We really ought to get that outdoor theatre knocked down. It's so ugly, so empty, so sad, standing there like a skeleton, the curtain flapping in the wind. I walked past yesterday, I could have sworn I heard someone crying.

Masha Maybe you did.

There's a pause.

Medvedenko Masha, I do think we should go home.

Masha (*shakes her head*) I'm staying here tonight.

Medvedenko Poor little fellow, he's going to be hungry.

Masha He won't be hungry. That's what Matryona is for.

There's a pause.

Medvedenko All I'm saying: a third night without his mother.

Masha Do you know, I think I preferred it when you philosophised all the time. It was actually less boring than baby, baby, baby, home, home, home. It's all I ever hear these days.

Medvedenko Please can we go back, Masha?

Masha You can go.

Medvedenko Your father won't give me the horses.

Masha He will. If you ask him. You just have to ask him.

Medvedenko Well then, perhaps I will. Does that mean you'll be home tomorrow?

Masha takes snuff.

Masha If it means you stop asking. Tomorrow.

In come Konstantin, with pillows and a blanket, and Polina with bed linen. They put them on the divan, then Konstantin goes to sit at his desk.

What's this about, Mama?

Polina His uncle's asking for a bed to be made up so he can be close to Konstantin.

Masha Here, let me do it.

Polina He's going backwards. Second childhood.

Masha does the bed. Polina reads the manuscript Konstantin is working on.

Medvedenko Well, I'm going to make a move then. Goodbye, Masha. Goodbye, Mama.

He has kissed Masha's hand, but when he tries to kiss Polina's she recoils.

Polina We can do without that, thank you very much. On your way.

Medvedenko Goodbye, Konstantin Gavrilovich.

Silently, Konstantin holds out his hand to shake. Medvedenko goes. Polina is looking at the manuscript.

Polina I have to say it's the last thing anyone expected, Kostya, that you'd actually turn into a proper writer. You've even got cheques coming in from the magazines.

She runs her hand through his hair.

Success suits you. You've become so handsome. If only you could find it in yourself to be a little bit kinder towards my Masha.

Masha (*making the bed*) Leave him alone, Mama.

Polina She's a good girl.

There's a pause.

Kostya, a woman doesn't need very much, just that from time to time you give her a kind glance. Believe me, I'm speaking from experience.

Konstantin gets up and goes out.

Masha And now you've upset him. What was the point of that? Interfering.

Polina Because I'm sad for you, Masha.

Masha And what use is your sadness, pray?

Polina It breaks my heart. I can see what's happening, I know exactly what you're going through.

Masha I'm not going through anything. Unrequited love, it only belongs in novels. You don't have to put up with it in life. It's perfectly simple, there's a practical way of dealing with it. You don't stand around waiting, like some ridiculous sailor expecting the wind to change. You don't do that. If love gets its claws into you, then you just have to prise them off. It's the only solution. We've got them to transfer my husband miles away. As soon as we move I'll be at peace. I can pull love out by the roots.

From two rooms away, the sound of a melancholy waltz.

Polina That's Kostya playing. Always a bad sign.

Masha dances a few silent moves to the waltz.

Masha The main thing, Mama, is to arrange it so I don't keep seeing him. That's all. Once Semyon's transfer comes through, then I promise in a month I'll have forgotten him. It's perfectly simple.

Dorn and Medvedenko push Sorin in his wheelchair through the door on the left.

Medvedenko I've now got six mouths to feed. With flour at two kopecks a pound.

Dorn Well, somehow you'll just have to manage, won't you?

Medvedenko Says the man who's rolling in money.

Dorn Hardly. Do you know how long I've been practising? Thirty years. Thirty years of dedicated service, my life given over to others, every day, twenty-four hours a day, and what did it get me? Two thousand roubles. And most of that I spent on my last trip abroad. So finally, at the end of it all, I'm broke.

Masha (*to her husband*) I thought you were going.

Medvedenko I was going. But I can't go without horses.

Masha (*lowering her voice, furious*) I just can't bear you hanging around me any more.

Polina, Masha and Dorn sit beside Sorin in his wheelchair on the left-hand side of the room, as Medvedenko wanders disconsolately to the side.

Dorn What was a drawing room now seems to be a study. It's different every time I come.

Masha It's good for Konstantin. It's good for his work. It means he can go and have a think in the garden whenever he needs to.

The sound of the watchman with his rattle.

Sorin Has anyone seen my sister?

Dorn She's gone to meet Trigorin at the station. She won't be long.

Sorin I don't like the fact you got my sister here. That means you must think I'm dangerously ill. Doesn't make sense, I'm meant to be dangerously ill, but nobody gives me any medicine.

Dorn What do you fancy? I'm sure we can come up with something. Valerian drops? Liver salts? Quinine?

Sorin Oh God, this man's idea of a prescription: moralising! It's unendurable.

He nods at the divan.

Is that for me?

Polina Yes, it's for you.

Sorin Then I'm grateful.

Dorn (*hums*) 'The harvest moon floats in the night skies . . .'

Sorin I keep meaning to say. I've got Kostya a great subject for one of his stories. It would be entitled 'The Man Who Wanted To'. *L'Homme Qui a Voulu.* When I was young, I wanted to be a man of letters – and it never happened. I wanted to speak well – but I spoke appallingly. 'As it were, as you might say, I mean, you know, unaccustomed as I am.' I couldn't ever finish a speech, it went on and on till the sweat was running in rivers down my face. I wanted to marry – and I never did. I wanted to live in town. Where am I? At the end of my life? Where am I? Well, there it is, there you have it.

Dorn Yes, unfortunately, the story's rather spoilt because you wanted to be a Civil Councillor Grade Four, and that's exactly what you were.

Sorin Yes, but I never aimed for that. It just happened.

Dorn You know, it isn't very dignified to be complaining about your lot in life when you've managed to survive well into your sixties.

Sorin Do you miss the point deliberately, or is it sheer stupidity? Why can't you understand? I still want to live.

Dorn That's just self-indulgent. Nature has laws. All lives end.

Sorin Yes, that's easy for you to say, because you're fulfilled. You're fulfilled and so losing life means nothing to you. But when the moment comes, just wait, you'll still be frightened.

Dorn The fear of death is an animal fear. We have to fight it. It's not rational, unless of course you believe in everlasting life and some kind of reckoning for one's sins. But as far as I know, you're not a believer. And what sins have you committed exactly? You served twenty-five years in the Department of Justice.

Sorin (*laughs*) Twenty-seven.

Dorn All right, even worse.

Konstantin comes in and sits at Sorin's feet. Masha watches him like a hawk throughout.

We're in Konstantin's way. We're stopping him work.

Konstantin Doesn't matter. It's fine.

There's a pause.

Medvedenko And, Doctor, of all the foreign cities you've visited, which was your favourite?

Dorn Genoa.

Medvedenko Why Genoa?

Dorn Without a doubt. In Genoa you leave your hotel, you go into the street at night and there are people everywhere. There's a warm river of people. And you begin to stroll among them with no particular aim, and there's a moment when you head this way, then you head that, and suddenly you start to feel psychologically that you're part of the crowd, there's no separation, you *are* the crowd. And at that point you think, 'Maybe there is such a thing as the soul of the world. Maybe it exists.' The soul that Nina Zarechnaya embodied in your play. Talking of which, what happened to her? Do we know? How is she doing?

Konstantin She's doing well enough.

Dorn I heard a rumour that her life was now quite disorderly. Do you know what that's about?

Konstantin Doctor, it's a long story.

Dorn Then summarise.

There's a pause.

Konstantin In brief: she ran away from home and took up with Trigorin. You heard that?

Dorn I heard that.

Konstantin She had a child. The child died. Trigorin fell out of love with her and abandoned her to go back to his previous arrangements. No surprise there. In fact, being the coward he is, he'd never let go of them. He'd somehow managed to keep both things going. So, piecing things together, I'd guess Nina's private life has not exactly worked out.

Dorn And professionally?

Konstantin From what I've heard, even worse. She made her debut in summer theatre near Moscow, then went to the provinces. At the start, I never missed a performance. For a while, I made a point of it. They always gave her leading roles, but really her acting was tasteless, she pushed too hard, her gestures were clumsy. There was no flow. There were moments when you'd get a glimpse of talent – she did a wonderful cry once, and there was one really good death scene. But it was just moments, really.

Dorn But if you glimpsed it, then there is a talent.

Konstantin Difficult to say. On balance, yes, probably. When I was in the audience she refused to see me afterwards, and the staff wouldn't let me into her hotel room. Which, knowing what her mood must have been, didn't surprise me. I wasn't going to insist.

There's a pause.

I don't know what else to say. When I got home, then I started getting letters from her. Intelligent, warm, interesting letters. She never said so but I could tell how unhappy she was. There wasn't a line that didn't give off tension and neurosis. She signed herself 'The Seagull'. In Pushkin's poem *Rusalka*, the miller keeps saying he's a raven. Well she keeps calling herself the seagull. And now she's here.

Dorn What on earth do you mean?

Konstantin In town. At the inn. She's been here for five days. If I could, I would go and see her. In fact Masha did try to see her, but she's refusing to see anyone. Semyon Semyonovich is convinced he spotted her in the fields yesterday after dinner.

Medvedenko It's true. She was heading back into town. I actually greeted her, I went up to her and invited her to come and see us. She said she would.

Konstantin She won't.

There's a pause.

She's been disowned by her family. Her father and stepmother have placed guards everywhere to keep her off their estate.

He crosses to his writing table with Dorn.

Easy, isn't it, Doctor, to philosophise on paper. Not so easy in life.

Sorin She was a wonderful creature.

Dorn Say that again.

Sorin I said how wonderful she was. Civil Councillor
Sorin confesses he fell in love with her for a while.

Dorn You old rogue.

Shamraev's laugh is heard.

Polina Sounds like the station party is back.

Konstantin Yes, I can hear my mother.

*Arkadina and Trigorin come in, followed by
Shamraev.*

Shamraev Truly, dear lady, you defy the laws of nature.
The rest of us grow old, we're all getting just a little bit
weatherbeaten, but you alone stay young. The clothes,
the vitality, the grace.

Arkadina Worming your way into my good opinion
again. You think I'm that gullible?

Trigorin Ah, Petr Nikolayevich, I can't believe it, not ill
again, please, no! We can't have that.

He turns, joyful, then shakes Masha's hand.

And Marya Ilinichna!

Masha You remember me?

Trigorin And married, I hear.

Masha Long married.

Trigorin Happy?

*He greets Dorn and Medvedenko, then nervously
approaches Konstantin.*

Your mother tells me that you're willing to put our past
behind you.

Konstantin holds out his hand.

Arkadina Boris Alexeyevich has brought the magazine with your new story in it.

Konstantin Thank you. It's kind of you.

He takes the book from Trigorin. They all sit.

Trigorin And news from your admirers as well. They send their respects. In Petersburg and in Moscow, I am always being asked about you. Everyone wants to know 'What is he like? How old is he? What colour is his hair?' For some reason they all think you're middle-aged. Nobody has guessed your identity. The pseudonym works perfectly. You might as well be the Man in the Iron Mask.

Konstantin Are you here for long?

Trigorin No, it's the usual absurdity. Back to Moscow tomorrow, I think. I have a story that's overdue, and then, oh, I'm backed up as usual. A contribution I promised to an anthology. There's always more.

As they talk, Arkadina and Polina set up a folding card table in the middle of the room. Shamraev lights candles and arranges chairs. From the cupboard, a game of lotto is fetched.

It's hardly welcoming weather. I've never known the wind so strong. Tomorrow morning, if it drops, the plan is, head straight for the lake and get some fishing in. Also: I need to take a good look at the garden and exactly where your play was performed, remember? I've been mulling over the idea of new story, and I need to refresh my memory of the exact spot.

Masha Papa, please let my poor husband have a horse. He needs to get home.

Shamraev (*imitating her*) Give him a horse, get him home! For goodness' sake, you know perfectly well they've just been to the station and back. I can't send them out again.

Masha You have other horses.

But Shamraev does not respond.

Oh, you're impossible.

Medvedenko It's all right, don't worry. I can walk, Masha.

Polina Walk? In weather like this? Come on, everyone.

Medvedenko It's only four miles. So, once more.

Polina is getting everyone round the table. Medvedenko kisses Masha's hand.

Goodbye. Goodbye, Mama.

Reluctantly Polina holds out her hand to be kissed.

I wasn't meaning to be a nuisance, it's just the baby. I have to get back for the baby. Goodbye.

He bows to them all, then goes out apologetically.

Shamraev I don't think he'll have a problem on foot. It's not as if he were a general.

Polina Come on, everyone, let's start playing. They'll be calling us in for supper in no time at all.

Polina has rapped firmly on the table. Dorn, Shamraev and Masha sit down to play. Arkadina speaks to Trigorin.

Arkadina This is what we do, when the autumn evenings draw in. We play lotto. It's funny, it's the actual set we had when our mother played with us as children. It's years old. Won't you come and join in before supper? It's a boring game, but it's one of those things that isn't so boring when you get into it.

Now she and Trigorin have joined the others. She gives them all three cards. Konstantin is leafing through the magazine.

Konstantin That says it all. He's read his own story, but he hasn't even cut the pages on mine.

He puts the magazine down on the desk, then heads for the door on the left. He passes his mother, kissing her on the head.

Arkadina Don't you want to join us?

Konstantin Forgive me, I'm not in the mood. I'm going out.

He goes out.

Arkadina It's ten kopecks to get in. Could you do mine for me, Doctor?

Dorn Yes, of course.

Masha Now if all the stakes are in, here we go. Twenty-two!

Arkadina Yes.

Masha Three!

Dorn That's me.

Masha Have you put it down? Seven! Eighty-one! Ten!

Shamraev Give us a moment. Not so fast.

Arkadina You wouldn't believe my curtain calls in Kharkov. Just thinking of them makes my head spin.

Masha Thirty-four!

The melancholy waltz starts up again.

Arkadina The students had organised a standing ovation. Three bouquets, two garlands and this, look.

She takes a brooch from her dress and throws it on the table.

Shamraev That really is something.

Masha Fifty!

Dorn Fifty-something, or fifty?

Masha Fifty.

Arkadina I had this astonishing costume. Give me credit: if I know nothing else, I do know how to dress.

Polina Kostya always plays when he's depressed.

Shamraev He's taking a hammering in the press, isn't he?

Masha Seventy-seven!

Arkadina The press! As if it mattered.

Trigorin It's not really working out for him. He still hasn't really found his voice. His work seems blurred, as if it were out of focus. At times it has a frantic quality. And no real people, not people who live and breathe.

Masha Eleven!

Arkadina (*looking at her brother*) Petrusha, are we boring you? He's fast asleep.

Dorn The former Civil Councillor Grade Four has lost consciousness.

Masha Seven! Ninety!

Trigorin I think it may be the environment. If I lived here, beside a lake, would I bother to write? I'd have had some sort of epic struggle, then at the end of it I'd have given up writing for fishing.

Masha Twenty-eight!

Trigorin My idea of heaven: a chub on a line. Or a perch.

Dorn Yes, but Konstantin has something. He really does. Something special. He thinks in images, and that's unusual. It makes for colourful writing, and it moves me deeply. It's just a pity that he doesn't have any structure, he just produces an effect, and we all know effect isn't enough in literature. Irina Nikolaevna, are you proud of having a writer for a son?

Arkadina You're not going to believe this, but I haven't actually got round to reading him. I never have time.

Masha Twenty-six!

Konstantin comes in silently and goes to his desk.

Shamraev You know, Boris Alexeyevich, we still have something belonging to you.

Trigorin To me?

Shamraev Konstantin shot a gull and you asked me to have it stuffed.

Trigorin That's strange. I don't remember that. I really don't.

Masha Sixty-six! One!

Konstantin opens the window and listens.

Konstantin It's so dark out there. I don't know why I feel so nervous tonight.

Arkadina Please shut the window, Kostya, there's a draught.

Konstantin closes the window.

Masha Eighty-eight!

Trigorin Ladies and gentlemen, I have to inform you, I have a full house.

Arkadina Bravo, bravo!

Shamraev Bravo, congratulations.

Arkadina The luckiest man alive. From birth.

She gets up.

And now let's all go and get something to eat. The famous novelist has not eaten all day. We'll resume after supper. (*To her son.*) Leave all that for now, Kostya, we're going to eat.

Konstantin I'm going to work. I'm not hungry.

Arkadina It's up to you.

She wakes Sorin.

Petrusha, supper.

Arkadina takes Shamraev by the arm.

So let me tell you, in Kharkov, end of play, this is what happened the moment the curtain fell . . .

Polina has put out the candles and now she and Dorn push Sorin off in his wheelchair. They all go out of the left-hand door. Only Konstantin is left, alone at his desk. He is preparing to write, but first he looks at what he has already written.

Konstantin New forms. New forms! All the time I talk about the need for new forms and yet when I read my own work, it's not new. Anything but. 'The poster on the fence proclaimed.' 'Her pale face, framed by dark hair.' Framed, proclaimed. It's nothing but cliché.

He scratches out.

I'm going to keep the bit where the hero wakes to the sound of the rain, and then I'm going to lose the rest. The description of the moon and the evening is just so long and overwrought. Trigorin has a formula, he can do it in his sleep. When he's writing, then the neck of a broken bottle glitters on the weir, and the shadow of the mill-wheel darkens. And there it is. You see it. The whole thing. Moonlit night. But with me, there's all the quivering light, the soft twinkling of the stars, the sound of the distant piano dying on the fucking evening air. It's unbearable.

There's a pause.

And, you know, I've begun to feel more and more that it's nothing to do with old form or new. Nothing at all. But that a person should write without thinking about form at all. It should just flow freely. From your soul.

At once a tap on the window, nearest the desk.

There's somebody there.

He looks out of the window.

I can't see anything.

He opens the door and looks out into the garden.

Somebody ran down the steps. Who is it? Who's there?

Now Konstantin goes out. The sound of him walking quickly away along the veranda. Then half a minute later he returns with Nina.

Nina! Nina!

Nina is in floods of tears. She lays her head on his chest to try and control herself.

Oh Nina, oh my Nina. It's you. It's you. I've been in agony all day, I had a feeling.

He takes off her hat and cape.

Oh my beloved, my beautiful, at last you're back. Don't cry, please let's not cry.

Nina There's someone here.

Konstantin There's no one.

Nina Please lock the doors or someone will find us.

Konstantin No one will find us.

Nina I know your mother is here. Lock the doors.

Konstantin locks the right door, then goes to the left, and puts a chair against it.

Konstantin It doesn't have a lock, I'll put a chair against it. I promise you, you're safe.

Nina gazes deeply into his eyes.

Nina Let me look at you. It's warm in here, it's nice. This used to be the drawing room. Have I changed too?

Konstantin Yes. You've lost weight. And your eyes are bigger. Nina, it's so strange that you've finally come to see me. You've turned me away so many times. And why's it taken so long? You've been here a week, I know that. I kept calling by, standing under your window like a beggar.

Nina I was afraid you hated me. I have a dream every night that you're looking at me and you don't recognise me. You have no idea. From the moment I got here, I've been walking on the estate, by the lake. So many times I've walked up to the house. But I could never find the courage to come in. Let's sit down.

They sit.

337

How wonderful to talk. To talk at last. Can we talk? It's nice here, so warm, so comfortable. Can you hear the wind? I remember in Turgenev somewhere he says, 'On nights like these how lucky a man is to sit under his own roof, in a warm corner.' I'm the seagull. No, that's not right.

She rubs her forehead.

What was I saying? Turgenev. 'And God protect those who wander alone in the cold . . .'

She starts to cry again.

Konstantin Nina . . .

Nina It's fine.

Konstantin Nina, you're crying again . . .

Nina It's all right, I promise you. It's all right. It feels good to cry. I haven't cried for two years. Yesterday, when it was dark, I went across to the garden to see if our theatre was still there. It's there. It's been there all this time. And that's when I cried for the first time, when I saw it. I felt a weight being lifted off me, I felt my heart clear. Look, I'm not crying any more.

She takes his hand.

And there it is, you're a writer now. You're a writer and I'm an actress. Even you and I have had finally to throw ourselves into the scrum. When I lived here, I'd wake up every morning, first thing I'd do is sing, like a child, full of joy. I was in love with you, I was in love with glory. And now? First thing tomorrow, up at the crack of dawn, and off to Yelets, travelling third-class, with the peasants. And waiting in Yelets, all the most cultured businessmen in town just longing to try their luck with me. Life's real, isn't it?

Konstantin Why Yelets?

Nina Because I'm contracted for the winter season. And I leave tomorrow.

Konstantin Nina, I've hated you, I've cursed you, I've taken your letters and your photographs and torn them into tiny pieces. But even as I did it I knew. I knew our souls are bound together for the rest of time. I don't have the strength to stop loving you. I can't. From the moment I lost you and I became a professional writer, my life has been unbearable. I suffer. That's all I do. Nothing else. My youth vanished. Suddenly I felt ninety years old. I say your name and I still want to kiss the ground on which you walk. No matter where I turn, I still see your face, that sweet smile that shone down on me when I was happy.

Nina (*bewildered*) What is he saying? Why is he talking like this?

Konstantin I have no one, I'm alone. It's as if I'm living in a dungeon, without any warmth, without any love. No matter what I write, it comes out stale and lifeless and gloomy. Stay here, Nina, I beg you. Or at least let me come with you.

Nina quickly puts her hat and cape back on.

Why not? Nina, tell me why not. Please. For God's sake.

He has to sit and watch in silence as she dresses.

Nina I've got horses at the gate. Don't come out, I'll go by myself. Can you get me some water?

She has begun to cry. He gets her a glass of water.

Konstantin Where are you going right now?

Nina Into town.

There's a pause.

Is your mother here?

Konstantin Yes. My uncle's been very ill. So on Thursday we sent her a telegram.

Nina Why on earth do you kiss the ground I walk on? Why? I ought to be put down like a dog.

She leans over the table.

You have no idea how tired I am. If only I could find peace. Some peace. I'm the seagull. No, that isn't right. I'm the actress. The actress!

Arkadina and Trigorin can be heard laughing. Nina runs to the door and looks through the keyhole.

So he's here too.

She returns to Konstantin.

It no longer matters. Truly. He undermined me. He didn't believe in the theatre, he mocked my ambitions, and slowly he infected me. I lost all my confidence. And there was all the torture of being in love, of being jealous, the constant anguish for my child. It killed my acting, because on to the stage walked a nothing, a non-person. I didn't know where to put my hands, I didn't know how to stand, I heard my own voice and it was horrible. You cannot imagine the hell of acting badly. I am – the seagull. No, that's not right. You remember that day when you shot a gull? A man happens to come along, catches sight of her, and for no other reason but that he can, he destroys her. A subject for a short story. No, that's not right.

She rubs her forehead again.

What was I saying? Oh yes, I was talking about acting. Well, it's all changed. I'm a real actress now, I go out

there and I couldn't be happier. It's like being drunk.
When I speak, when I move, I feel myself to be beautiful.
And in some way, the act of coming back here has been
so good for me. I've had time to walk and think, to
think and walk, and I've replenished myself, my spiritual
resources. I've understood something at last, Kostya.
When we work, if we act or if we write, it mustn't be for
glory, it mustn't be for fame, none of the things I used to
dream about, it must be about the ability to endure. To
carry your cross and have faith. I have faith. And now
things don't hurt so much. When I think of my vocation,
I'm not afraid of life.

Konstantin You have a vocation. You're lucky. You
know where you're heading. I'm still trapped in a sort
of chaos, a chaos of crazy dreams and half-felt images.
I don't know who or what it's all for. I have no faith.
I have no vocation.

Nina is listening for the others.

Nina Shh . . . I've got to get going. Goodbye. When I'm
a great actress, promise you'll come and see me. Please?
And now, it's late. I can barely stand. I'm exhausted. I
need to eat.

She squeezes his hand.

Konstantin If you stay then you can eat here.

Nina No, it's not a good idea. Don't see me off, I'll go
by myself. The horses.

She gestures out to where they are.

So she brought him with her, did she? Fair enough, it
doesn't matter. When you see Trigorin, don't tell him
I was here. I love him. I love him more than ever before.
A subject for a short story. I love him, I love him with
all my heart. To the point of despair. Oh Kostya, do you

remember how happy we were? How bright, how warm, how full of joy our life once was? The feelings we had, like beautiful flowers. Remember? I know it by heart. 'Humans, lions, eagles, partridges, deer, geese, spiders, the fish swimming silent at the bottom of the sea, micro-organisms too small to detect – in a word, everything that lives, everything that has life, everything that is – everything has lived out its cycle and died. In its place, nothing. For thousands of years, the moon has shone down useless on an empty world. The cranes no longer wake and call to each other in the meadows. In the lime groves, the May beetles are silent.'

Impulsively Nina embraces Konstantin and runs out through the door to the outside. Konstantin is silent. Then:

Konstantin It wouldn't be good if someone saw her in the garden and told Mama. It might upset Mama.

Systematically now he tears up all his manuscripts and throws them under the desk. Then he unlocks the right-hand door and goes out. Dorn tries to open the door on the left.

Dorn Strange. Someone's jammed the door.

He comes in and puts the armchair back in its proper place.

It's like an obstacle race.

In come Arkadina and Polina, then Yakov with the alcohol, and Masha, then Shamraev and Trigorin.

Arkadina Put the red wine on the table. Boris Alexeyevich likes beer. We'll all have a drink while we play.

Polina And you can bring us some tea while you're at it.

She lights candles, then sits at the table. Shamraev has led Trigorin to the cupboard.

Shamraev Here, this is what I was talking about just now.

He takes out the stuffed seagull.

It was you who asked me to do it.

Trigorin Really?

He stares at the bird.

I don't remember. I don't remember at all.

From the right, offstage, the sound of a gunshot. Everyone is startled.

Arkadina What on earth was that?

Dorn Don't worry. Something's exploded in my medicine chest. I'm going to check.

He goes out. After half a minute he returns.

As I thought. It was a bottle of ether which burst.

Arkadina sits at the table.

Arkadina My God, that scared the life out of me. For a moment it reminded me . . .

She puts her hands over her face.

I was gone for a moment there.

Dorn has picked up a magazine and is leafing through it. He goes over to Trigorin.

Dorn I don't know if you saw this article published in here a couple of months ago. A report, a rather *urgent* report. From America, as it happens. And I wanted to ask you . . .

343

He has put his arm on Trigorin's back to lead him down to the front.

Because this is a matter of particular interest to me . . .

He drops his voice, low.

Get Irina Nikolaevna out of here. Doesn't matter where. The fact is, Konstantin Gavrilovich has shot himself.